Southern Illinois University Press

Carbondale and Edwardsville

A
POLITICAL
PASSAGE

The Career of Stratton of Illinois

David Kenney

Library of Congress Cataloging-in-Publication Data

Kenney, David, 1922–
   A political passage: the career of Stratton of Illinois.
   Bibliography: p.
   Includes index.
   1. Stratton, William G. 2. Illinois—Governors—
Biography. 3. Legislators—United States—Biography.
4. United States. Congress. House—Biography.
5. Illinois—Politics and government—1951–
6. Illinois—Politics and government—1865–1950.
I. Title.
F546.4.S77K46 1990   328.773'092 [B]   89-11587
ISBN 0-8093-1549-1

The paper used in this publication meets the minimum requirements of
American National Standard for Information Sciences—Permanence of Paper
for Printed Library Materials, ANSI Z39.48-1984. ∞

Contents

	Illustrations	vii
	Preface	ix
1.	Father and Son	1
2.	Young Congressman	14
3.	State Treasurer	25
4.	Anchors Aweigh	36
5.	Back to Congress	48
6.	Wilderness Years	64
7.	State Treasurer Again	93
8.	First-Term Governor: First Biennium	105
9.	First-Term Governor: Second Biennium	126
10.	The Case of the Errant Auditor	137
11.	Second-Term Governor: Third Biennium	152
12.	Second-Term Governor: Fourth Biennium	166
13.	Years of Trial	180
14.	After Politics	204
	Notes	217
	Bibliography	234
	Index	237

Illustrations

Following page 72

The future governor, with father and brother, 1918

William G. Stratton at twenty

Campaigning in Lake County, 1940

Congressman Stratton and family, 1941

On Okinawa, 1946

Illinois congressmen

As state treasurer, 1951

The house at 437 Vine Street, Morris, 1951

Campaigning in Chicago, 1952

Inauguration day, 1953

"Open House" in 1953

Sandra and Diana Stratton, 1953

Governor Stratton with Stillman Stanard and Glen Palmer

The governor's mother, Congresswoman Marguerite S. Church, and
    Mrs. Stratton's sister, 1955

A 1955 celebration

Stratton, Adlai E. Stevenson, and Samuel W. Witwer

Illustrations

With Orville Hodge

Campaigning in 1956

With Jack Dempsey and Richard M. Nixon, 1956

"Opening day—the first ball," 1957

Governor and Mrs. Stratton with the Clark Gables

With Paul Powell, 1957

The mature Stratton, 1958

Stratton in the Soviet Union, 1959

With Queen Elizabeth, Prince Philip, John Diefenbaker, and Mayor Daley, 1959

With President Eisenhower, 1960

Helicopter campaign tour, 1960

Shirley Stratton, 1960

The Strattons, 1964

Preface

The performance of government at the state level in the United States is important to each one of us and to the federal system. What state government does determines the extent to which most of us can be educated, the ease and safety in which we travel, and the quality of our lives in general. The governors of the states are important public officials, and their skill or their lack thereof in legislation and administration has a profound influence on the degree of success they achieve.

Few governors, other than those who gain greater fame by running for president of the United States, receive much attention from scholars. We can profit from knowing more about them—how their lives were turned toward politics, the goals they seek and the tools they employ, and the strengths and weaknesses of their administrations. It is hoped that this study of the political life of a midcentury governor of one of the most significant of the fifty states can help to fill that void.

My attention was first fully directed to Governor Stratton when I had the opportunity to teach a course in Illinois government during his first term. Since then I have taught the course a number of times, and have been deeply involved in public affairs in Illinois as both an elected and an appointed official. The hold that Illinois government and politics have on my imagination has never lessened. It is a world all its own.

Many persons have assisted me in the writing of this book. Governor Stratton kindly assented to be interviewed, and talked with me at length on several occasions. The official collections of his papers and photographs, in the Illinois State Historical Library and in the Illinois State Archives, were the primary research sources. Dr. Roger Bridges, formerly of the Historical Library, facilitated my work there. Cheryl Schnirring, Gary Stockton, and Mary Michals of the Historical Library staff were unfailingly courteous and helpful during the many months I spent at work there. Personnel of the Archives and of the Illinois State Library were always cooperative and expert in guiding me to relevant materials. The memoirs published by the Oral History Office of Sangamon State University were a priceless resource.

Grateful acknowledgment is extended to the Illinois State Historical Library for supplying, with permission to use, the photographs that appear as illustrations in this book.

On a more personal level I benefited greatly from many conversations about Illinois politics with my longtime associate and treasured friend the late James E. Helfrich. My uncle, Craig Templeton, for many years a practitioner of politics, has always been generous in sharing his understanding with me. During my ten years of residence in the state capital at Springfield I benefited from literally hundreds of conversations with persons engaged in and observant of the political scene, many of them bearing old scars from it, and others fresh wounds. For a time during 1986, Sylvia Van Bergen, then a graduate student at Sangamon State University, assisted me in research. Kathryn Koldehoff has provided me with invaluable editorial assistance and advice. Karen Clayton skillfully typed an entire draft of the manuscript in one of its later stages. My wife, Wanda, typed several chapters of an earlier version and provided the setting in which the project could take root and grow. My debt to her is greater than I can say. My colleagues in academic political science, both at Southern Illinois University and on other campuses, have cheered me with their interest in my work. Not one of these persons, of course, has any responsibility for the shortcomings of this book.

A
POLITICAL
PASSAGE

1

Father and Son

William Grant Stratton was governor of Illinois for two terms, from 1953 to 1961. Earlier he served two terms as state treasurer, and two as congressman-at-large from Illinois. In neither case were those terms consecutive. There was hardly an election in Illinois for twenty years when he was neither on the ballot nor safely in office. He went to Congress in 1941 at the age of twenty-six, and for the next two decades he pursued public office unceasingly. He appears to have been a competent congressman, an honest treasurer, and by most accounts, a good governor.

It is evident that his political life began when he was a child. His father, William Joseph, was such a great influence upon him that the father deserves attention here.* For a time the older man, even after his death, completely overshadowed the younger. When he first became active in politics, William Grant was often called "young Bill Stratton," to distinguish him from his father, and later "Billy the Kid." Eventually he gained the maturity that allowed him to aim beyond his father's office and to seek to be governor and more.

William Joseph Stratton, the governor's father, was born in 1886. *His* father, John, had emigrated as a child with his family from England directly to Illinois in 1850.[1] He became a farmer in Lake County and sold cordwood, and ice cut from the lakes during the winter months. He kept a livery stable and, at times, as many as forty horses. John Stratton married Mary O'Boyle, who was Irish and Catholic, prospered,

---

*Neither Stratton, father or son, used his full middle name, simply the initial. However, as long as William Joseph figures in this account, to avoid potential confusion the full names will be given when more than the last name is needed.

and headed a large family. Some of their children were raised as Catholics, some were not.[2]

The scenic Chain O' Lakes region, in Lake County, where the Stratton family lived, was within fifty miles of Chicago. It was a popular vacation choice for Chicagoans at the turn of the century, but roads were poor, and their access to it was mainly by rail. An old friend of the family recalled in 1941: "I spent many happy hours at the Stratton Farm.... way back in the early 1900s.... The Stratton Bus Line (Horses and Dirt roads) met the trains at Ingleside and Lake Villa at that time to convey passengers and baggage to the various summer hotels."[3]

William Joseph Stratton seemed destined for politics. An often-told but little-documented tale has two Lake County politicos visiting one day in the kitchen. "I could take the next man we see and make him a political winner," one said. At that moment the young William Joseph entered the room, on his rounds delivering ice.[4] Legend does not report what steps were taken to fulfill the prophecy. But we do know that William Joseph's mother once remarked when he was a young man, "Oh, Will, he is going in for politics."[5]

William Joseph was elected to the board of Ingleside's one-room rural school before he was twenty-one. As a board member he took part in the decision to employ a young teacher named Zula Van Wormer, who lived in Trevor, Wisconsin. Within a short time, in 1908, William Joseph and Zula were married. She was a well-educated and intelligent person. Her range of interests included literature, drama, music, athletics, natural history, and fortunately, in view of her husband's career, politics.[6] She quickly became a community force in Ingleside, active in the Parent-Teacher Association and Methodist church, and a leader in the campaign to secure a bond issue for the improvement of the Ingleside school. Wiliam Joseph and Zula had two sons, William Grant, the future governor, born on February 26, 1914, and Charles Kerwin almost two years later.

While he claimed "farming" as his vocation during his twenties and thirties, William Joseph Stratton was diligent in politics and held a series of increasingly important party and public positions. In addition to his service on the Ingleside school board, he was elected to the county board as a township supervisor and held that position for fourteen years. During part of that time he chaired the board. He was an elected member of the Lake County Republican Central Committee for sixteen years, and its chairman for eight. His importance in Republican politics was recognized in the state capital by 1917, when he was appointed deputy state game warden by Governor Lowden,[7] and by 1922 he was known as "the Republican boss of Lake County."[8]

Father and Son

Len Small of Kankakee was elected governor in 1920—a Republican year in Illinois. William Joseph Stratton sided with Small and was promoted to the position of chief game and fish warden. He was thirty-four and had an impressive presence—six feet in height, handsome, well-groomed, trim, and muscular. In a portrait of the time his hair was dark, his features sharply cut, with a slight cleft in the chin. His gaze was clear, direct, and level. In this and other pictures he had a half smile on his lips, and invariably a pleasant look.

William Joseph Stratton's next step up the political ladder followed a crisis involving Governor Small. In 1922 the governor was charged with keeping interest earned on state funds when he was state treasurer and was indicted.[9] He managed to get a change of venue for his trial, from Sangamon County to Waukegan, in Lake County, where his friend William Joseph Stratton was a political force. The trial brought statewide notice to Stratton. After the governor was acquitted, several of the jurors began work in state jobs.

In office for a second term, Governor Small supported the creation of a new Department of Conservation in 1925. Its first director was William Joseph Stratton, appointed by Small. At thirty-nine, Stratton had achieved one of his ambitions, and his new income allowed him to provide a better life for his family. He worked hard in 1925 and 1926 at launching the new department for which he was responsible. He was eager to win statewide elective office, and to position himself for a later try at becoming secretary of state or governor. In 1926 he sought but failed to be nominated for state treasurer.

In 1928 Len Small wished again to run for governor. He wanted a third consecutive term, a prize that was unprecedented in Illinois. After twelve years as secretary of state the popular Louis L. Emmerson felt that his turn to be governor had come, and the long-continued struggle between the two for supremacy within their party came to a head. William Joseph Stratton was not a bystander.

The logic of events placed Stratton on Emmerson's side. He wished to run for secretary of state, but he could not hope to beat the popular Emmerson in the primary. If Emmerson were to run for governor, however, then the door would be open for Stratton. Such a pairing was in their mutual self-interest. Initially, Stratton thought such an arrangement would have Governor Small's approval.

Stratton began a campaign for nomination for the office of secretary of state, believing he had the backing of the governor. He sought to enlist his friends in his cause, but then he learned that Small had other plans for the statewide ticket. William Grant Stratton recalled in 1943, when he was facing a similar situation, the events of 1928.

I can remember just as well as if it was yesterday, when Leslie Small [the governor's son] called my father and said, "Bill, you can't buck the ticket, you would probably better not go on." He was told that if he would only step out they would make him and his family comfortable for a long time to come. And I can remember his words that night ... "I appreciate the generosity of your offer, but I could never face my friends ... if I sold out. I would [rather] risk an honorable defeat."[10]

The weight of the governor's office and his leadership of the party were against William Joseph Stratton. At odds with the governor who had appointed him, he resigned from his position as director of the Department of Conservation to make the race for secretary of state. The name recognition he had achieved, and the friends made, during more than a decade of conservation work, and the political involvement over a longer period, including the statewide campaign of 1926, now had their payoffs. Years later, many still carried the deputy game warden badges that he had widely distributed.[11] He was active in the Masonic Lodge, and associates there were helpful to him. He enjoyed hunting and had gained many friends while following that sport. Claude E. Clinton of Olive Branch, near Cairo, wrote to William Grant Stratton in 1949, "Your father ... and myself were great friends ... he come [sic] to my home here and goose hunted with me."[12] Perry Conn, a hunting companion from Quincy, perhaps best identified William Joseph's greatest political strength when he wrote in 1950, "Having each person feel he had known you all your life, that was your father's big asset."[13]

In spite of Governor Small's opposition to his candidacy, William Joseph Stratton had no serious challenge in the primary. Nineteen twenty-eight was again a Republican year. Emmerson, backed by Stratton for governor, won in the general election with a plurality of 425 thousand votes, while Stratton was the winner by 269 thousand. His strength was downstate, everywhere except in Chicago and the urban Democratic enclaves in a few other counties.[14] At last he had achieved statewide elective office, after more than twenty years in politics. The position provided much patronage, name-enhancement, and a vehicle that could carry him to higher office. Now he was able to provide still more comfortably for his wife and two teen-aged sons.

William Joseph Stratton was deeply engaged in 1929 and 1930 in the administrative and political tasks of his office. His routine was not all work, however, for he continued to pursue the interests of a lifetime. In 1957 the noted conservationist Louis Barkhausen wrote to William Grant Stratton: "I am enclosing several photos taken in 1930 of your father, who was a great duck hunter. He shot with me at my place at

Cuba Island many a time," Barkhausen remembered. "Sometimes he came over alone and took his limit."[15]

Despite such interludes, the work of the secretary of state was heavy, and by the end of 1930 political cares had begun to pile up. Stratton hoped to go from that office, after one or two terms, to the governor's chair, after the example of his ally Lou Emmerson. Depression came in 1929, however, and the party in power was paying its political price. In the off-year election of 1930 the long dominance of Republican candidates was clearly broken. An ambitious politician of the party had good cause to be concerned, and as the depression deepened in Illinois in 1932 it became clear that Republican candidates would find the going difficult in November. Stratton was on the ballot, but as anticipated the general election proved to be a great success for Democratic candidates, from top to bottom of the state ticket. Although he was the leading vote-getter for the Republicans, Stratton lost the office of secretary of state to state Senator Edward J. Hughes of Chicago by fifty-nine thousand votes. It is the opinion of William Grant Stratton that his father was "counted out" in the Chicago wards.[16]

In 1933 William Joseph Stratton was out of state office, appointed or elected, for the first time in sixteen years. He continued in politics, however, rather than turning to some other endeavor. Staunchly partisan, he lent his name, prestige, and campaign efforts to the top of the party ticket in 1934. With the state and national tide still running strongly Democratic, he must have known that defeat was probable. He was beaten by John Stelle of McLeansboro for the office of treasurer.

Republicans had no better success in 1936. Stratton ran again for secretary of state, but this time was defeated much more soundly by Hughes. He no longer led the ticket; his political star was setting. He was broken in health and finances, his resources exhausted by fruitless campaigns, "the victim of party-wide defeats," as his son later remembered.[17]

William Joseph was not in good health thereafter and was not able to go on the state ticket in 1938. Instead he attempted to win the Republican nomination for county clerk in Lake County. His economic situation must have been grim for him to seek a county position after having been a leader in Republican politics for thirty years. His health did not allow him to campaign, and he was beaten in the primary.[18] Only four years earlier he had led the Republican state ticket. Soon after, on May 8, he died of complications following gall bladder surgery. Worn out and impoverished by repeated political defeat, he was only fifty-two.

His political fortunes rose and fell with those of the Republican party, but in another time it is quite possible that he would have become governor. Employment in state government, while he was active in it, was almost entirely through the patronage system, and he accepted that fact as a given of political life. That he had a reputation for honesty, that he was a ready listener, and that he was willing to accept the suggestions of wiser heads[19] were traits that would have endeared him to many. And indeed his circle of friends and acquaintances was large. William Joseph Stratton must have had an unusual capacity for friendship; years after his death he was still widely and fondly remembered.

Beyond doubt, the foundation of his son's political career rested upon his accomplishments, and his death in one sense opened the door to his son's entry into politics. There was still in Illinois a Bill Stratton with political ambitions, only now it was the younger man rather than the older. Results of the 1938 election were cheering to Republicans, for Illinois appeared to be returning to its traditional political loyalty. It was a time for William Grant Stratton to think of running for public office.*

In one sense, Stratton had been trained in politics from infancy onward. Long after he left the governor's office, he recalled being allowed by his parents to hear the talk when political associates visited their home.[20] "I was reared in an atmosphere of politics," he wrote in 1941. "My ambition, from the time I can first remember ... was to be engaged in public life and affairs. It was [one] instilled by the life around me."[21] Stratton's mother encouraged her sons to read worthwhile books, and he stated in 1960 that his early ambition "was stirred by a great interest in reading ... history and biography."[22]

One of Stratton's vivid early memories is of his father taking him to see Governor Small. The governor kindly suggested that "Willie" be left in his office while his father took care of other matters. That was done, and for almost an hour the eight-year-old boy sat in the governor's office while Small talked on the telephone and conducted other business. Stratton still clearly remembers that experience, and feels that it helped motivate him to a life of politics.[23]

William Joseph Stratton took his son with him into other political settings. An old friend of the family wrote the governor in 1959, "I can remember when you used to come up to the court house with your father when he was a member of the Board of Supervisors," and you were "a little boy." Another friend wrote in 1950, "How well I remember first meeting you with your father at a political rally in Peoria."[24]

There is no doubt that during the early, formative years of his son's life the influence of William Joseph Stratton was of great importance. While he was not educated beyond the public schools of Lake County, he read widely and owned a number of books. He kept a collection of

---

*From this point forward references simply to "Stratton" will be to the younger man. When reference is to his father the full name will be used.

Indian artifacts, which his son remembered and credited with interesting him in archaeology.

The influence of his mother upon Stratton during his childhood years was also unusually strong. Zula utilized her skills and experience as a teacher while keeping William out of school until he was nearly eight. He learned to read and write at home before he and his brother Kerwin entered the Ingleside school.[25] A picture taken of the entire school in 1922, when William and Kerwin started the first grade, shows forty-four pupils of varying sizes. The two Stratton boys stand side-by-side, both wearing neckties. Few others were similarly adorned. Tousled blond hair lay across William's forehead.[26]

A person with the character and personality of Zula Stratton, having her son much in her company during the impressionable childhood years, teaching him to read and write at ages when children usually are under the tutelage of a professional in a school setting, must have had a substantial formative influence upon him. A great deal of later evidence bears out that conclusion.

As Stratton grew older, the influence of his father and the political world continued to be strong. Years later, he recalled that "as a boy, it was my privalege [sic] to travel extensively with my father on his many missions in the interest of the infant and struggling [Conservation] Department." William had "many fond memories of visits to the game farm with my father and the thrill of seeing the deer and pheasants."[27]

With William Joseph Stratton in the governor's cabinet during the 1920s, the family was in comfortable circumstances. During summer vacations William and Kerwin enjoyed the out-of-doors. In 1945 a glimpse of a golf course reminded Zula, she wrote to Stratton, "of you boys playing golf when you were so young. Remember how we used to go to Pistauqua Heights three times a week at least? And swimming every day, and tennis and canoeing."[28] In spite of such distractions, William completed the elementary grades in five years, with the benefit of his mother's instruction at home, and at twelve entered Warren Township High School at Gurnee. One of his teachers recalled him later as a "chubby little freshman" in her English class. Midway through his father's term as secretary of state, William finished high school at sixteen and entered the University of Arizona.

It is not surprising that he chose to major in political science, in view of the solid grounding he had already received in practical politics. Later he wrote, "I was literally born into politics and raised in an atmosphere of campaigning." Popular legend to the contrary, he did not campaign with his father in 1926, 1928, and 1932, for he was in high school and then college during those years. He did visit state and county fairs with him during the summers, and attended some political meetings.[29] He learned to know the state and many of his father's political associates. Later he acknowledged that "I gained much of my political knowledge from [my father]."[30] He was well prepared to begin the formal study of politics and government.

Zula Stratton was not in the best of health in 1930 and spent some time during the winter months in Arizona. For that reason the university at Tucson was the family's choice for William. Kerwin later joined him there, and their mother kept house for the two.[31] There is also reason to think that William himself might have been of uncertain health at that time, and that the Arizona experience was for his physical benefit as well his mother's.[32] In any case, the close relationship between the two continued. Kerwin spent one school year at Tucson, then continued his education at North Central College at Naperville, Illinois, where he eventually captained the baseball team.

Tucson in 1930 was almost a frontier town. It had a population of about twenty thousand. Arizona had been a state for only eighteen years, and land near Tucson could still be homesteaded. William's life at the university was uneventful, though apparently satisfying to him. During his first year in Congress, his secretary, John O. Graham, who had also been a student at Arizona in 1930–31, wrote to the Alumni Association: "While at the University, Bill didn't go out for any extra curricular activities. He played tennis quite a bit and served two years in the Arizona National Guard. . . . [He] was a member of Delta Chi, but held no office in his chapter." Stratton recalls that he took part in intramural baseball, softball, and volleyball, as well as tennis. Outdoor sports could be enjoyed throughout the winter.

One of his fraternity brothers, John M. Burton, wrote to Stratton in 1944, "I recall one day at the [fraternity] house when we made a 'deal' that I would be your Adjutant-General when you were elected governor of Illinois."[33] Apparently Stratton, before he was old enough to vote, was ambitious for high political office, so it is surprising that he did not take part in campus and fraternity politics. Perhaps his being two years younger than most of his classmates was the reason.

Stratton's membership in Delta Chi was meaningful to him. He continued the association for many years, attending alumni meetings in Chicago, and in Washington during his service in Congress. He often visited the chapter house at the University of Illinois in Urbana, when as governor he attended football games there. In 1955 became a life member of the Delta Chi alumni association. He also continued his association with the University of Arizona's alumni group for many years after his graduation. His experience in the National Guard was less well documented, for during his time in the Navy he sought to have that service credited to him, and there was difficulty finding any record of it.

While his father was waging the political wars of the early 1930s, Stratton was making his way into the adult world. His work at the university was completed in 1934, earning him a bachelor of arts degree in political science. He returned to Illinois and on September 4 was married to Marion Hook of Gurnee, who had been a friend when he attended Warren Township High School. She was a graduate of Stephens College, in Missouri.[34] At twenty, having lived with his mother during college years, Stratton may have been emotionally ill-prepared for marriage and all of its responsibilities. Before marriage, however, economic realities had to be recognized, and Stratton found a job with the Northern Illinois Public Service Company, a subsidiary of Commonwealth Edison. Times were hard and jobs not easy to get. His father assisted him in securing the interview that led to his employment.

Later Stratton recalled that "it was a time when economic conditions were extremely difficult. Pay was unbelieveably [sic] low, if a job was available at all."[35] His wage was ninety dollars a month, and while his title was "traveling sales trainee" his first assignment was reading meters in Calumet City.[36] Soon he was assigned to Joliet, in Will County, to the bookkeeping department of the company's installation there, where he also worked as a floor salesmen.

With the end of 1936 Stratton was transferred to Morris, in Grundy County, for its area an old and pleasant county seat village, located on the Illinois River and the Illinois and Michigan Canal. Stratton called Morris home for the next thirty years. Natural gas service was newly available there, and Stratton's work was as a salesmen and promoter of gas appliances and furnaces.[37] No doubt the increased responsibility and opportunity for greater earnings were welcome, for a daughter, Sandra Jane, was born in 1936.

Stratton liked his selling job because it helped him meet many people,[38] easing his entry into politics. As early as 1936 he was a Young Republican "captain" in Joliet. At a tense meeting in 1943 between Republican county chairmen and Stratton, then state treasurer, Alfred F. Schupp, the chairman of Will County, declared: "God damn it, I want to talk politics. I recall, Bill, you coming in [in 1936] and, I says, 'Who the hell are you?' And you said, 'My name is Stratton, Bill Stratton.' At that time you were ambitious, and still are. You wanted to get started right, and I . . . told you to go back and get in touch with the committeeman."[39] Stratton followed Schupp's advice and became active in the politics of his precinct and of Will County and then of Grundy County. His work there and in the broader Young Republican organization led to associations that were important to him in later years.

When his father died in 1938, Stratton was living with his family in a small rented house in Morris and still working for Northern Illinois

9

Public Service Company. He had joined the Lions Club, the Eagles, and the Methodist church, and enjoyed outdoor sports—golf, tennis, and hunting—and bowling, when his time and means permitted.

The depression lingered on in Illinois, and Stratton was still earning only a meager wage. The birth of a second daughter, Diana Joy, in 1939, must have made him even more eager to enlarge his income. The two positions of congressman-at-large attracted his attention. Illinois had two such positions because in the past its rapidly growing population had caused its allocation of seats in the United States House of Representatives to be increased, while the internal politics of the General Assembly had prevented any redrawing of district lines to allow all representatives to be elected from districts. Both incumbents were Democrats, and there were no would-be candidates on the Republican side with strong claims on the nomination. After his father's repeated candidacies in the 1930s, the name Bill Stratton was widely known. Years later Stratton observed that in 1940 he did not wish to "waste" the name recognition his father had earned.[40]

Experienced politicians with whom Stratton sought counsel advised him to run in the 1940 primary for congressman-at-large for the experience it would provide, since against a large field of more seasoned candidates he would hardly have a chance of nomination.[41] They did not anticipate the level of commitment and vigor, nor the potency of the name, that Stratton would bring to his candidacy. He filed his primary petitions on February 14, 1940, quit his job, and went campaigning.[42] He was twenty-five years old.

The Illinois in which Stratton sought to be elected to Congress in 1940 contained the geographical center of the population of the United States, and itself was home to almost eight million persons, third among the forty-eight states after New York and Pennsylvania. It comprised fifty-six thousand square miles. To campaign across such an extensive state, with such a large population, was an ambitious undertaking for a young man with meager personal resources, no job, and only limited hope of gaining contributions.

Photographs of the period show that Stratton was dark and slender, careful of dress and grooming when he posed for formal portraits, with some difficulty making his gaze meet the camera eye. An air of pensiveness is often present, but no negative mood marked his campaign.

Stratton hired his cousin, Howard Dibble, to help him with driving the old car in which they also often spent the night. His strategy for campaigning was already clearly formed. He visited as many counties as possible and, before the year ended, had been in at least 95 of the state's 102. He called on Republican county chairmen, other party leaders, and newspaper editors. He built upon the name recognition that he found and took nothing for granted. He also took care to follow closely after Republicans Dwight Green and Richard Lyons, who were contesting for the gubernatorial nomination. Associating himself with neither of them, he took advantage of the public reception of their views to adjust his own. In that way he was able to attract followers of each.[43]

There is no doubt that Stratton's 1940 campaign was conducted on the most frayed, even broken and knotted, of shoestrings. Thomas B. Littlewood observes that "part of Springfield folklore are stories about how various men in high places befriended Stratton years ago when he was scrambling and didn't have money for a train ticket to Chicago."[44] As George Thiem reports: "One legend has it that ... when Stratton arrived in Danville on a hand-shaking tour, he looked so seedy that GOP businessmen took up a collection to buy him some new clothes. [Stratton remembers it as only a new hat.] At another time, according to the late Charles Allison ... top assistant to Senator Brooks, Allison invited Stratton to dinner in Chicago's LaSalle Hotel. Stratton came in a shabby suit and tennis shoes. He was thin and so hungry he ate two full meals."[45] Stratton denies that he ever wore tennis shoes in such a situation.

In spite of such problems, when the votes in the April Republican primary were counted, Stratton had the highest total, by a wide margin, of any of the fourteen candidates for congressman-at-large. He received 372,000 votes, out of a total cast of 1,144,000. By comparison, there were 1,504,000 voters on the Democratic side. Clearly the general election in the fall would be no easy contest. Second Republican to Stratton, and thus in contention for one of the two positions of congressman-at-large, was Stephen A. Day, with 236,000 votes.

Such a large primary field had been to Stratton's advantage. Because votes were divided among fourteen, it enabled him to win decisively with less than one-third of the total. His name was important—many thought they were voting for his father. Willard Ice, a contemporary of Stratton, an attorney, and for many years a valued employee of the Illinois Department of Finance—the Department of Revenue building in Springfield is named after him—recalls that in 1940 "we all felt that Bill Stratton himself was an unknown, elected more than anything on his father's name."[46]

The advantage of name recognition carried on into the fall campaign, but then it was against limited and formidable opposition—Day on the Republican side, and the incumbent Thomas Vernor Smith, a professor at the University of Chicago, and Walter J. Orlikoski, a Chicago alderman, for the Democrats.

Prospects for the Republican ticket in 1940 seemed brighter than they had been for a decade. Fear of involvement in a European war strengthened opposition to the Roosevelt administration. Many opposed the third term that Roosevelt was seeking, and in Wendell Willkie he faced a formidable contender. Democratic governor Henry Horner, elected in 1932 and 1936, was dead. Small and Emmerson were gone from the Republican scene, and with them some of the factionalism that had weakened their party for many years. New leadership had appeared.

Heading the Republican ticket for the United States Senate seat was C. Wayland "Curly" Brooks. He and William Joseph Stratton, both active Masons, had been running mates in the 1930s and in adversity had formed a strong friendship. Brooks was born in West Bureau, in Bureau County, Illinois, in 1898, the son of a Congregational minister. As his father's work took him from church to church, Brooks attended public schools in Dixon, Peoria, Kewanee, Neponset, and Wheaton. He entered the University of Illinois in 1916, and a year later enlisted in the Marine Corps. He won a battlefield commission in France, and was wounded seven times. His father and two brothers also served overseas, and his older brother died in service. Brooks himself received the Distinguished Service Cross and Croix de Guerre, among other decorations. He was active in the American Legion. To a generation that had served in and remembered the First World War, he was a certified military hero.

Brooks attended the University of Chicago after the war, and received a law degree from Northwestern University in 1926. He was admitted to the Illinois bar in the same year. He was an assistant state's attorney for Cook County for seven years and became noted for his work against organized crime during a time—the Capone era—when Chicago was a center of underworld activity. After leading the Republican ticket in 1936 for governor, a strong showing in a decidedly Democratic year, he chose to seek election to the Senate in 1940, for the balance of the term of the late J. Hamilton Lewis. His friendship and support were to be important in Stratton's career.

The Republican candidate for governor in 1940 was Dwight H. "Pete" Green. His career and political involvement were similar to Brooks'. Born in 1897 in Indiana, he served in the First World War and attended Stanford University soon after it ended. He received a law degree from the University of Chicago and was admitted to the Illinois bar in 1922. After 1925 he was associated with the Bureau of Internal Revenue and became a special assistant to the United States attorney for northern Illinois in the prosecution of underworld figures, including Al Capone, in tax fraud cases. He achieved a notable reputation in that activity and served as the United States attorney from 1932 to 1935. In 1939 he ran a surprisingly strong race for mayor of Chicago. Like Brooks he was a Mason and active in the American Legion.[47]

In the company of candidates of the stature of Brooks and Green, and in a year of Republican resurgence in Illinois and nationally, Stratton must have sensed the good chance he had to win election to Congress. As the core of his campaign he adopted a strong isolationist position. As his father had, he ran as the downstate candidate and assailed the Democratic Kelly-Nash organization of Chicago and its two candidates for congressman-at-large. On the whole his campaign positions were those one would have expected, given his background and experience. He had grown up in a home in which opinions were strong against Democrats, Franklin D. Roosevelt, and their domestic and international policies.

The war in Europe became more real in the summer and autumn of 1940, with Dunkirk, the fall of France to the Nazis, and the battle of Britain waged in the skies. Fear of involvement and isolationist feeling were strong in the American Midwest and affected the choices of voters as they went to the polls on November 5. The results in Illinois were favorable to Republican candidates for the first time in a decade. Green was elected governor by 257 thousand votes, while Brooks won the Senate seat by a slim margin of 21 thousand.

For the two positions of congressman-at-large, Stratton was the leader with 2,050,000 votes. The other Republican candidate, Day, was close behind with 2,020,000, while the Democrats Smith and Orlikoski had 1,968,000 and 1,914,000. Stratton's greatest strength, as expected, was downstate. He did well in the collar counties ringing Cook, and had respectable totals in Cook and in Chicago.

Stratton, at twenty-six, was thus elected to the Congress of the United States as his first public office. He was the youngest member in 1941, and was sometimes called "the baby of the House." Because he was elected at-large from a populous state, while most members of the House were elected by districts, he also was able to claim the largest vote. He was well-educated, politically sophisticated, and widely acquainted among Illinois officeholders and other politicians.

As 1940 ended, Bill and Marion Stratton and their daughters, age four and two, closed their modest rented house in Morris and left for Washington, D.C., to make their home near the nation's capital. "Young Bill" was taking a giant step along the political pathway that was so attractive to him.

Young Congressman

Early in 1941, Stratton rented a home for his family in Alexandria, Virginia, and began his work as a freshman congressman. As the youngest member of Congress, he attracted national attention. In April he went to New York City to receive at a luncheon the Advertising Club's "Award of the Rake," given for "the simple virtue of making one's mark in the world by dogged digging into a pursuit." Nine other young men were so honored, including bandleader Artie Shaw and Oren Root, Jr., who had organized Wendell Willkie's campaign for the presidency in 1940.[1]

In 1941 Metro-Goldwyn–Mayer released a motion picture starring Robert Taylor as the outlaw Billy the Kid, and so titled. The name seemed appropriate, and "young Bill Stratton," the "baby of the House," became known to many as Billy the Kid. The name stuck with him for years. It served to imply not only youth on his part but was also intended by some who used it to suggest outlaw inclinations. Stratton was still thin at the time, with dark hair combed back in a pompadour. He favored blue pinstriped double-breasted suits, with the wide lapels of the time, worn with a vest and often with a colorful necktie. A gold watch chain completed the statesman's uniform.[2]

At the core of Stratton's small Washington staff were John O. Graham, who served formally as his secretary, and Marion Keevers, who was to be secretary and later executive assistant throughout his career as a public official. Both were friends of Stratton's from Young Republican days. Graham, of Freeport, Illinois, had been a student and basketball player at the University of Arizona in 1930 when Stratton began his college work there. He was active in politics during the 1930s in Freeport and Stephenson County. Keevers, of Coal City near Stratton's home in Morris, had been Young Republican chairwoman for the twelfth congressional district and Grundy County, and junior Republican national committeewoman. She had worked as a secretary in Morris, Chicago, and Springfield before going to Washington with Stratton. Cheerful and competent, with a positive attitude toward her work, she was to be of much value to Stratton for many years to come.[3]

The avoidance of war was Stratton's first aim, and it was as an isolationist that he was principally known during his first year in Congress. One of his first letters as a member of Congress went to one of the leading Midwest voices of isolationism, Colonel Robert R. McCormick, publisher of the *Chicago Tribune.* He asked that the *Tribune* be sent to him and suggested that it and other midwestern newspapers should be delivered to Washington earlier in the day to counteract the influence of the "Eastern interventionist papers."[4] At that time the endorsement of the *Tribune* was considered essential to candidates running statewide on the Republican ticket.

Stratton's isolationist views, and his critical feelings toward President Roosevelt, led him to actions that earned him, unfortunately for his reputation, the greatest public notice of his first term in Congress. On July 9 he obtained leave from the House of Representatives to extend in the *Congressional Record* his remarks of that day, to include an excerpt from the May 2 *American Guardian,* the publication of George S. Viereck, a propagandist and registered agent for Nazi Germany.

Stratton then had the material in question printed on one side of a postcard. It read:

ROOSEVELT TOURS, INC.

*

EXTENSION OF REMARKS OF

HON. WILLIAM G. STRATTON

of Illinois

IN THE HOUSE OF REPRESENTATIVES

Wednesday, July 9, 1941

*

Article from the American Guardian

*

Mr. STRATTON. Mr. Speaker, under leave to extend my remarks in the RECORD, I include the following article which appeared in the May 2, 1941, issue of the American Guardian. This article is very appropriate at this time, when the administration, in repudiation of its pre-election pledge, is now urging Congress to repeal the present law restricting the service of the National Guard and draftees to the Western Hemisphere.

The article follows:

(From the American Guardian of May 2, 1941)

ROOSEVELT TOURS, INC., ANNOUNCES

FREE TRIPS ABROAD!

"Excursion to Belgrade, Cairo, Buenos Aires, and all corners of the earth.

"Luxurious American flagships.

"All expenses paid—including Bethlehem bayonet, Goodyear gas masks, Du Pont grenades, hospitalization, knotty-pine coffin, dignified white cross, and gold stars for mothers.

"No passport required.

"We have left no stone unturned in our untiring efforts to make this unique trip a reality for this summer—the best that big money can buy is being rapidly made available.

"For further information inquire at the White House or our branch offices at Wall Street and Downing Street.

"'See the world through a gun sight.'

"We plan, you go."

(NOT PRINTED AT GOVERNMENT EXPENSE)

Stratton then placed his congressional frank, his free mail privilege, on the address side of the card, and sent four thousand copies to Republican national headquarters, "for addressing and mailing to the precinct committeemen of Illinois." There is evidence that other copies were distributed in bulk, for further individual mailing.

Stratton knew how strong antiwar feeling was in Illinois, and was attempting to capitalize upon it at the precinct level. Such a position was compatible with his personal feelings and his campaign postures. It also served to make him acceptable to Colonel McCormick and the *Tribune.* But Stratton's actions did not escape criticism at home. In a letter to Edward Lindsey, editor of the *Decatur Herald,* objecting to a critical editorial of October 27, he defended his issuance of the cards, saying:

there is nothing mysterious about these cards. I pay for them, and the law states that they may be shipped by me either in bulk or individually to ... whomsoever I designate.... I have no control over these cards after they leave my office, and people may read them, burn them, or dispose of them as they see fit.... It is through the Congressional Record that the people may know the undistorted views and opinions of the Members of Congress.... Perhaps there are those who do not wish the public to be informed ... but ... I shall continue to exercise my duty by using the means ... provided to the people's representatives for public presentation of issues so vital to every American.

Lindsay apologized for the editorial's having stated that Stratton distributed franked *envelopes* in bulk—which could then have been used for mailing any sort of material—but declared that with the substitution of "cards" for "envelopes" the editorial stood as originally published. "The card you sent," Lindsey wrote, "which indicates that you used your privilege as a congressman to spread upon the Congressional Record clipped matter from the American Guardian ... is even more disappointing than your abuse of the franking privilege. In that instance the ideas and arguments were not even your own."[5]

In the Viereck matter, Stratton's choice of source material was not judicious, and distribution of the cards in bulk to an associate of Viereck's, as it was alleged he had done,[6] was not wise. But as he pointed out to Lindsay it was not an unlawful action and the material in question, which he had openly inserted in the *Congressional Record,* reflected his strongly held views. In any case the incident did not seem to do him grave political harm. It did earn him the disfavor of many Jews in Illinois and elsewhere because of Viereck's role as a Nazi agent.

Foreign policy was not the only arena for Congressman Stratton; he quickly became involved in the whole range of concerns of his constituents, including price control, allocation of scarce materials, location of defense plants and shipyards, and veterans' claims. These were not policy issues for him, but rather matters in which he was often asked to intervene on behalf of constituents. In the policy sphere he was opposed to repeal of the Neutrality Act, the arming of merchant ships, convoy duty for the Navy, lend-lease aid to Great Britain and Russia, and extending the period of service for draftees and National Guardsmen. In these issues his positions were consistent with his chosen role as an isolationist. He also opposed the St. Lawrence Seaway project on the grounds of its cost. An anti-poll-tax bill was one of his keen positive interests, reflecting his training as a political scientist, and he stayed on in Washington in October until it was voted upon. He favored extending the life of the House Un-American Activities Committee.

He also supported Senate Bill 860, which would have prohibited "the sale of intoxicating beverages and the location of vice establishments in the vicinity of training camps." The Woman's Christian Temperance Union and church groups were active in promoting it, and Stratton was strongly for it. "I am unalterably opposed," one of his form responses read, "to placing temptations before the youth of our country serving in our armed forces, and will do everything in my power to combat these evils." (One wonders if he felt the same when he was serving in the Navy a few years later.)

In his first year in Congress Stratton displayed firm and consistent views, as an isolationist and against President Roosevelt and the New Deal. His speech file shows that he relied heavily on information from the Republican National Committee, the House of Representatives Republican Caucus, the America First Committee, and statements and speeches of other Republican members. He was cautious in his dealings with labor and sensitive to special interests such as the Townsendites and the postal workers' lobby. The detail of his work as a congresssman received careful attention.[7]

Stratton displayed unusual political maturity and sophistication for one his age who had not held previous office. He sent hundreds of letters of thanks to party workers and other supporters after his election. He knew the value of political contacts, of the regular renewal of friendships, of thanks given, of not offending other politicians, of the significance of others' turf, and of offering the olive branch of reconciliation when feelings were ruffled. He had sound political instincts. From the time he arrived in Washington he paid careful and continuing attention to Illinois politics.

Another young man might have caught Potomac fever and sought a career in Washington, but it was soon clear that Stratton's eye was on state office rather than a continuing seat in Congress. Although it was certain that Illinois would lose one of its at-large House seats in 1942, Stratton could have beaten Stephen Day, the other incumbent, and he knew it. Instead he was intent on winning the Illinois office his father once had held—secretary of state. Since it was not up for election in 1942, the logical post for him to seek was state treasurer, which was. The constitution prohibited the treasurer from succeeding himself, so there was no incumbent to contend with for nomination or election. It was an office for which William Joseph Stratton had run twice, without success.

In May 1941 Stratton informed officials of the Illinois Republican party that he intended to run for state treasurer, sending a letter to each of four thousand downstate precinct committeemen.[8] By getting his hat in the ring early, he was attempting to discourage other Republicans from seeking the nomination. He argued that his statewide candidacy and victory in 1940 were evidence of strength that would help the party ticket.

Another indication that Stratton had his eye firmly fixed on Illinois in mid-1941 is that he and his wife Marion bought a house in Morris at that time. An elegant, Italianate structure at 437 Vine Street, in a good residential neighborhood, had become available for back taxes plus whatever the Grundy County National Bank had in it. It was a three-story house, with stucco over brick, and with a mansard roof and twin columns flanking the entrance. It had been built in 1869 by Lyman Ray, an early lieutenant governor of the state.

The price of the house was eight thousand dollars, more than the Strattons could manage, so their friend Senator C. Wayland Brooks loaned them half that amount, and they borrowed the balance from the bank.[9] It was to be a home address and political headquarters for Stratton for a quarter of a century, though he lived in it only occasionally. It was a long way up the ladder from the modest rented quarters that had previously been the Strattons' home in Morris.

Vine Street was graced with a number of large, old houses, interspersed with more modest ones. The Stratton's new home at 437 was one of the finest. Next door was a house of the prairie school of architecture, said in local legend to have been designed by associates of Frank Lloyd Wright, if not by the master himself. The street, only a few blocks long, was lined with graceful elms, with their branches arching to meet above it. It was a suitable home for an aspiring politician, from which he might eventually go to the governor's mansion or other high office.

Stratton was deeply involved in the patronage of Illinois politics in 1941. At that time most state jobs were filled by the party and officials in power, and under that system service to party and to successful politicians was more important than merit and qualifications. Stratton knew fully the importance of the patronage system. To a friend who was seeking a state job early in 1941 he wrote: "jobs with the State Civil Service have been more or less [in] name only. . . . Civil Service . . . has been abused so that I would not know of any branch of it where it could be considered really permanent."

Lacking any patronage jobs to dispense in Washington—"under a Democratic Administration it is impossible for any Republican to get any patronage or jobs down here for their friends," he wrote—Stratton turned to the state system for the influence so important to his ambition to win state office. After eight years of a Democratic administration in Springfield, Republicans in 1941 had been hungry for the many jobs that the election of Dwight Green as governor opened to them. There were thousands of applicants. Stratton corresponded frequently in patronage matters with Green and John T. Dempsey, who was chairman of the

Governor's Advisory Committee on Employment. That title was a euphemism for the Governor's Patronage Board, and the realistic Stratton often used that designation in correspondence. Dempsey was also chairman of the Cook County Republican Central Committee. In addition to state jobs, the location of defense plants and employment in them were patronage matters.[10]

Stratton's correspondence in 1941 with political figures in Illinois also touched upon the factionalism that persisted in the Republican party, and his chief concern was gaining the nomination for treasurer. Stratton was aligned with the group that included Senator Brooks, state Attorney General George Barrett, and state Auditor Arthur C. Lueder. Governor Green and those around him represented another faction, which included the incumbent treasurer Warren Wright and Richard Yates Rowe of Jacksonville. One of Stratton's correspondents late in 1941, as he sought support for treasurer, was William W. "Smokey" Downey, who was to play a significant role in his political life for many years to come.

Smokey Downey grew up in Lincoln, Illinois, where his father was involved in county politics. "Raised in a political atmosphere," as he put it, he became a journalist and was attracted to the nearby state capital. There he was employed by the *Illinois State Journal* by 1928 and covered the police, courts, and eventually statehouse political happenings. He was fired in 1938 because he publicly criticized the *Journal* editor, Emil Smith, for what Downey felt was less than full attention to the illegal gambling for which a then "wide-open" Springfield was noted. He was hired by Lake County's Richard Lyons, who was running for the United States Senate, to promote the Republican slate downstate. After Lyons lost, Downey helped state Representative Hugh Cross of Jerseyville become Speaker of the House in 1939, and managed Cross's successful campaign for lieutenant governor in 1940. It was then that he became acquainted with Stratton.[11]

Downey was still working for Cross when he responded to an inquiry from his friend Stratton with a lengthy letter of political gossip and advice, in October 1941. Downey thought Warren Wright would run for the United States Senate, and he advised Stratton that

> Dick Rowe is definitely a candidate for Treasurer. Personally, I still think you are a way out in front. Don't forget, this is not the time to be out in front too far. Stay in Washington, keep your feet on the ground, shoot plenty of correspondence to these county chairmen. Above all, people who are trying to get their sons or brothers out of the army, move heaven and earth in trying to help them. Crack the Tribune a couple of

times, especially about not wanting to send an army of American boys to foreign soil until such time as England sends her own soldiers to fight her battles.

Downey then concluded his letter on a more personal note, which suggested that he and the congressman's staff, as well as Stratton and his wife, were well acquainted.[12]

Another one of Stratton's regular political correspondents in 1941 was Glen D. Palmer, of Yorkville, Illinois. Palmer had known Stratton since he was an infant, and recalled bouncing him on his knee. He had helped William Joseph Stratton in each one of his campaigns and, as an employee of the Department of Conservation when the elder Stratton was its director, had developed the state's first game farm at Yorkville. He had helped William Grant Stratton in his primary and general election campaigns in 1940 and now supplied political information to him in Washington. Palmer hoped to help Stratton win the treasurer's office, and to fill a position in it. He was an agent for the Northwestern Mutual Life Insurance Company, but was chronically short of funds. Later he borrowed money from Stratton in small amounts from time to time.

By April 1941, Stratton had made it clear to Palmer that he intended to run for treasurer. Already the two had their eyes on the 1944 contest for secretary of state, and Palmer wrote Stratton that he believed that Warren Wright, of the Green faction of the party, would be Stratton's principal opponent for the nomination. They were looking beyond the two-year term as treasurer, which Stratton hoped to win in 1942.

In a detailed report of political events in January 1942, Palmer informed Stratton that he

saw Ike Volz, who told me he was never happier than to see you get by the way you were going to do. Said you know Bill is just like the old man. An early announcement that some said was too early scared the pants off opposition. I said where did he get that idea. Ike said following his Fathers [sic] methods. Then we both laughed and Ike said I guess we both know about that and are in the same boat with a future winner.[13]

That proved to be true for Palmer, as he worked for Stratton in the treasurer's office and later for eight years in his cabinet.

Another Illinois correspondent of Stratton's while he was in Washington was his mother. She was living in Libertyville, in Lake County, and planning soon to move to a small house on one of the lakes. Their letters suggest a loving, kind relationship. Stratton sent her money from time to time. In May 1941 she wrote him a letter which is revealing of the family's finances.

> Dear Billy:
> ... I want to thank you for the very nice Mother's Day gift. ...
> Seeing Congress of the U.S. on your check was an added thrill.
> ... I owe approximately four thousand dollars less than I did a year ago ... I have a thousand dollar insurance policy, also around five hundred dollars owed to me, and $20,000 is a conservative estimate of the value of the property.
> Yesterday I paid off $166.00 back taxes ... I'm going to try very hard this summer to sell enough of the vacant [space] to put the house in good repair.
> ... Things look pretty good, and now that I've got the mortgage off the acreage I feel like a new woman.
> ... Love to you all and thanks so much for everything you do for me.
>
> Mother[14]

Stratton's mother had retained a lively interest in public affairs. In 1941 she visited Washington with a group of women to lobby against the lend-lease arrangement for providing war materials to Great Britain and Russia, and also, no doubt, to show off "my son the congressman" to her friends.

Stratton formally announced his candidacy for state treasurer on January 7, 1942. It had been known for months that he intended to do so. Apparently he had been able to secure the support of Governor Green and the Republican organization. Stratton had stressed his own experience in running and winning statewide two years earlier. By seeking another office, he was leaving the single remaining position of congressman-at-large to the incumbent Republican Stephen Day. He used that as an argument for recognition of his candidacy for treasurer.

Although Stratton continued his work as a congressman and did not campaign widely in Illinois before the primary election, he did pay increasing attention to his candidacy and to Illinois personalities. He was concerned with the smallest details of his primary campaign. To the R. E. Shaw Printing Co., in Dixon, Illinois, he wrote: "enclosed herewith find corrected proof of Primary Petition which is o.k. as changed. I would like the print of 'State Treasurer' a little larger, but not quite as large as William G. Stratton."[15]

One of Stratton's regular correspondents in early 1942 was William Peterson, of Springfield, a friend from Young Republican days. Stratton had continued to attend YR functions, such as the state convention in

1941. Peterson was employed in the state auditor's office. He was deeply interested in helping Stratton become state treasurer. He relayed political gossip, such as the alleged sale of jobs in a Springfield munitions plant, and also hard political news and offers of campaign assistance. One of his letters is illustrative of a political practice of the time. It read:

> Just a note to apprise you of current events.
>
> Today something broke which has been anticipated for the past several weeks. [State Treasurer] Warren Wright in a ruthless request asked all employees . . . for a flat 5% of their yearly salary—payable during this day—before the day was out.
>
> Most of the employees are in the lower income bracket and there is desparation [*sic*] in their hearts.
>
> What this means, you will understand more greatly than I, in not only Wright's campaign [he was running for the Senate nomination], but also the one you are more really interested in [secretary of state in 1944].[16]

As a public official Stratton never practiced that kind of sandbagging.

Apparently Stratton had full organization support in the April 14 primary and had done his homework well. Out of a Republican turnout of 937 thousand he gained 625 thousand votes and won in every county. With the nomination safely in hand, he could resume his attention to issues in Congress, and begin his campaign for November's general election.

Stratton's political correspondence increased substantially after the primary election. He wrote a great many letters of thanks to persons who had assisted in his campaign in one way or another—to county chairmen, precinct and ward committeemen, and others. He acknowledged messages of congratulations and offers of support. Would-be jobholders flooded him with supplications, even though the treasurer's office offered relatively few patronage positions. Stratton's political file for 1942 was as bulky as his congressional file, and as carefully and professionally tended. From it it is apparent that he had a wide circle of friends and many acquaintances and that he was outgoing and popular.

At midsummer the Strattons moved back to Morris, leaving on July 18 the house they had rented in Alexandria. As a result of the political life he had chosen, they were to spend little time together as a family during the next seven years. He immediately set about campaigning around the county fair circuit, and traveled to and from Washington during the balance of the year, visiting in Illinois as much as his time permitted. His secretary, John Graham, remained in Illinois after mid-

July to manage the campaign there, and the two were much in correspondence.

Stratton recalls that the 1942 campaign took him into every county.[17] That is probably not literally true, but the evidence shows that he campaigned actively and extensively taking nothing for granted, as was his habit. Already, one of Stratton's political characteristics was evident. He sought always to emerge from campaigning without accumulating grudges that might harm intraparty unity or impede cooperation with members of the opposing party in a legislative setting.

When November came in a year only narrowly Republican, Stratton led the ticket and won with a plurality of 254 thousand votes, beating W. D. Forsyth of Springfield. Senator Brooks won election to a full term by a plurality of 203 thousand, and Stephen Day was returned as congressman-at-large by 86 thousand. Stratton did reasonably well in Cook County, but his margin of victory was downstate. At twenty-eight he was the youngest man ever elected to major state office in Illinois. As 1943 began, he was eager to begin his work as state treasurer and to take the next step toward his larger ambitions.

State Treasurer

Before he took office Stratton had already decided upon the domestic arrangements he would make while treasurer. His father's friend
Earl Benjamin Searcy informed him that "your dad [as secretary of state]
always lived at the [Abraham Lincoln] hotel," and Stratton replied that
he had "decided to live at the Abraham Lincoln and go home to Morris
over the weekends."[1] His presence in Springfield during much of each
week was essential; and who would occupy the fine home in Morris if
not Marion Stratton and the children?

The demands of the patronage system upon the new state treasurer
were heavy. By his own appraisal, Stratton was "inundated" with job
applications. He paid personal attention to all patronage appointments.[2]
It was a disadvantage for him to be able to reward so few of the many
who had helped him—the classic politician's dilemma—for from the
start of his term as treasurer, he had his eye fixed on the office of
secretary of state, and patronage was important toward that end. From
his correspondence it is clear that he was quite active politically.

Jobs were only one form of patronage. The business of the state
was another. In 1942 Stratton exchanged letters with Orville Hodge of
Granite City, about Hodge's help in his nomination for treasurer. After
Stratton won, Hodge solicited some of the treasurer's bonding business
for his insurance agency. Stratton replied, "Dear Orville, ... you may
rest assured you will receive your share of the bonding." Apparently that
was a conventional way of rewarding political supporters. In another, a
considerable number of bankers and insurance agents were paid "for
your services," Stratton wrote, "during the turnover of the Treasurer's
Office ... [in] checking out the accounts of my predecessor."[3] In such
a setting it is not surprising that Stratton gained the reputation of being

a patronage politician during his first term as treasurer. Many who were employed did little or no work, in the tradition of the time.

Regarding the responsibilities of the treasurer, Stratton was diligent in attempting to make a good record. He turned to Rupert F. Bippus, a Chicago attorney and an old friend of his father, among others, for counsel. Stratton was inclined to look to persons who had been associates of his father. In addition to Bippus, Senator Brooks and Glen Palmer come to mind, and others served in a similar capacity as time went on.

Throughout the 1940s Bippus was one of Stratton's most helpful advisers. He was born in Chicago in 1890 and was educated in its public schools and the Kent College of Law, also in Chicago. From 1915 to 1922 he was an assistant city prosecuting attorney. He served Secretary of State William Joseph Stratton as commissioner of securities from 1931 to 1933. He retained a great affection for the older Stratton, and undertook to aid the younger during his campaign for Congress in 1940. Bippus offered much practical political advice.

The Bippus letters, scattered through the Stratton collection, are literate, detailed, informative, and refreshing. In one, written in 1942, he saw Chicago's Mayor Kelly losing support by closing the saloons. "A democrat can't turn reformer in a city like Chicago," Bippus believed, "and especially one who has licensed more saloons and permitted more gambling than any other mayor the city has ever had. The democratic party here thrives on the support of the drinking and sporting element."

After Stratton was elected treasurer in 1942, he named Bippus to "represent him in matters of banking, finance and securities" as chief collateral clerk—principally a political post. Stratton directed Bippus and C. Guy Willard, chief revenue clerk, to carry out a study of the accounting methods employed in the treasurer's office. Accordingly, they submitted a detailed report on May 11, 1943, in which they stated that there had been little change of procedure for "many years," in the face of a greatly increased work load and many more dollars handled.[4]

In June Stratton drew upon that report in contracting with Pearce and Granata, a Chicago accounting firm, "to proceed immediately with the work of putting into effect my proposals for modernizing and improving the system of accounting and keeping of records in the Office of the State Treasurer."[5] In a speech prepared for "Aurora radio" Stratton claimed credit for modernizing procedures in the treasurer's office after "27 years of no substantial change." Among the new procedures was the practice of microfilming all state warrants (checks), a record that proved to be important in the discovery of embezzlement by State Auditor Orville Hodge during Stratton's first term as governor.

State revenues were substantial during 1943 and 1944, since the wartime economy was strong, employment was high, and a scarcity of materials prevented capital spending. Thus Stratton was able to point to a growing reserve, which was invested in United States securities. Such an investment strategy also allowed him to allocate the purchase of war bonds by the state to county and other quotas. That was good politics. It gave him the opportunity to make many friends in the banking community and among volunteer citizen leaders of war bond drives.

Many letters of thanks appear among Stratton's papers as a result of his policy of crediting state war bond purchases to group and local quotas. Illustrative of the political credit to be derived from such a practice is a letter from Gust Maggos, who was chairman of the American Hellenic War Bond Drive. He wrote: "After meeting you, and discussing the State's bond purchase program, I realize I have met the man who can make it possible for our Society to make its national quota.... The eyes of every member of the Order of Ahepa in our nation will be turned upon you ... in anticipation of the huge bond purchase which I trust you will announce in the near future."[6] Such gratitude, magnified many times over, contributed much to Stratton's political capital.

It is interesting to note the state of Stratton's personal finances while as treasurer he was handling and investing millions of dollars of the state's money. Study of his checkbook stubs for the years 1943 to 1948 sheds light on his financial condition. The picture that emerges is one of a lower middle-class young family of the time, living on a salary, having little left at the end of each month despite a frugal life style. Stratton controlled the family checkbook, writing checks each month to his wife for household expenses and paying other bills as they came due. He also regularly sent checks to his mother, to Senator Brooks in repayment of the sum the Strattons had borrowed when the house in Morris was purchased, and to the Grundy County National Bank as mortgage payments. The house was a considerable expense. A pony called Mischief was purchased for Sandra and Diana, and regular payments were made for its board. Stratton's bills at the Abraham Lincoln Hotel were heavy, and in August 1943 he rented an apartment at the Ann Rutledge for seventy dollars a month.

Each month the Stratton checkbook balance fell to near zero. It is the record of a family struggling to get by, with the usual expenditures and limited income. The pony for the children was clearly a luxury and was still remembered by Diana more than forty years later. Stratton must have been aware of the irony of his handling millions for the state while his family found it difficult each month to live on his salary. He was maintaining two homes and providing at least a portion of his campaign costs.[7] Undoubtedly he was receiving contributions toward his political expenses, but that money did not pass through his personal account.

Just as Stratton had decided during the first few months of 1941 to seek state office rather than reelection to Congress, so he made the decision by mid-1943 to run the next year for secretary of state. To serve in the highest office his father had held was his long-time ambition.[8] The man who ousted Stratton's father from the office of secretary of state in 1932, Edward J. Hughes, was still in that position in 1943. In addition to seeking the office his father had held, Stratton may also have had the desire to replace the man who had defeated his father. In any case, he announced quite early his intention of seeking the Republican nomination. Throughout 1943 he traveled widely within the state on official duties and to political events. In July he informed all Republican precinct and ward committeemen of his intention to run for secretary of state. His political files were well organized, and it is clear that his attempt to gain his party's nomination was much more than simply an amateur effort.

Stratton felt that he had Governor Green's support. In December 1943 he told the Executive Committee of the Illinois Republican County Chairmen's Association that after the election in 1942, Green said, "'Bill, I feel that you will be the next Secretary of State.'" Stratton "consulted with [Green] in July," and told the governor of his plans. "'Well,' he said, 'it doesn't make any difference to me, Bill. I don't oppose it.'" With that assurance, Stratton proceeded with plans for organizing and funding his primary campaign.

Then "some two months later.... Senator [Brooks] called [Stratton] and said, 'Bill, the Governor had me in Springfield last night and he said you were definitely out of the picture.'" Stratton said, "I could hardly believe the Governor would do that." Stratton credited Brooks with telling him that the governor "suddenly changed his mind. He was fearing if I was elected there would be undue influence" by Brooks on me.[9]

Apparently Green felt that if Stratton were secretary of state he would defer to Brooks in patronage matters, and as a result Brooks would be in a better position to challenge Green's leadership of the party. Stratton's friend and ally Smokey Downey, who was by then a lieutenant in the Navy, wrote to Stratton on September 15, 1943, with information that Lieutenant Governor Hugh Cross had no intention of running for secretary of state in 1944. Downey continued:

> From what I gathered after talking with ... [Cross] it seems as though Green is definitely of the opinion that Brooks controls you body and soul, and that if you were in the Secretary of State's office you would have no say-so about the running of the office. Hugh is not of this same opinion, but you had

better get busy and stop some of those clowns out there from poisoning the Governor's mind along these lines.[10]

Green preferred Arnold P. Benson, a newspaper editor from Batavia and majority leader of the state Senate, for the Republican nomination for secretary of state. He offered Stratton the party's endorsement for the office of clerk of the Supreme Court, a relatively minor post, which carried a six-year term. Stratton felt it was a dead end and did not wish to seek that office.

Rupert Bippus wrote Stratton a long letter on October 22, 1943, scolding him sharply for his intransigence in continuing his intention to run for secretary of state. He chastised Stratton for rudeness in discussion of the matter with members of his staff and newspaper reporters, including Glen Palmer, John Graham, and Bill Peterson of the treasurer's office, George Tagge, veteran political analyst for the *Chicago Tribune,* and reporter Charles Wheeler. Bippus invoked the memory of "the gentle, kind and considerate at all times, Bill Stratton [the elder] who everyone in Illinois either loved or let alone because he never hurt anyone's feelings, particularly his friends." Bippus reported that Senator Brooks had said "that he had gone as far as he could for you, but he could not break with the Governor. That you must tell anyone who asked ... that, while he had done all he could for you, when the Governor and all the other state officers had taken the position against you, that he [Brooks] then asked you to accept the Supreme Court Clerkship." He reprimanded Stratton for ignoring the advice that friends were trying to give him. "To go very far politically is not something that just happens.... Your father never won by chance.... No matter how much you rode in the seat beside [him] before you were 21, you still were not a season[ed] campaigner in those days." He concluded by pleading with Stratton to do nothing that would be harmful to his future or to his father's good name.[11]

In spite of this advice and of the feelings of Governor Green and Senator Brooks, Stratton confirmed with Republican precinct committeemen, in a letter of October 28, his intention to stay in the primary contest for secretary of state. Then on December 6 he forwarded his petitions to them. He was encouraged by many of his friends to stay in the race and by mid-December he was deeply committed. Withdrawal then would have been an embarrassment and a serious blow to his ambitions.

On December 15 the Illinois Republican County Chairmen's Association unanimously adopted a resolution endorsing a slate for the primary election that included Benson for secretary of state. It also directed the association's executive committee to call upon Stratton to plead with him for "unity and harmony" and to offer him slating for clerk of the Supreme Court. The meeting took place on December 16 in the treasurer's office. The committee made its purpose known. Stratton replied that he welcomed this first opportunity to present his case to an agency of the party. He felt that he had been "an accepted candidate" until late October. He had been in most of the counties, had had a good reception, but then Governor Green turned thumbs down.

Stratton reviewed his political record and said, "I thought we were doing a pretty fair job in dealing with you gentlemen on patronage and things of that kind. I have handled all of it personally." He recalled his father's 1934 and 1936 campaigns for the Republican ticket in a losing cause. "He lost every nickel he had," Stratton said. He also recalled that his father faced a situation similar to his, in 1928. The elder Stratton had initiated a campaign for secretary of state, believing he had Governor Small's support. When he learned that he did not, he refused a lesser offer, and continued his candidacy. Stratton concluded, "I am afraid that has to be my position."

The discussion continued, with Stratton rejecting the idea of running for Supreme Court clerk, which he felt was "a minor political office." He expressed doubt that any agreement made in 1943 would hold after six or twelve years—"it is pretty hard to get them to hold for three or four months." He pointed out that if he "made a deal" he would lose the confidence of many in the party. John T. Dempsey, who was chairman of the Cook County Republican Central Committee, suggested that if Stratton had made patronage promises, that could "be adjusted."

Then Alfred F. Schupp, the veteran chairman from Will County, said to Stratton: "You talk about political friends. You can talk about your friends in Springfield, etc., but that is bullshit. The thing is this: you want a certain job ... think it over damn seriously." Stratton replied: "Now we are down to bedrock." He expressed the hope that whoever wins, it could end amiably. "That is the nice thing about living in this country, gentlemen."[12] The meeting ended with tentative agreement for further discussion, but with the chairmen returning to their homes about the state, it seemed unlikely that another meeting would occur.

The time was full of stress, for before December ended, Stratton's brother Charles Kerwin died unexpectedly of an allergic reaction to one of the medicines used in treating common colds. After an unsuccessful try for election to the state legislature and a venture into selling insurance, Kerwin had been teaching and coaching football at Fox Lake. Perhaps the shock of his brother's death caused Stratton to recall the boyhood days when their father was secretary of state and strengthened his resolve to continue in the race. In any case, by January 3, 1944, he had made the decision to go on with his campaign.

On that date Stratton made a formal response to the Executive Committee of the Republican County Chairmen's Association. He pointed out that he had announced his candidacy in good faith, confident that he had the governor's approval, and stressed his record of strong statewide wins in the general elections of 1940 and 1942 and good performance as treasurer. The governor should not, he felt, have attempted to "purge" him. Was it not the governor who was creating disunity, rather than Stratton? The primary election, he observed, should be a tool of the voters to choose in each party a preferred candidate for each office, not a tool for party leaders to use in enforcing their will. Stressing his service to the party, "just as my father before me," Stratton pointed out that many persons had urged him to run, and he felt an obligation to his party and its members to do so. "Gentlemen, I have concluded to carry my fight direct to the people ... and to the people ... I promise that this important office will not be used for political dictatorship."[13]

Stratton received many letters of support. Often they invoked memories of his father. Typical of them, but with an amusing twist at its close, was one from Frank Phillips, a Republican precinct committeeman in De Kalb, who wrote:

> I want to congratulate you for having backbone enough to not let a political machine run your business. I know that there are others up in this neck of the woods that are for you. I had a great deal of confidence in your father and I think you are a chip off the old block. I saw Mr. Bensons [*sic*] petition in a tavern here, which I think is a poor place for a petition although I frequently go in them myself.[14]

Stratton waged an intensive primary campaign. From February 22 until March 24 he was continuously on the road. He visited fifty-one communities in the first two weeks, and the weeks that followed were similar in pace.[15] Given the highways of the time, and Stratton's reluctance to travel by air, it must have been an exhausting experience.

While Stratton was attending to duties in Springfield and campaigning downstate, his friend Rupert Bippus was looking after the campaign in Chicago and offering advice. On January 17 he wrote Stratton that in an upcoming meeting in Springfield for Republican women "you should expect some women visitors to ask—'why is the young man not in the military service?' You should tell Marion [Keevers] just how you want her to handle such inquiries."

On February 23 Bippus reported in much detail on campaign headquarters in Chicago, giving evidence of the intrigue and paranoia that are often found in such operations. "None of your important men trust each other or even seem to respect one another," he wrote. He was optimistic, however. "Sentiment is growing for you up here and ... it looks awfully good," he concluded.

On March 9 Bippus wrote to Stratton that two top-level operatives "said they were unable to raise any funds whatever, and almost everyone they called on gave them the answer that you were not on the regular ticket [thus] ... they ought not to, or do not want to contribute." He complained that "money is hard to raise in this campaign." Apparently Bippus worked hard at fund-raising. Early in March he reported to John Graham that "I have been hounding George Larson ... since November. This week I rode him hard. Last night he brought in $500.00. The promise was $1000.00. If he thinks that settles things, he is in error. I will worry him into a nervous breakdown."[16]

The campaign was pushed hard in Chicago during the last ten days. Stratton proposed reductions in auto license fees and the sales tax, in view of the high levels in the state treasury. That was clearly a demogogic pose, as those funds would be needed for long-deferred capital projects and the rehabilitation of veterans when the war was over, and he knew it.

In a news release Stratton charged that "the Statehouse machine has brought all its payroll 'Charlie McCarthys' to the foreground to deceive the public.... These manuevers are those of desperate machine politicians staging a P. T. Barnum parade."[17] To a gathering of ward and precinct workers in Cook County, Republican party chairman John T. Dempsey declared: "I don't need your votes: the Governor doesn't need them: the other candidates are as good as nominated, but if your wards and precincts don't carry Arnold P. Benson, don't a damned one of you come to me for any patronage for four long years. Not for a dime! That's all!"[18] Following that order, the campaign in Cook County concluded about as one would have expected. In news columns and editorials the *Tribune* was also on Benson's side.

When primary election day came on April 11, Benson received 401 thousand votes to 303 thousand for Stratton, and he won both in Chicago and downstate. Stratton observed that "the day was anything but good and it rained over the entire state all day, consequently a very light vote was cast. Of course the Governor's organization vote got out and mine did not. Had it been a decent day I believe I would have won."

Navy Lieutenant Smokey Downey wrote from overseas to Stratton soon after he learned of the primary election results. It was his opinion that

Any fellow, as young as you are, who can single handed go up against the big guns in a primary, as you did, and cause them to put their best pressure, yes and funds, out to beat you certainly has nothing to be ashamed of. Remember, Bill, you are plenty young and we all have a long time to live so don't let it get you down. We will be around when some of those "regulars" will be on the sidelines begging for consideration. . . . Those guys will always need the help of us young fellows. . . . Keep your chin up and we will all work out something in the brighter days to come.[19]

Stratton's friend Ruppert Bippus chided him again, however, for his intransigence and urged him to make peace with Green and Brooks.

Stratton feels that his independent stand in bucking the organization slate in 1944 earned him respect and was crucial to his later success.[20] Edward Pree, who was Stratton's administrative assistant during his first term as governor, stated in his memoir that in 1944 Stratton "developed a reputation for independence and the courage to take on the regular organization. People sympathized with his ambition to follow in his father's footsteps." Pree remembers that Stratton "used to say that 1944 was the key . . . the basis for the wide support, personal following, that he developed later on, the key to his whole political future."[21]

Before another candidacy could be planned Stratton still had a number of months to serve as treasurer. The most pressing task after the primary was to trim personnel costs so that the appropriation for the fiscal year ending on June 30 would not be prematurely depleted. A number of persons who had been put on the payroll prior to the primary were terminated soon after. Clearly some of them were doing no useful work for the state. They were political operatives for the most part, who had little expectation of any lengthy tenure. Thus Stratton did not foster any ill will by terminating their employment. It was a grand game of fiscal musical chairs as he attempted to make his appropriation and legitimate personnel needs come out even.[22]

If one of Stratton's objectives in wishing to run for secretary of state in 1944 was to defeat Edward J. Hughes—the man who had won that office from his father twelve years before—it is ironic that Hughes died on June 28. Even if Stratton had survived the primary, he would have been denied the satisfaction of running against him.

Hughes' death made two appointments necessary: one by Governor Green of a secretary of state; and one by the Democratic State Central Committee to replace him as a candidate. It is surprising that the governor chose *not* Arnold Benson, who was the Republican candidate and who would have benefited politically from serving as the incumbent from July until the November election, but instead Richard Yates Rowe. Almost as remarkable was the Democrats' choice of a candidate. The nod went to Edward J. Barrett, who had been both state treasurer and auditor during the 1930s, but who was serving in 1944 in the Marine Corps in the Pacific. It almost seemed as if neither party wanted to win. If Stratton had won the primary election, he might have been appointed secretary of state in July. One with his political instincts would have sought that end.

After a brief period of uncertainty about Stratton's position regarding the support of candidates of his party, it became clear that he would do so. The *Chicago Tribune* reported on August 7 that Stratton, "whose aloofness caused Republican leaders some concern after his defeat in the ... primary, last night declared himself 100 percent for Governor Green and the entire ... ticket.

"I am happy," Stratton stated, "to cooperate in every way. I shall do all I can to reelect Governor Green and the entire ticket. I am not merely saying this; I am proving it by action. I have no personal quarrel with the governor and never have had." On October 10 he wrote to the Republican treasurer of Logan County, saying "as you perhaps know, I have been out doing what I can for the ticket over the State."[23] There is no evidence in his papers, however, of the kind of effort he had made in his own behalf in February and March.

The general election, on November 7, 1944, proved in Illinois to be a toss-up between the two major parties. In his bid for a fourth term as president Roosevelt carried the state by 140 thousand votes over Thomas E. Dewey. Green won a second term as governor by 72 thousand; Democrat Scott Lucas was elected to the United States Senate by a margin of 217 thousand votes over Richard J. Lyons; Democrat Edward J. Barrett, still overseas in the Marine Corps, beat Arnold Benson for secretary of state by 116 thousand votes; for congressman-at-large, Democrat Emily Taft Douglas defeated Stephen Day by 191 thousand. Republican candidates won the offices of treasurer, lieutenant governor, auditor, and attorney general, all by slim margins.

That Benson was beaten in the contest for secretary of state, while other Republican candidates for statewide office were winning, made it possible for Stratton's supporters to assert that he would have won if he had been the candidate. (The contrary, of course, could never be proved.) It was obvious that he fully intended to be back in the political wars before long.

By early December 1944, Stratton had applied to the Navy for a commission. As an elected state officer he was not eligible for military service until he completed his term. He had been sensitive for some time about his lack of a military record, even though he claimed service in the Arizona National Guard while he was a student in college. Assistant Treasurer John Graham had already taken a civilian job in Washington,

D.C., in the Navy Department. He would never again be a member of the Stratton team, since he apparently fell out of favor as a result of inappropriate behavior in 1943 and 1944. Stratton's executive secretary, Marion Keevers, was also in Washington as secretary to Congressman Evan Howell, who represented the Illinois district in which Springfield was located.[24] The group that had worked closely together for four years was going its separate ways.

Anchors Aweigh

Soon after leaving the position of state treasurer in January 1945, Stratton went into the Navy. His first duty was at Cambridge, Massachusetts, where he was sent to Harvard University for training. From there he went to Camp Perry at Williamsburg, Virginia, and then to the Naval Personnel Depot at San Bruno, California. On July 30 he was flown to Hawaii and from there to Guam, and on to Okinawa, where there was a naval supply depot. Stratton, a lieutenant junior grade, earning $166.67 per month, plus $16.67 "sea pay," served on Okinawa as personnel officer with "collateral duty" as legal officer. Even though the war with Japan ended soon after Stratton reached Okinawa, there was much to do and duty hours were long and often arduous.

While stationed at Okinawa his only contact with family, friends, and supporters came through the mail, and his most faithful correspondent while he was in service was his mother. She expressed her ambition for him to be governor and then president of the United States. At the time she was living near Ingleside in a small house she had bought in 1944 and was selling building lots from property she had inherited from her husband. She was anticipating better times ahead when she wrote "it would be rather nice to own my little home all clear, owe no one, and have a car again. Sounds like a beautiful dream, doesn't it? Well, it's what I've been trying for, for a long time. And I think your father would be awfully pleased if he could know that comfort and security were finally achieved. . . . It wasn't any fault of his that there were so many years of worry and want."

Stratton also received and kept a number of letters from his wife and daughters. Those from Marion were quite practical, almost business-like in tone. They began "Dear Bill" and ended simply with her name. She reported selling the family car "for $1225, two pheasants, and a slab of bacon." In a time of meat rationing, she found the latter quite welcome! There was baseball and football news, and the information that she was canning vegetables, and that money was in short supply. Marion also sent political gossip and clippings.

Stratton's daughter Sandra, who was nine, reported, "I rode [the pony] Mischief one day last week." She sent news of her friends and school. She asked if Stratton had seen any Roy Rogers movies on Okinawa. One letter closed, "I am writing to you because it is a language requirement." Diana was six years old and just beginning school. In the fall, in her mother's hand, she bragged "I can read a few words now."

Stratton's mother, always sensitive to political news, in September sent a clipping about Richard Yates Rowe's seeking the Republican nomination for treasurer, which she thought Stratton wanted. She was a baseball fan too, and in late September sent a *Tribune* sports page, which reported that the league-leading Cubs had just beaten the second-place Cardinals in ten innings, four to one. (On the last day of the month they clinched the pennant, their sixteenth [and to date, last], then lost the World Series to the Detroit Tigers four games to three, Stratton learned in later letters.) She had just gotten a new electric stove, and hoped for a new furnace before winter came, "a nice little oil burner— I'll certainly appreciate it, after cutting wood for ten months."

Marion's letters were less frequent and less affectionate than those from Stratton's mother. She often seemed to be out of sorts, and her letters were remarkably matter-of-fact for a young woman writing to her long-absent husband. In late October she reported raking leaves and planting bulbs. And "I've moved the furniture around in the south living room five times in the last week trying to get it to look comfortable and it still isn't anything to talk about."

In the fall of 1945, with a primary election coming soon, the political pot began to bubble. Early in October, Stratton's mother sent him a *Tribune* clipping of a George Tagge column. It recalled that when Stratton left Springfield in January 1945, he was thinking of running for treasurer in 1946. Even so, Republican Richard Yates Rowe was busy lining up support for that post. Friends of Stratton had been urging Governor Green to slate him for the congressman-at-large seat held by Emily Taft Douglas, Tagge reported.

Again, in November, Mrs. Stratton offered political news and enclosed a Tagge column in which it was reported that "word from Okinawa that William G. Stratton will not consider suggestions that he run for congressman-at-large opened the field for others. Stratton wrote ... that under no circumstances would he be a candidate" for Congress. Tagge reported that Stratton "still intends to run for state treasurer against the Green entry, who is likely to be Richard Yates Rowe of

Jacksonville." Mrs. Stratton was still hopeful that her son would run for treasurer. She wrote that "the Governor would surely lack common sense if he repeated his tactics of . . . [the 1944] campaign."[1] It appeared that another confrontation between Green and Stratton was in the making.

Stratton was receiving news of political doings from a number of sources. His old friend and former chief clerk in the treasurer's office, Glen Palmer, wrote late in October. He sent clippings detailing the formal announcement by Rowe of his candidacy for treasurer. "The boys are getting just a bit anxious to start the campaign," he reported. "I think all of your old bunch are going all out for you." There had been much illness in Palmer's family in 1945. "Sure will be glad [to] get back on a payroll if possible," he suggested to Stratton. "Believe me I think of the red dog games a lot of times when I am trying to keep two nickels in my pocket. [I] am broke about all the time." His interest in helping Stratton win office was understandable.[2]

Stratton, before he left the United States, had put together a team to look after his political interests. His objective was to secure endorsement from the governor for the nomination for treasurer, if that could be done, and to conduct a primary campaign in opposition to the organization choice, if it could not. The team included George Storey of Washington, Illinois, who was Republican chairman of Tazewell County; Dwight Davis, a veteran politico from Rushville; George Perrine from Aurora; Earl Madigan of Lincoln; Rupert Bippus; and Glen Palmer. A meeting of the Stratton team in September went poorly. The chief problem was lack of a statewide organization.

Another meeting of the Stratton team took place on November 9. In addition to those mentioned above, others present included Chester Todd and Andrew Fasseas of Chicago, and Charles Burgess of Aurora. Perrine informed the group that he had conferred with the governor but had gained no useful information. "Of course you and I know," Storey wrote, "how practically impossible it is for one to get anything definite out of him." Then a few days later State Superintendent of Public Instruction Vernon Nickell "delivered a message" from the governor, to Perrine, intended for Stratton, to the effect that "if you would run for Congress the Gov. would support you for Secretary of State in '48."

The Stratton team disagreed on the course to follow. It was learned that neither Senator Brooks nor the *Tribune* would support Stratton for treasurer. All except Madigan felt that he should run for Congress. Storey reported that "nothing . . . has been done in all of these months toward setting up a real statewide organization. I could see nothing but defeat for you under such circumstances."

One can imagine the difficulty Stratton was having, one-third of the way around the world on Okinawa, in trying to decide what to do. He sent many early Christmas cards, and in a number of them he asked for political information and for opinions about which office he should seek. The homemade card showed a mantel with stockings labeled "Marion," "Sandra," and "Diana" on one side of a body of water, and on the other a palm tree and a stocking marked "Bill." It produced considerable correspondence and comment, which allowed Stratton to gain the benefit of a number of separate opinions. That was its intended purpose.

Earl Madigan replied from Lincoln, "Received your Christmas card five minutes ago.... You probably will never be able to realize how much it was appreciated by this Irish family." A long letter of political news and analysis followed. In the months and years that lay ahead, Madigan proved to be one of Stratton's most perceptive advisers.*

Republican state Senator Charles W. Baker of Davis Junction wrote expressing the hope that Stratton would "be home in time to run for Treasurer. Politics sure is rotten I am getting Damn sick of the way things are going [sic]. I guess it won't be any better until Green and [Mayor] Kelly get out."

On December 1, Rupert Bippus informed Stratton that the "plan I have been working on has now developed to point [sic] where it is necessary we talk direct." He suggested a phone conversation but there is no evidence one took place. Bippus wished to fill the place of Stratton's primary adviser.

On December 11, Perrine, Bippus, and Todd jointly wrote a letter to Stratton. Readers of these pages have already become acquainted with Bippus. Todd was a young Chicago businessman. Perrine was a politically active attorney from Aurora, a member of the Republican State Central Committee. They enclosed three copies of a "declaration of candidacy" for the position of congressman-at-large, and three envelopes, one addressed to each of them. They strongly advised him not to seek the office of treasurer but instead the position in Congress for several reasons: the Illinois Republican delegation in Congress, including Senator Brooks, and Vernon Nickell, Lieutenant Governor Cross, and Smokey Downey all favored such an arrangement; the Republican organization throughout the state approved it; money would be hard to raise; the Cook County Republican organization was too dependent on state patronage to oppose the governor's wishes; the *Tribune* would not support Stratton for treasurer; and a primary campaign with him on Okinawa would be

---

*"This Irish family" has proved to be quite a political one. In 1972 Earl Madigan's son Edward was elected to the United States House of Representatives, and eighteen years later continued to serve there, and in 1986 Earl's son Robert was elected to the Illinois Senate.

difficult. His three friends also informed Stratton that the governor had told Perrine "that he had nothing personal against you and that if you would be a candidate for congressman at large he would welcome you into the picture in 1948." Perrine said that when he talked to the governor he "mentioned that certain fellows would have to be taken care of in any picture that would entail a change of position on your part and he agreed to that." "For your personal information this has to be it," they concluded. They asked that a signed declaration of candidacy be sent separately to each of them, one on each of three days, to guard against loss in the mail.[3] The situation was one in which Stratton had little choice but to seek the nomination for Congress. Still he delayed making the final decision.

Stratton's mother was continuing in her letters to express the hope that he would run for treasurer, while Marion's letters reflected little interest in which office her husband might seek. She informed him instead that the winter had brought much cold, snowy weather, that coal was hard to get, that she had bought a Christmas tree and second-hand bicycles for the girls, and that the family had Christmas dinner at home.[4]

Bippus wrote on December 28, in alarm because he had not received Stratton's declaration of candidacy. He, Perrine, and Todd had released to the newspapers word that Stratton would run for Congress. Bippus admitted that the incumbent, Emily Taft Douglas, would be hard to beat in November, and that she might step aside in favor of her husband Paul (later a United States senator) who had left positions as economics professor at the University of Chicago and member of the Chicago City Council and gone into the Marine Corps as a private early in the war. He was wounded and promoted to major. Bippus was trying to review all the facts of the matter, for the time for filing petitions was growing short.

Bippus then turned to more personal matters. All was not well with the Stratton's marriage. "Bill," he wrote,

> you may hear things about conditions at home. Marion seems so weary and discouraged when she talks to me if there is the slightest indication of gossip.... There are more gossips ... to the square inch in Grundy County than any other like area....
> I just don't believe that you and Marion can ever continue to live in that County. I don't hesitate ... to tell her that I hear gossip and also tell her she can't fool anybody ... I think it really hurts her when I talk to her like that. . . . I think since 1940 your ambitions have certainly come ahead of Marion and the children. I know you don't mean that, Bill. You just have

faith until you get back and start your life anew—domestically, socially, politically and every other way.

Apparently Bippus took seriously his intention to advise Stratton as his father might have. The strain of Stratton's long absences from home, while he was treasurer and now while in the Navy, was endangering his marriage.

Chester Todd wrote on January 7, 1946, also to urge the return of the statements of candidacy. "There are a couple of guys in this town who are your friends and would like to help you get someplace in politics but if you don't help us help you we are helpless." He concluded, "If they get lost in the mail you have not only made a damn fool of yourself but also of your friends who stuck their necks out and made the deal."

Within a few days Stratton returned the signed declarations of candidacy for Congress. That decision elicited a number of expressions of approval. State Representative Henry J. White of Somonauk wrote, "More power to you Bill and you better hurry back—H[ell] is popping around the battle scarred elephant here in Illinois, he needs some blood transfusions." Dr. Austin Kingsley of Jacksonville had a different view of the matter. "Listen to me," he wrote, "do not be a candidate for Congress against Emily Taft Douglas—they are just putting you against her to passify [*sic*] you. . . . The trade is on and don't let them kid you . . . I have talked to big republicans and democrats and I know what I am talking about."

Charles Burgess was also dubious about Stratton's chances. "No one but a Republican woman can beat Mrs. Douglas," he wrote. Defeat would end Stratton's career and he should stay out of the contest in 1946. Burgess wanted Lieutenant Governor Hugh Cross to run for governor in 1948, with Stratton for lieutenant governor or treasurer, and for governor in 1952. "I think you're the kind of man we need in public office," Burgess wrote, "but I don't think you're taking the right steps to arrive at the right place at the right time."

Burgess, an industrialist, had emerged in politics almost overnight in 1944. He had so impressed fellow Republicans that he quickly became dominant in his party's affairs in Kane County. He was being mentioned as a potential candidate for United States senator or governor. That scenario was not to be, but for the next twenty years he was one of Stratton's most influential advisers and, by Stratton's appointment, filled important public positions.

John Graham, formerly congressional secretary and assistant treasurer for Stratton and now a lieutenant (jg) in the Navy, had also been on the Christmas card list. He responded on January 8. He had been in

Springfield when it became known that Stratton was going to seek the nomination for Congress. Graham reported that Governor Green had told George Perrine to see that Stratton made that decision. Green "was plenty pissed off at Perrine [whom he had appointed to the Illinois Commerce Commission]," Graham wrote, "and I understand laid the law down to him last month." When Stratton made his decision known "all hands breathed a sigh of relief." Graham concluded by making a pitch for his former job when Stratton returned to Congress. Later in the winter Graham was out of the Navy and employed by the State Department. He was looking for other work and complaining that Stratton had answered none of his letters. During a visit to Chicago he had "made a touch" for one hundred dollars on Chester Todd.

George Perrine wrote to Stratton on March 19, offering much the same information that Bippus had already provided. Obviously each wished to appear to be Stratton's principal agent. Perrine and Downey had been touring downstate and talking for Stratton. Governor Green was cooperating fully: "The Governor has taken care of everything we have asked him to in regards to patronage," Perrine assured Stratton, "and the deal is . . . that anyone who is one of your No. 1 men will be taken care of." The governor was paying billboard costs for Stratton. "He has assigned a car to us—Earl Madigan is driving," Perrine went on. "Earl is now on the Governor's payroll for $300 a month in Public Works and Buildings. This leaves him free to work with me at all times." Perrine asked Stratton to let him make all press releases. He was confident that 1946 was going to be a Republican year.[5]

Stratton spent an uneventful seven months on Okinawa, except for the September typhoon, when he was living in a tent. He thought and talked a great deal about Illinois politics during his time on the island. Letters in 1947 and 1948 from his friend D. C. Christenson, who had been with him on Okinawa, and who was still in the Navy as a lieutenant commander, suggest the content of some of the discussions. The Stratton Christmas card was a carefully planned move, in Christenson's recollection, to bring Stratton to the attention of a number of persons in Illinois who were important to him and to gain information from a number of sources, independent of one another, so Stratton could have the most complete picture of political conditions at home.

Apparently Stratton told Christenson that when he became president of the United States, Christenson could be his naval aid. In 1948 Christenson wrote to say "just give me a buzz whenever you are ready for that Naval Aide that you said you might need someday, and I will be glad to shoot the breeze with you on the fantail of a yacht over a highball while cruising down the Potomac." When he learned that Stratton was running for secretary of state in 1948 Christenson wrote, "most happy to hear the good news about your future moves in Illinois. That is the job we wanted on Okie."[6] The top supply officer on Okinawa inscribed a picture he had given to Stratton, "to the Senator."[7]

Life for Stratton on Okinawa had been much like peacetime life in the service at any remote outpost. After work hours were over he enjoyed the company of an affable circle of young officers. Kent Randall of Blackwell, Oklahoma, wrote late in 1946: "haven't had a good gin rummy game since I last saw you." In 1948 Christenson wrote Stratton that he had "recently been sorting out some of my Okie pictures and find quite a few with you leaning on that quonset hut bar.... I ... remember with a smile the wild jeep ride one dark night after much revelry in the Club when old Doc Nanny fell out of the jeep. Also remember the Capt's dilemma about the little tent back in the hills?"[8]

Years later, after Stratton had completed two terms as governor, Clyde Byerly wrote from Pennsylvania to say, "I cheerfully remember 'Let the people rule, let the people pay' and much more pleasantries from our Naval careers.... At least once a year I tell the story about the Shore Patrol and the pelvic bone from the Red Cross and the 'sleuth' who solved the crime." Stratton replied at length and cordially. "What a pleasure," he wrote, "to hear from you and be reminded of those old rollicking days!"[9]

Stratton left Okinawa and was at sea enroute to the United States when he learned that he had been nominated for a seat in Congress in the April 9 Illinois primary. He won a smashing victory, with 368 thousand votes to a total of 70 thousand for his three opponents. He arrived in Norfolk, Virginia, on April 29, 1946. When he was released to inactive duty on June 7, his papers show that he was five feet, nine and one-half inches tall, still slender at 146 pounds, with brown hair and blue eyes.

Stratton's primary election victory elicited many letters of congratulation, advice, and supplication. Charles Burgess wrote on April 10, saying that if Stratton could win in November he would be the next governor. Burgess warned that victory over Mrs. Douglas would come hard, since "some Republicans," including state officeholders, would support her. "The partial sell out to the Kelly machine is still going on," he declared. "The Republican Party in the state of Illinois is lower than a snakes hips and its [sic] getting lower every day."

Earl Madigan and John Graham were quick to claim places on the Stratton bandwagon. Madigan was proud that Logan County had gone strongly for Stratton in the primary, and his precinct especially so, by 205 votes to only 9 for the three opponents! In vain, Graham was bidding strongly for a place on Stratton's team. On April 18 he wrote advising that Mrs. Douglas had a voting record that was "radical" and "leftist" but that Republican women would still tend to support her.

Graham was eager to recover his old job as congressional secretary, but Stratton had not forgotten Graham's inappropriate behavior while assistant treasurer. Graham made a point of saying that he had not had a drink for several months. Stratton replied to the effect that Graham should not participate in his campaign. Graham wrote expressing his disappointment. In his behalf he "realized," he argued, "that my actions were not above reproach when I was in Springfield. I drank too much, slept too late and didn't make any bones about going around with Erma. As far as that goes, I guess none of us used our heads. . . . I got a divorce without any fan-fare and married Erma. I feel I have atoned for my wrong-doing on that score." He had quit drinking and learned how to get to work on time. "Somewhat hurt" that he was not to be in the campaign, he still hoped to be secretary to Stratton. He asked for a prompt reply.

While Stratton was in Washington in May, with Governor Green, to host a party for the Illinois congressional delegation, he visited briefly with Graham. Apparently Stratton suggested that he might arrange a job for Graham, on one payroll or another. Graham wrote in June to remind him of it. Then in late July he wrote again. No job opportunity had come to him, he was in financial distress, and "embarrassed" to be writing to Stratton again. He reargued his case for being admitted to the Stratton team. "I have no other means of livliehood [*sic*]," he pleaded, "nor did I have any other income than that which I received from you; I have therefore, not much to turn to except you. . . . I went into the Navy as I thought it might help our organization, all I got out of that was dysentery. Please let me hear from you, Bill." His letter was marked "file." There is nothing in the record to suggest that it was ever answered.

John Graham did not again play a significant role in any of Stratton's campaigns, nor did he gain a position in any office that Stratton held. While Stratton displayed a high degree of loyalty to many of the persons who served him faithfully, he could be decisive in ignoring the pleas of those, like Graham, who had been associated with him but who had fallen out of favor.

Early in June, Richard Yates Rowe, who was the Republican candidate for treasurer, wrote to Stratton suggesting a campaign strategy. He proposed that the candidates for state office make the county fair circuit in July and August, then for five weeks beginning immediately after Labor Day, take a caravan into every downstate county, with the last month of the campaign to be spent in Cook County and Chicago.[10] That was essentially the plan Stratton followed in 1946 and in later campaigns.

It was generally recognized that Representative Emily Taft Douglas was a formidable opponent. She was the daughter of the noted sculptor Lorado Taft; and while her husband Paul had yet to gain fame as a

United States senator, he was a well-known economist, former Chicago alderman, and Purple Heart veteran of World War II. Mrs. Douglas was a prime target of some Republicans in the Congress and of the Republican National Committee. Charles Burgess urged an attack on her as one who "votes on the Communists [*sic*] dictate." He referred to her as a " 'Red New Deal' Democrat with a definite Communist voting record." There were not many women in Congress in 1946, and the contest between Mrs. Douglas and Stratton attracted wide attention. Ed Pree recalls that "it put [Stratton] . . . in the spotlight nationally."[11]

Upon Stratton's release from active duty, and after a brief visit with his wife and daughters, he immediately began an intensive round of campaign appearances. Not in office nor gainfully employed, he was conducting his campaign with only meager resources. His checking account balance in Springfield's First National Bank on June 2 was $114.73. Throughout the rest of 1946 that account reflected ordinary household expenditures, board for the pony Mischief, dues to the Morris Lions Club, insurance premiums, taxes, and in September and October political obligations—$1635 to the Midland Advertising Agency, in three installments, and $619.50 to the Morrison Hotel in Chicago, where Stratton had his headquarters during the last four weeks of the campaign.[12] Undoubtedly other political debts were paid in cash. It is evident that day-to-day living expenses for the Stratton family came from political contributions. The candidate had to live, and without other income, contributions for political purposes were his only source of funds. He also found it necessary to borrow money. Some assistance in the campaign was donated. For example, Smokey Downey, who was out of the Navy and working for Lieutenant Governor Hugh Cross, felt that the party was not helping Stratton, and volunteered his assistance in both the primary and general election campaigns. Years later he recalled that he had liked Stratton personally and could see his potential for higher office.[13]

It is evident that Stratton, in the 1946 campaign, was trying to find a broader philosophy than he had displayed in his earlier term in Congress. In a news release he stated that "we must stand ready . . . to help and encourage the forces of decency and humanity throughout the world while remaining steadfast in our opposition to those doctrines whether called Communism, fascism, or imperialism which seek to deny the rights and dignity of the human being."[14] In 1941 he hardly would have expressed himself in that way. In matters of this sort, Rupert Bippus was an influential adviser.

As a part of his campaign, Stratton paid for subscriptions to *The Republican* magazine and sent them to a number of Republican women's clubs, county chairwomen, and other women of influence. He received a number of letters of thanks—most of them thoughtful and articulate, obviously coming from the kind of opinion leaders he hoped to reach to offset the appeal Emily Taft Douglas had for women.

One letter of another kind illustrates a different sort of mind-set with which Stratton had to deal. Its writer, of Chicago, was

> concerned with the meat situation, food, housing, cars, etc. I want the times we had when I was a child 40 or 50 years ago we were happy then.... Then comes the Colored Race, I do not hate them or dislike them, but do not care to live next door to them, or mix with them, why not give them a Southern State all of their own they would be a lot happier so would we. Why don't we refuse to help the world, mind our own business, and that will be the end of all wars.

The caravan of Republican candidates through downstate counties began on September 3. From October 9 to 12, Stratton was in Chicago campaigning with Governor Green. From October 14 to November 4, he was headquartered at the Morrison Hotel in Chicago. As he campaigned, Stratton was attempting to find issue positions with which he could be comfortable and with which the voters could be reasssured. The general issues of the campaign, as seen by Republicans, were the meat shortages, the Communist threat, the rights of labor, reducing the expenditures of government and the size of the bureaucracy, and the housing shortage, which was severe as millions of veterans returned to civilian life. Stratton blamed price controls for shortages of meat, housing, and materials.

In Chicago on October 21 he linked Emily Taft Douglas's name to Moscow and communism. He referred to a broadcast from Moscow on October 20 which urged "election of [CIO-Political Action Committee]-backed candidates. . . ." Stratton declared that "the intimate connection between Communism, the PAC and PAC-backed candidates such as Mrs. Douglas has been brought out into the open. The pink badge of approval so graciously extended by Stalin is the direct result of Mrs. Douglas' voting record during the past term of congress. It is a matter of record that Mrs. Douglas followed the Moscow party line on twelve important bills in which the PAC was interested."

In a speech on WENR radio on October 31, however, Stratton did not link Mrs. Douglas' name to communism, nor did he make any implication of such an association. He saw the main issue as one of "regimentation" against "freedom" and "home rule." He was opposed to the New Deal and its bureaucracy. The Communist threat disturbed him. He wished to see the costs of government lowered and a 20 percent reduction in income taxes. He also stated that official corruption should be uncovered.

In Bloomington, late in October, he expressed support for the United Nations Organization, soundly managed aid to other nations, self-determination for all nations, cooperation with other great powers, and no domination by any great power. He felt that "the maintenance of a strong, solvent, free America is the basis of our greatest contribution to world order."[15] This speech is a fair reflection of Stratton's views at that time. It also clearly indicated a progression from his thought while in Congress in 1941 and 1942. Since that time, he had had the broader experience of state office, military service, and travel abroad and the added maturity of five eventful years, coming at an age when his opinions were still being formed.

As the campaign neared its end, Stratton advertisements were placed in the state's leading newspapers and in a number of labor publications. The costs of such advertising were not great. Radio was little used and, of course, television not at all. It was clearly a low-budget campaign. However, in a time when Stratton did not travel by air, the investment of his time and energy in ground transportation was great.

The general election was on November 5. It resulted in a strong Republican resurgence, as voters blamed their problems on Democratic incumbents. Richard Yates Rowe won the office of treasurer with a plurality of 479 thousand votes; Vernon Nickell was elected superintendent of public instruction by 520 thousand; while Stratton trailed the party ticket with a margin of 367 thousand over Emily Taft Douglas. Only Stratton was running against an incumbent. He did much better than many expected him to and the fact that it was a distinctly Republican year brought him victory.

Years later, in writing his autobiography, Paul Douglas remembered that in 1945 and 1946 "Emily was making a splendid record in Congress." Working against her reelection were the strong public desire for rapid demobilization, which she was cautious about, a widespread fear of Russia, strengthened by Communist infiltration of unions and liberal organizations, and meat shortages due to price control. It was a "pork chop" election. Emily was "attacked by both right and left," Senator Douglas recalled, and lost her seat in Congress while leading the ticket of her party.[16]

Charles Burgess wrote to Stratton on election day. "You didn't specifically accuse Mrs. Douglas of being definitely affiliated with the Communist regime," he charged, "and then follow up and prove by disclosing her voting record. I am really sorry you didn't do this." On the next day, when the election returns were known, he wrote to say, "Next to you I believe I am the happiest man in Illinois."[17] There were times during the next two years when he was less pleased with Stratton.

5

Back to Congress

In December 1946, Stratton rented an apartment on Sixteenth Street in Washington, D.C., for eighty-nine dollars a month. He was to live there alone when Congress was in session while his family stayed in the house in Morris—a situation little different to them from his tour of Navy duty.

With the end of World War II and the return of servicemen to civilian and political life, there were many new faces in Congress. Altogether seventy veterans were elected in 1946. In addition to Stratton, other newcomers who were to gain future fame, by one course or another, included Senators John W. Bricker, Henry Cabot Lodge, Jr., and Joseph R. McCarthy and Congressmen Richard M. Nixon and John F. Kennedy. Bricker was fifty-three, Lodge was forty-four, McCarthy thirty-five, Nixon and Stratton both thirty-three, and Kennedy twenty-nine. Nixon, like Stratton, had won election in 1946 while implying Communist connections on the part of his opponent, a strategy of many Republican candidates that year.

U.S. News & World Report said of Stratton, not altogether correctly, that he "brings a resolute isolationism and conservatism back into the House as the result of the only state-wide contest [for Congress] in Illinois. . . . He defeated Mrs. Emily Taft Douglas, who, in a single term in the House, had acquired a considerable reputation as a liberal. Mr. Stratton's campaign emphasized the Communist menace."[1] It is an indication of the national attention Stratton attracted to note that he was one of only a few freshmen congressmen, out of many, who were named in this analysis.

Upon Stratton's return to Congress, Marion Keevers had come from her position as secretary to Congressman Evan Howell to assume a key position in Stratton's office, the role she had filled in his earlier public positions, in Congress and as state treasurer. Bill Peterson resumed work for Stratton in the Illinois end of the operation. Stratton helped John Graham get the job of majority printing clerk in the House.

Stratton had no lack of friends in Illinois who were eager to advise him. Rupert Bippus and Charles Burgess were regular correspondents. Smokey Downey continued to offer advice while he was administrative assistant to Lieutenant Governor Hugh Cross. He suggested that Stratton offer special services to all Navy veterans in Illinois. "You would certainly be making quite a hit," wrote Downey,[2] himself a former Navy officer.

Stratton had hardly settled into his congressional term before advice about the next office he should seek was coming in. Earl Madigan wrote in March about constituent matters and included some political talk. He had been sounding out Republican opinion from Rockford to East St. Louis and had picked up some interesting news. "I feel a campaign coming on," he said.[3]

Glen Palmer also wrote in March chiding Stratton for not answering Vernon Nickell's letters. "Bill," he said, "I had hoped you had got over that habit of not writing your friends." Stratton was diligent with routine political correspondence but often lax with personal letters. Palmer had recently cooked Sunday dinner for Nickell. The menu was pork roast and boiled potatoes, "so I gave him a Hell of a good jolt of liquor so the food might taste a little better," Palmer wrote. Nickell too had been an associate of Stratton's father.

Palmer wrote again after the Chicago mayoral election in April, which ended badly for the Republican candidate, Russell Root. Following a trip to Springfield, where "things are really starting to boil," Palmer reported that he "didn't hear a single person say Green can be Governor [again]. . . . Personally I cannot see where he has a chance. . . . Cooney Becker [formerly state treasurer] spent ten minutes telling me what a S of a B Green was."

Palmer saw as potential Republican candidates for governor in 1948, in addition to Stratton, Attorney General George Barrett, Director of Conservation Livingston Osborne, Conrad Becker, Treasurer Richard Yates Rowe, and Congressman Everett Dirksen. He had heard of no one but Stratton for secretary of state. On the Democratic side for governor he reported talk of Senator Scott Lucas and Secretary of State Edward J. Barrett, but neither Adlai E. Stevenson nor Paul Douglas was mentioned.[4]

George Perrine agreed with Palmer about the impact of the mayoral election upon Green's prospects. "You asked me in your last letter," he wrote to Stratton in April, "to . . . analyse [sic] the effect of the Chicago morality [sic] election upon Mr. Green's aspirations. It's a little early to make an accurate analysis, Bill, but I would say that Green's national picture has been deflated almost entirely." Charles Burgess agreed that

Green had "lost a great deal of prestige as a result of the Chicago election. . . ." He urged Stratton to run for governor in 1948 and believed he was the only Republican who could win. He thought the Democrats might run Chicago Mayor Martin Kennelley.[5]

Earl Madigan felt that the Centralia mine disaster was a great discredit to Governor Green.[6] Occurring on March 26, it had claimed more than one hundred lives. The *St. Louis Post Dispatch* alleged that Green's Department of Mines and Minerals had been "shaking down mine operators for campaign funds, using the mine safety inspectors as collection agents!"

Madigan agreed that the Chicago mayoral election had reflected badly on Green and said that downstate county chairmen had been asked to send workers into Chicago during the campaign. Many had refused. Sinon Murray [a Republican leader in Chicago] "stopped this order in . . . Auditor Lueder's office. [Treasurer] Richard Yates Rowe told people to ignore it." Madigan felt that more than half of all "working, thinking" state employees would seek new jobs if Green were nominated in 1948. The descriptive phrase most often heard by Madigan of Green was "dead duck." Rowe was willing to run for governor, but Green would not let him.[7]

Glen Palmer continued to be a faithful correspondent. On June 17 he reported that after "listening around the Capitol and Abe Lincoln [Hotel] I think [Green] has slipped more than ever." Members of the General Assembly "are not following his requests." In July Palmer informed Stratton that Sam Parr [of the Department of Conservation] wanted to have him judge in an "agricultural show, in order to get you before the public, and plans on one of his dinners and Poker parties. . . . Then the latter part of November 'Sunshine' Graeffe, who works in conservation and incidentally is the fellow who raised the red setter dog I have, wants us to come to Springfield for a couple of days quail shooting."[8]

While Stratton's friends were keeping him abreast of political happenings at home, he was deeply involved in his duties as a member of Congress. A carefully kept file of responses to constituent views suggests that he was more systematic and often more noncommittal than he had been during his first term. Over and over he replied that the matter in question would "receive my careful consideration." Matters that were most often called to his attention were the reduction of income taxes (which he favored), public housing (he supported the Taft-Ellender-Wagner bill, which passed), the peacetime draft, civil-service salaries and retirement (he generally favored higher salaries), rent control, and the fate of displaced persons in Europe. Other concerns often called to his attention included labor issues and rates for postage to foreign countries.

Stratton's "case work"—requests for assistance of some sort in contrast to comments upon proposed legislation—was filed by county, suggesting future political use. The most common subjects were veterans' problems, immigration matters, requests for government publications and copies of particular bills and reports, complaints about mail service, and appointments to the service academies.

Stratton did not introduce many bills in 1947 and 1948; one, however, HR 2910, attracted more attention than would a dozen on more routine subject matters. It concerned the admission of "displaced persons" (DPs) from Europe to the United States. Introduced on April 1, 1947, it proved to be controversial, attracting both support and opposition in considerable measure.

As Stratton explained it, HR 2910 would admit up to one hundred thousand displaced persons of twenty nationalities to the United Strates each year for four years. It proposed no changes in the traditional "quota system" for controlling the flow of immigration. National quotas had often gone unfilled during the war—the displaced persons admitted would simply be within those unused quotas. Those admitted would have to be "mentally and morally sound" and would have to have sponsors who would guarantee they would not become public charges. Stratton reported a "heavy demand" for copies of the bill.[9]

It was estimated that, at the end of World War II, eight million persons in Europe were "displaced"—separated from their homes for one reason or another, often having no homes to which they could return. They included liberated slave laborers, concentration camp inmates, and others whom the swirling currents of war had caught up and deposited in strange and often hostile settings. Approximately six and one-half million such displaced persons were able to return to their homes when the war ended—the balance remained separated from their prewar locations. A majority of them were Poles, Yugoslavs, and Baltic peoples who did not wish to return to territory dominated by the Soviet Union. Many were Jews. Ukrainians, Greeks, and Czechs were also among the displaced.

The *Nation* reported that "a bill for dealing with the problem in the only simple, intelligent, and morally defensible way has been introduced in Congress, not by a broad-minded liberal but by Representative William G. Stratton of Illinois, a Republican isolationist of the McCormick school and a one time member of America First. The Stratton bill has its weaknesses. ... But by and large, it is a remarkably good measure." The *Nation* supported it. Coming from a "conservative," the bill was well received by other congressmen of that stripe. It received a good reception elsewhere.[10]

The journal of Catholic opinion, *Commonweal*, reasoned that, with much of Europe in ruins following World War II, the United States was fat and prosperous and many of its people were uncomfortable over their relative wealth. As a result,

> we indulged in a rather prolonged moment of self-righteousnes. We were, for a few months, inclined to do only the necessary for an ungrateful Europe. . . . We translated this huffiness to our legislators, and the result has been a delayed attack on some of the most demanding problems of European recovery. It has surely been one of the telling reasons for our dragging approaches to a solution of the agonizing condition of Europe's displaced persons.

At last, according to *Commonweal*, the Stratton bill had appeared partially to correct that condition. It did not feel that the bill would be seriously opposed in any quarter and urged letters to congressmen in its support. "Perhaps the Congressmen would feel more at ease about their votes on the Stratton Bill if they were told that the American people have passed through their period of injured feelings and are quite willing to take up the rich man's burden, no praise solicited."[11] Reactions to the bill, however, were not as uniformly favorable as *Commonweal* predicted.

One can imagine the favorable reception such legislation would have in highly ethnic Chicago. On October 29, 1946, just before the election, the Jewish Community Council of Peoria sent Stratton a letter urging the admission of displaced persons to the United States. A "fact sheet" of three pages was included. This may have served to set Stratton thinking about the matter. At least he placed the letter in his file.

During the spring of 1947 Stratton sought data and opinions to help him deal with the problems of displaced persons and their admission to the United States. He went to the highest levels of authority for assistance. In writing to his friend Vernon Nickell on April 10, Stratton reported that his "bill on displaced persons has developed considerable support, although, of course there will be those who are opposed. I really believe that we have something here that may be helpful for a number of reasons. As you well know, there are several angles involved in a proposition of this kind."

Certainly there was not a singleness of purpose behind the displaced persons bill. George Perrine wrote on April 18. He observed that

Your coming out for the immigration of displaced persons caused considerable downstate comment . . . you have picked up some support in Cook County among certain foreign element groups. I would be a little cautious in how I approach this program. If it is limited by some selection method, then I don't think anyone objects to it. The only thing that we see so far is this: most people feel that it will make it possible for several thousands of Jews to be moved into this country. . . . Now, nobody in Illinois, outside of the Jews, wants any more Jews in this country.

Perrine felt that the selection of displaced persons to be admitted could please Illinois voters who had friends and relatives so favored. He knew two people in Aurora who wanted to get relatives out of eastern Germany. "They are not Jewish but on the other hand are good German people," he wrote. Their admission would win friends for whoever made it possible. Those remarks would seem to qualify Perrine, who later was to serve in Stratton's cabinet, as anti-Semitic. It is Stratton's opinion that he was reporting the feelings of others rather than his own. There is little doubt, however, that they would have been echoed by many Illinoisans of the 1940s.

Rupert Bippus wrote Stratton on July 9 to express concern that the displaced persons bill "might not do you any good downstate. I assume you thought this all out. In any event the die has been cast." Perrine wired later in July: "Sincerely suggest you drop any and all further activity in regards to immigration of displaced people. Womens clubs and other civic clubs seem to be totally opposed. . . . It is hurting considerably downstate."

But not all who wrote Stratton on this matter were opposed. One letter read: "Dear Congressman: Frankly I was 'agin you' in the last election; in fact I thought it was a near calamity when Mrs. E. T. D. was defeated. However I am beginning to think I had you underrated, in as much as you are certainly to be commended for this humanitarian move, which I think is going to win you the support of a good many right minded people." Frank L. Sulzberger of Chicago, who had served on the Public Aid Commission with Stratton, wrote: "Dear Bill: I just want to tell you how pleased I was to see that it was you who introduced the bill . . . to give a few of the D.P.s a chance to come into this country."

Andrew Fasseas wrote early in June to express approval, especially of the credit earned among Jews and ethnic groups generally. As publisher of *The Greek Star,* a newspaper printed in Chicago in Greek as well as in English, Fasseas was sensitive to ethnic opinion and well qualified to evaluate it. Earlier in the year he had written Stratton advising him of Jewish interest, in Illinois, in his taking a stand on the matter of Palestine as a Jewish homeland. Perhaps Stratton was attempting with the displaced persons bill to recover some of the standing lost among Jews six years before in the Viereck matter (which is described in Chapter 2). Fasseas wrote again on June 18 to say: "I have contacted some of the highest ranking Jewish Americans. They feel that since you have introduced the bill in Congress there exists [none] of the ill feeling that their people had for you before."

Letters and petitions on the displaced persons bill were carefully sorted and filed: from Illinois, pro and con; from other states, pro and con; and from abroad. The bulk of them was clearly on the side of its passage. There were petitions from displaced-person camps in Europe. An especially touching one came from such a camp in Germany. It was signed by forty-nine persons from Latvia and Estonia; for each, detailed information about age, education, and former occupation was given. All were skilled adults, eager for a new beginning for lives shattered by the dislocations of war, and not wishing to place themselves under Russian rule. Their spokesman eloquently, though not fluently, addressed Stratton:

> Dear Sir: At first we wish you a happy New Year and God bless you in your hard and responsible work.
>
> We the former in mates of D.P. Camp Pegnitz, Bavaria kindly require you, as the first initiator of the new low of emigration, for we know that you are our friend and defender. We have not forgstten your proklamation not to lose caurage and patience this proclamation has strengthened our caurage and trust to you ... We kindly request you with a common petition if it is possible to support ... emigration for the below mentioned persons. We should be honored to find our new home just in your state which has given so famous son as your dear Exelence.
>
> Abaut our miserable conditions here in so called D P Camp you are sufficiently informed.

The arguments for and against the displaced persons bill, which were presented in letters to Stratton, are easily summed up. Many who were in favor stressed the moral, or idealistic, argument—"the least we can do." Others saw the bill as a means of reuniting divided families. Some were impressed by the skills that could be added to the labor force, through selective admission. Those who were opposed feared the competition for scarce housing, the entrance of Communists and "too many Jews," and the threat of "un-American ideas."

Stratton replied to many of the letters. He pointed out that the traditional quota system of regulating immigration would not be weakened; that only mentally and morally sound persons would be admitted; that all admitted would have sponsors and "guaranteed" housing; that a limit of one hundred thousand per year for no more than four years would be admitted; and that the United States was itself a nation of immigrants and their descendants.[12]

Hearings on the bill were held in June and July. They helped to consolidate favorable opinion. The American Legion had at first been opposed but changed its stance in October. Other groups that were in favor included, but were not limited to, the Council of Jewish Federation and Welfare Funds, the American Federation of Labor, the American Farm Bureau Federation, Catholic War Veterans, the League of Women Voters, the Northern Baptist Convention, the American Civil Liberties Union, and the United States Chamber of Commerce. No final vote was taken on the proposal during 1947.

Stratton left with his family on July 30 for a two-week vacation in Panama, a popular destination for members of Congress since they could be guests of the Panama Railroad Company, a United States government-owned corporation, and members of their families could accompany them at modest rates. This was almost Stratton's first opportunity to be out of Washington in seven months. He had played golf from time to time and participated in the baseball game between House Republicans and Democrats. His family had visited him at Easter, but those activities appeared to have been his only relaxation until the trip to Panama.

Already Stratton was making plans for getting his campaign for secretary of state in 1948 off the ground. He took with him to Panama a list of persons—most of them with political utility to him—to be remembered with post cards. He was campaigning even while out of the country on vacation. Marion Keevers wrote Stratton in the Canal Zone that Charles Burgess was concerned that he "had announced." She reported that she "told him you hadn't. Sounds like the old pot is boiling." On August 3, Burgess sent a telegram to Stratton in the Canal Zone informing him of an "important conference Chicago yesterday. Decision regards opposition slate deferred pending your return. Give no interviews anyone until see me eighteenth." Indeed, it did seem as if the "old pot" were boiling.

Stratton returned to Morris soon after his trip to Panama, and on September 1 a news release was widely distributed announcing his candidacy for secretary of state. It was probably a trial balloon, intended to elicit responses from Governor Green and other public and party officials. Stratton was referred to by the *Lincoln Courier* as the "bad boy of Republican politics."

In early October the Strattons went to Missouri for a fishing trip in the Ozarks with Congressman Parke Banta. Marion Stratton reported to Marion Keevers, in Washington, on October 13, that "Wm. didn't get too many fish, but ... we both had a very enjoyable few days." A week later she reported that "Wm. has appointments scheduled for practically every day during the next five weeks." He has "a touch of cold or flu ... but you know Bill, he hates to rest." Apparently Marion Stratton was helping with congressional work while her husband was at home.[13]

By early November the decision to go for secretary of state had been made. Earl Madigan had written to Stratton on November 6, when it still seemed that Governor Green might back Richard Yates Rowe. Madigan predicted that in a primary contest Stratton could win and recounted support that he had enlisted. "They dare not fight us," he declared, "and if they do they are going to be a sick bunch of pols." While Green might have preferred to back Rowe, who had already announced, this time he had no choice.[14] A disruptive primary fight in 1948 would have reduced any chance he had to get on the national ticket. So, unlike 1944, he eventually endorsed Stratton.

Stratton wrote to Glen Palmer on November 5. "Couldn't resist trying out the new [campaign] stationery on you. This will prove ... that we are now in business. Unfortunately we were not able to obtain this stationery as soon as I might have liked due to raids made on funds by certain voracious gin-rummy players from the north."[15] Stratton and his associates must have been avid card players, especially of gin rummy. Among his papers there are numerous references to the game.

Even though Stratton's chief concern from August until November was the decision to run for secretary of state, the displaced persons bill continued to be a significant matter for him. Many of his friends were still opposed to his involvement with it. Charles Burgess wrote on August 3, while Stratton was in Panama, to say that "among the vet groups— this bill has done more harm than good for you. That is the local opinion of *your* friends." Paul O. Lewis of Chicago expressed the thought that "your sponsorship of the bill to bring in D.P.s is objectionable to me and to many others.... Perhaps, this move on your part was to attract some of the Chicago votes. If so I am certain the net results will not be as anticipated." Stratton replied that "the bill ... was introduced in an attempt to solve a special problem resulting from the war and our subsequent occupation of Europe. You can be sure that no hasty action will be taken."

On December Burgess wrote again to say that "if Mrs. [Eleanor] Roosevelt's statement is correct in which she says she was a part of the group which asked you to introduce the [DP] Bill, and if you knew she was ... then I am sorry to say, Bill, that you and I are parting company so far as politics are concerned, although I hope I can remain your personal friend." Burgess concluded with the hope that Mrs. Roosevelt had spoken falsely. Correspondence in January showed that he was still allied politically with Stratton, and he was still critical of the displaced persons bill.[16]

Stratton made an eloquent appeal for support for the bill in an address to the organization called United Service for New Americans, on January 11, 1948. His speech was titled "Delayed Pilgrim's Progress." Its implication was that the displaced persons were the "pilgrims" whose progress in life had been delayed. In it he reported that the displaced persons bill had the support of more than one hundred and fifty national organizations. All of the major religious groups were in favor. Other groups and individuals had testified to the good character and work habits of those seeking entry. While HR 2910 was pending before Congress, Stratton told his audience, private groups were helping to secure the admission of displaced persons, and several of the states were setting up commissions to be of assistance. Congressmen visiting Europe had become convinced of the quality of many of the persons who were living in DP camps. "The hopelessness and frustration," Stratton declared, "the sufferings of our delayed pilgrims can and must be ended now. We have waited, argued and debated long enough. The path is clear and open. I urge you all to do everything in your power to join me in pressing for immediate and definite action."[17]

Apparently Stratton was holding firm in his support of the bill, in spite of the continued objections of a number of his advisers and friends. One of them wrote on January 21, saying "your bill . . . to allow thousands of immigrants to enter the U.S. is simply killing Wm. G. Stratton in Illinois." Charles Burgess wrote Stratton a bitter letter of criticism on April 1. His friends had elected Stratton as an isolationist, Burgess believed, and his vote for the European Recovery Program, or Marshall Plan, was a betrayal of that trust. Burgess continued:

> Those people who went out of their way to give you this support are justified now . . . in feeling that you have traded that support and friendship for the support of a minor number of Internationalists and of the Jewish element. You told me when you returned from Panama last summer, after having introduced the Stratton Bill . . . that your entire reason for the introduction of such legislation was gaining the support of as many of those Internationalists who had supported Mrs. Douglas as you could attract. You stated that you felt your support of the Stratton Bill would gain more votes than you would lose.

Burgess charged Stratton with taking positions on the displaced persons bill and the Marshall Plan simply to maximize his support by the voters in 1948—not an unreasonable thing for a member of Congress to do. Burgess continued:

> You probably believe that your ... supporters of the past several years are all so solidly Republican that they will in November vote a straight ... ticket and therefore you will lose little of their support and at the same time pick up the votes of those people who were opposed to you when you ran against Mrs. Douglas. You may be surprised. Loyalty to an individual in politics among people who seek no personal financial job or patronage can be stretched just so far. You have imposed upon that loyalty to the breaking point.
>
> Any man who will vote against his best judgment for the purpose of seeking support from a faction whose beliefs he is diametrically opposed to is not a safe man to become Secretary of ... State. ... I hope Eddie Barrett beats you—and I'm predicting that he will.

Such words from a respected supporter must have been disturbing to Stratton. He marked Burgess' letter "did not answer—file." Burgess wrote again on April 3 to say "you must have heard from the hometown folks. I see on the final passage of the Marshall ERP Bill you refrained from voting. [In 1989 Stratton did not remember it that way.] Well, that is further indication of your recently acquired habit of inconsistency."

Later in April Burgess informed Stratton that he should not attempt to do any fund raising in Kane County, where Burgess was party finance chairman. "Solicitation of funds for your personal campaign expenses will not be welcome," he warned, "in fact, word has gone out to refuse to make any contributions." A portion of the amount that Burgess raised for Republican candidates generally would provide "some funds" for Stratton. Burgess was clearly deeply disturbed by his friend's actions.[18]

Nevertheless, Stratton continued his public posture of support for the displaced persons bill. On April 21 he spoke about it to what Rupert Bippus, who arranged the appearance, described as the "largest B'nai B'rith lodge in Illinois." In May Stratton wrote to the editor of *Collier's* magazine, commending him for an article on the subject. "We Americans cannot dismiss this topic as one represented by statistics only," he stated, "we must think of it in terms of human beings."[19] It is probable that Stratton had in fact told Burgess he was backing the displaced persons bill only to pick up a few votes. Even so, his support of the proposal went well beyond the minimum effort he might have made. His recollection in

1989 was that he never wavered, publicly or privately, in his support of the DP bill.

A displaced persons bill was passed by Congress on June 25, 1948. Due to the complexities of the legislative process, it was not, by number, the bill that Stratton had introduced and backed. Still, its content was much the same. As Public Law 774, it permitted the admission of up to 220 thousand persons during fiscal years 1949 and 1950, without regard for immigration quotas. Special preference was to be given to farm workers and to persons whose homelands had been occupied by a foreign power. In a thoroughly Republican document, prepared by Senator Robert A. Taft, PL 774 was spoken of approvingly. "By authorizing the admission of more than 200,000 displaced persons," it read, "we have not forgotten that America is still regarded as a haven for the oppressed."[20]

The displaced persons bill was a significant matter in Stratton's personal and professional development. It was one that the Stratton of 1941 would have opposed strongly. No doubt he hoped to gain votes from his support of it; but it is also clear that he continued that support when valued friends opposed it, and threatened the withdrawal of their friendship unless he gave it up. It could not have been easy for him to persevere in its behalf.

Stratton filed for the Republican primary for secretary of state in January 1948. Governor Green sought nomination for a third term, in the face of wide opposition and indifference within his party. Lieutenant Governor Hugh Cross had wished to run for governor and would have been stronger in November than Green.[21] He did not want a primary fight, however, and withdrew from the race and from politics, which allowed Green to slate his ally Richard Yates Rowe for lieutenant governor, clearing the way for Stratton to run for secretary of state. Green and Stratton remained on cordial terms during 1948.[22]

With an agreed-upon slate, Stratton was unopposed in the April primary and had no need to return to Illinois to campaign. Green was nominated for a third term; Senator Brooks for a second full one. They were to be opposed by two newcomers to the state electoral scene, Adlai Stevenson and Paul Douglas. The stage was set for the general election in November.

There is no doubt that Green faced strong feeling against a third term. Part of it was general, against a third term for any governor—recall Republican feelings against Roosevelt's third term and efforts in behalf of the Twenty-Second Amendment—and part was particular, against a third term for Green. He had been badly hurt politically by events of 1947 and the accumulation of political liabilities. According to longtime legislator Charles Clabaugh, "Pete [Green] got on the bottle" and was at times ill-prepared to concentrate on policy issues.[23] It is apparent that Green was not a strong presence at the top of his party's ticket.

Stratton returned to Illinois for the state Republican convention early in May, where he visited with his mother. She wrote on June 2, saying, "You don't know how much I enjoyed seeing you at Springfield. And it was such a pleasure to be where there were political goings on. Guess I'll never get that out of my system. Anyway, why should I want to?"[24]

Marion (still not enchanted by political life) and the girls completed the picture of a happy family circle when Stratton attended the Republican National Convention in Philadelphia. It still seemed possible, if not likely, that political lightning might strike and Governor Green be nominated for vice-president. In that case it would be necessary for the Illinois Republican State Central Committee to select a candidate for governor to replace Green, and who would have a better chance for that honor than one already on the state ticket? But none of it came to pass.

Stratton found it necessary to return to Washington briefly when President Truman called what he described as the "do-nothing Eightieth Congress" back into session on August 3. When that highly political event ended Stratton was ready for campaigning in earnest. His plan was conventional, and his team was coming together. Bippus anticipated a close contest; and Bill Peterson, who wrote to Marion Keevers late in August that "it kind of gives me a kick—we're all like the old-time fire-horses—ready to run when the bell sounds," believed Secretary of State Eddie Barrett would "be a tough baby to knock off." Glen Palmer also sounded a warning note.

Charles Burgess continued to be disaffected. He was still bitter over the displaced persons legislation, and felt that without Stratton's backing, it would never have been enacted. He charged Stratton with having

> the poorest voting record ... in support of Republican measures of any Congressmen from ... Illinois.
>
> This all adds up, Bill, to what you told me in defense of the Stratton D.P. Bill—that you were doing everything you could to attract the votes of those Fellow Travelers, Left wingers, radicals and others, who had supported Mrs. Douglas. ... You felt you could gain a percentage of those votes without losing too many of the votes of your friends.
>
> I hate to say it, Bill, but I don't know who is the biggest liability to the Republican vote in ... Illinois. It's pretty evenly divided between you, Green and [Chicago leader Sinon]

Murray.... Murray is the #1 liability. You're the #2—and Green is the #3.

Burgess' greatest concern over the admission of displaced persons from Europe was in regard to housing. He felt that veterans who were having difficulty finding homes would turn against the Republican party because of Stratton's sponsorship of the original displaced persons bill. He chided Stratton by saying, "Of course you entered the service in the last war only for the purpose of being able to claim the servicemen's support, and you could have had it 100% if you'd gone down the line with such legislation as was beneficial to the servicemen."

Burgess concluded by stating that while he would not bring the matter up publicly before the November election, "I am going to use this against you at every opportunity with any future Primary Election in which you may be entered." The political rupture between Stratton and Burgess seemed complete, although Burgess had stated earlier to the press, "I am not opposed to Stratton as Secretary of State ... as I am supporting the entire ... ticket.... I am opposed to the position which Stratton has taken in what I construe 'selling his friends down the river.'" Stratton marked Burgess' long letter "file," and there is no record of any response to it.

By mid-August, Stratton had begun a busy round of campaign appearances. The downstate Republican caravan took place the latter half of September and into October. There was little time for Stratton to spend with his family during the campaign. A photograph, which appeared in the *Mt. Pulaski Times-News* for October 21, shows that the girls were rapidly growing up—they were open-faced, smiling, seemingly happy, with clear, direct gazes into the camera. Marion was pleasant in appearance, neat, and attractive. Stratton seemed the proud and attentive father.

Andy Fasseas, a leader of Chicago's Greek community, had continued to be a loyal supporter, and when Stratton spoke on the "Greek-American Radio Hour" he identified Fasseas, who introduced him, as "my right-hand associate" in this campaign, and as being of "wise counsel" since 1940. Stratton was always sensitive to the levers of electoral power, so far as ethnic groups were concerned.[25]

A poll of Illinois voters released on October 30 showed Republican Tom Dewey a sure winner over President Truman and Governor Green and Senator Brooks in close races. However, when the polling places closed on November 2 and the votes were counted, the results were very different. Truman beat Dewey by 34 thousand votes. Paul Douglas routed Brooks by a 408-thousand plurality, and Adlai Stevenson overwhelmed Green by 572 thousand. Stratton did somewhat better, but lost to Eddie Barrett by 362 thousand votes. Democrats won the offices of auditor, treasurer, attorney general, and lieutenant governor as well. Clearly the voters were tired of the incumbent team of Green and Brooks, and sent Stratton down to defeat with them. He was an incumbent too, with a name long known as an officeholder at the state level. Stratton ran about even with Barrett downstate, but he lost decisively in Chicago.

Again Stratton had suffered disappointment in seeking the office that he had so earnestly coveted for at least seven years. It was not to be his fate to seek it again.* Of the many persons who wrote to him following the election, most blamed Green for the defeat of the Republican ticket. M. B. "Tiny" Overacker, county clerk of Sangamon County, wrote to say "we are all feeling quite blue but as the old football coach use to say 'Let's get ready for the next game!' . . . The people just weren't voting for the Republican Party this time."[26]

That analysis was faulty—many *were* voting for the Republican party, as the support for Dewey and Republican candidates for the University of Illinois Board of Trustees indicated. They clearly were voting *against* Green and Brooks, and to a lesser degree Stratton. But Overacker, as a practicing politican in Sangamon County, was hardly in a position to charge the defeat to party leaders. Ed Pree, Stratton's administrative assistant when he was governor, states that in 1948 "Governor Green . . . took the whole ticket down with him."[27] Fred Selcke, county clerk of nearby Menard County, was of the same opinion. He offered to help Stratton run for treasurer in 1950 and was of much help to him then and in his campaign for governor in 1952. John Graham, still in Washington, felt that "Green was too big a load to carry." Even though he was no longer on the Stratton team, he pledged future loyalty. He too suggested a try for treasurer in 1950 and may still have had hopes for an appointive post under Stratton. Earl Madigan wrote from Logan County, saying "our defeat was hard to take . . . for some young guys who had a lot pinned on the outcome. I know that you are the chief loser. I failed you miserably in this County. I am looking around for a business to get into but this looks like a rough deal. . . . Good luck to you, Bill." He invited Stratton to come see him at any time.

Stratton replied in a philosophical vein. "All our friends, including yourself, worked hard and did everything possible . . . but there were

---

*One day in June 1986 I met by chance Secretary of State Jim Edgar on the Southern Illinois University campus in Carbondale. Edgar said, "I understand you are working on a book about Bill Stratton—I would like to read it." "You know, of course," was my response, "that Stratton's father held your job at one time." "Yes," Edgar answered, "Bill told me once he had always wanted the job his father had. He tried twice to be elected to it, and couldn't. He said he had to settle for being governor."

62

forces at work over which none of us had any control. . . . Naturally we hated to see the party lose, but it may well be that we will be able to play an even larger part in the Republican rebuilding than we did in the previous ten years." To a friend in Woodstock, Stratton wrote, "it was tough to lose the State Administration with its jobs for so many loyal workers. However . . . 'one battle does not make a war' and the Republicans will win again in this state." In a postelection exchange of letters with state Senator Victor McBroom of Kankakee, Stratton was cheerful and optimistic, as he invariably was following a loss at the polls.

It was clear that Stratton was looking toward to the future and was not demoralized by defeat in 1948. Many of his correspondents urged him to run again in 1950 or 1952. After spending two weeks in the sunshine at Tucson, he returned to Washington to wind up the details of his office there.[28] He had no intention of concluding his political career. With the end of his congressional term in January, however, he was out of office and out of income—there were debts remaining from his campaign and no funds with which to pay them. Stratton had no law practice, nor did he have a family business to which he could return. Many felt that his political life was ended.[29] He, in 1949, did not consider seriously any vocation other than politics. He returned to Morris to an uncertain future and a marriage which was dissolving. It was a wilderness time for William Grant Stratton.

6

Wilderness Years

With 1949, Stratton faced one of the crossroads of his career. State government had gone Democratic, and there was the strong possibility that it might remain so for the next eight years. With a family to support, he had to consider finding employment in the business world. He had an offer from the Franklin Life Insurance Company, one of Springfield's largest industries, but the lure of the business world could not match that of politics. Stratton remained in Morris and was soon considering his next try for public office.

He was not the only Republican to have come on hard times. Earl Madigan, who lost his job in the auditor's office when Arthur Lueder was defeated, wrote: "Dear Bill:—Well, two days of trying to sell Jeep-Kaiser-Frazer cars. Exactly no sales. A rough deal—chum. But, I know that you too, probably have your own troubles.... You never have written any of the fellows." In a later letter, he chided Stratton for not replying. Stratton's habit of neglecting personal correspondence when it was not immediately useful to him was still evident. However, at this time he no longer had an office staff or typist.

Apparently Stratton's eventual reply mollified Madigan, for he wrote again in April: "Dear Bill;—Have you forgotten that you still have some friends that are interested in you ... ? Before long I believe we should have a conference." He offered some political news from Logan County and concluded: "I have contacts (good ones) all over downstate Illinois. We are not too old to start all over again. Let's hear from you." By that time Madigan was proprietor of the Yellow Cab Company in Lincoln.[1]

During the winter and spring of 1949 the Strattons' marriage of fifteen years was coming to an end. After the beginning of his campaign for treasurer in 1942 he and Marion had spent little time together. He had been in Springfield, in the Navy, or in Washington from 1943 until

1949, while his family continued to live in Morris. The little time he was not actually living elsewhere, he was campaigning—still away from home—evidently an unsatisfactory arrangement for Marion and himself.

Joseph Immel, who as a leading Chicago Republican assisted Stratton in his 1952 campaign for governor, recalls that "it was not a very good marriage." He felt that Marion Stratton would not or could not accept political life.[2] Given the circumstances of having two small children and a large, old house in Morris, which they had envisioned as the base for a political career, the Strattons probably felt that they had little choice other than to live apart, and for the most part they did. That such an arrangement had harmed their marriage, which became apparent when Stratton returned to Morris in 1949, could not have been surprising.

Family life was further stressed by Stratton's lack of income; times were hard. The final checks he wrote to his wife were for fifty dollars on March 29 and ninety dollars on May 5, both marked "household," and twenty dollars on May 5, memoed "hairdo."

Stratton sued for divorce on grounds of desertion, and the decree was soon granted. He was in arrears in child support payments by October. At that time Sandra and Diana were living with their mother in Joliet. Her attorney wrote requesting payment, for the girls needed glasses and dental work.[3] They continued to live with Marion until Stratton became governor, then he wished them to have the experience of living in the executive mansion, and they became part of his household until they were grown. Even while the girls were in his care he continued to make child support payments of one hundred and fifty dollars a month to Marion until Diana was twenty-one. In the divorce settlement Marion was given a note for one-half of the amount that they had paid for the house in Morris. There was little else to divide. The note was paid in full during the first year that Stratton was governor, $4,000.00 plus $418.17 simple interest at 3.5 percent.

The summer months of 1949 must have been hard ones for Stratton. He was living alone in Morris, with only a slim chance of returning to office in 1950. He placed in his file, for whatever reason, a penciled sheet of gin rummy scores, for "Glen" (probably Palmer) and "Bill," with notations of the amounts won and lost: $3.54, $1.38, and so forth, by the players who once had handled millions for the state. One can imagine the political talk that accompanied the fall of the cards.

Also in the file were penciled notes that reveal some of the anguish through which Stratton must have been passing. Apparently he thought of himself, in the words of the popular song of the time, as "the daring young man on the flying trapeze." "Once I was happy, but now I'm forlorn,/ like an old coat that is tattered and torn" certainly symbolized his feelings at that time. And "betrayed by a maid in her teens," to follow the words of the song, perhaps expressed his feelings about his former wife, whom he had known during their teen years, and who was hardly older than that when they were married. "His movements are graceful, the girls he does please," may have been his estimate of the impression he made on other women at that time.[4]

But it was not Stratton's style to remain long in a depressed state. Friends offered advice about his political future, including John Graham, who counseled Stratton not to go into the 1950 primary for treasurer unless he could be certain he would win—defeat would be disastrous. "In 1952," he wrote, "I'd think you could safely run for either governor or secretary of state—whether you run in 1950 or not. The only danger would be from Dick Rowe in case he run [sic] in 1950 for treasurer and would happen to get elected." Still hopeful of returning to the Stratton team, Graham offered to help in the 1950 campaign if it materialized. He added, "heard about your divorce. Too bad it had to happen, but I feel I know the situation. Keep your feet on the ground now, so the snipers don't have anything to smear you with."

Stratton's reply reveals clearly his political intentions and his analysis of the condition of his party.

> I definitely will be a candidate for State Treasurer. Si Murray is making a definite bid to take over [as state boss] by running Louie Nelson from Chicago for treasurer. You can readily see ... how important it is that we make this fight in 1950. It can well develop into quite a battle on grounds where we were always most at home—the Independent [Republican] position against the domination of the Cook County gang. Looks like some interesting months are ahead.

Stratton knew that a struggle was going on for control of the Illinois Republican party and that if he did not make a decisive move in 1950 he would probably be left behind permanently.

Before campaigning for the primary election began in earnest, Stratton had time during the summer for more personal matters. As an officer in the Naval Reserve, he took a refresher course in "general supply" at the Great Lakes Training Station during the latter half of June. He was a member of the Executive Committee of Governor Stevenson's Commission on Displaced Persons and gave it some attention. His former secretary, Marion Keevers, was employed in Chicago by The Fair department store, in its executive office, and Stratton saw her during the summer.

On September 12 Louis Nelson wrote asking for Stratton's help in seeking the nomination for state treasurer. Nelson was then the treasurer of Cook County—the first Republican to hold that office in twenty years—but he could not legally succeed himself. Nelson had impressive credentials: he was a veteran of World War I, a graduate of the University of Wisconsin, a longtime Proviso Township School Board member, and the president of the First National Bank of Maywood. In addition, he had the backing of Chicago Republican leader Sinon Murray. It was obvious that Nelson was a strong candidate, but Stratton was determined to make the race himself. By November 1 he was ready to announce his candidacy, and had forty-three hundred copies of a letter to that effect printed by the Copy Cat Printing Service in Joliet for $27.74, paid on delivery. Given his credit rating he hardly could have had them in any other way.

On November 10 Stratton formally announced his candidacy to "neighbors and friends assembled in the living room of his home at Morris." To make his announcements there had been his custom since 1941, as it would continue to be until 1959. This time he spoke critically of "the cynical, discredited men whose chief ambition is to get control of the office of State Treasurer in 1950 in order to use it to elect their man governor in 1952," which was not very different from the use that Stratton eventually made of the office, one he no doubt intended in 1949. He stated that "his campaign will be fought to rebuild the Republican party."[5]

Among many other old friends, Marion Keevers offered encouragement and assistance. She was in touch with Stratton in early December, offering and asking for political news. She also sent a New Year's greeting, on which Stratton noted—"No reply necessary—Saw 1/24/50—WGS." Marion wrote again in February, with political gossip and news of an increase in salary and a new apartment.[6] There is no doubt that her friendship and support were important to Stratton at this time.

It was essential that he win the primary in 1950 if he were to continue to be a viable politician. There was no strong statewide party organization, nor was there an incumbent governor of the party to endorse one of the seven persons seeking the nomination. "It was a wide open primary ... in the true sense."[7] Stratton recalled in 1956 that "in '50, when I ran in the primary ... I had the organization against me."[8] There was hardly an organization capable of such action. Without an endorsement, Stratton had to go directly to the people.[9] He went "everywhere" and had the experience, name recognition, and personal appeal to make victory possible. His father's following was still strong, so "a name like Stratton made the difference."[10]

A short time before the primary election Stratton called his friend Smokey Downey from the campaign trail in Pinckneyville to say "I've got these guys beat!"[11] That confidence would probably have perplexed Louis Nelson, who had the support of most of the party's county chairmen, as well as that of Si Murray and other leaders in Chicago and the ward and township committeemen in Cook County.

Given the circumstances, Stratton found money hard to raise early in 1950. Ed Pree recalls that generally "he didn't have big money to run with. In those days, he was hampered by lack of funds."[12] Personal finances continued to be a difficult problem for Stratton. He borrowed nearly five hundred dollars on his life insurance policy, which was probably all it was worth. Money must have been especially short in the weeks just before the primary. In lieu of a birthday visit and a cake, Stratton's mother sent him a check on February 26. "Dear Bill:" she wrote. "Maybe this will help until your other money comes.... Well, dear, you have been a real joy to me these thirty-six years, and I just hope you'll have lots of blessings in your years ahead. Lovingly." He repaid that loan promptly.[13]

Stratton came out of the April 11 primary a clear-cut, if not a majority, winner. He gained 290 thousand votes, to 214 thousand for Louis Nelson, 126 thousand for Jim Simpson, and 123 thousand for four others together. He did well in the collar counties surrounding Cook, except for his birthplace, Lake. It was also the home county of his opponent Jim Simpson, who was a member of a well-known family and who had served a term in Congress. Stratton did well downstate, but lost in Cook County.

The *Chicago Daily News*, in an editorial on April 12, expressed its pleasure that in Cook County, the "regular" Republican slate, led by William N. Erickson, president of the Cook County Board, triumphed in the Republican primary over a faction headed by John T. Dempsey, "Gov. Green's old patronage boss," and Sinon Murray, who was "in close alliance with the hoodlum-dominated west side bloc that has disgraced the party in recent sessions of the legislature." Murray's support of Louis Nelson, the *Daily News* believed, had hurt Nelson in his race against Stratton, just as former Governor Green's support had hurt Jim Simpson. Stratton "is his own man," the editorial concluded, "and he plays a lone hand politically." That reputation probably helped Stratton substantially in the seven-man race for the nomination for treasurer.

After the primary the usual round of congratulatory messages came in. Leslie P. "Ike" Volz, who had long been active in the Republican party and had handled patronage for Governor Green, wrote on April 14:

My sincere congratulations on your amazing performance Tuesday.... No one that I talked to ... gave you a look-in, so your victory was a most pleasant surprize [*sic*]. I wish your dad ... could have been here to see it.

Knowing you ... you must be having the time of your life. Before the primary hardly anyone would give you a tumble—

or a thin dime. Now you're the fair haired boy and everybody is trying to "kiss in."

I don't suppose anybody was ever nominated to an important office who was as free from obligations as you are. I hope you will stay that way, Bill.

Former Governor Dwight Green, who had backed another candidate, wired, "Your victory confounded all the experts and you will have to tell me sometime how you did it." That message must have given Stratton more than just a little satisfaction. Charles Burgess, apparently still annoyed with Stratton over the displaced persons act and other positions of his in Congress, nevertheless sent his congratulations. "I actively supported Nelson, as you know," Burgess admitted. "[But] the primaries are over." Evidently he was ready to bury the hatchet, and invited Stratton to a dinner in Washington, D.C., which he was hosting for candidates in Illinois for Congress and the state offices. Stratton attended.

Other old friends who wrote included George Storey, who exclaimed: "Well! You surprised the natives. My Good Wife said, when we came in late the night of the primary—'I can just hear his little chuckle.'" Others in those years mentioned that "little chuckle." (It can still be heard.) Storey then indulged in some political talk and distinguished between "true Republicans" and "syndicate gamblers" in Tazewell County. The latter term was a reference to the Si Murray-John T. Dempsey-west side bloc wing of the party.

Stratton's general election campaign in 1950 was modeled after those of earlier years, though this time there was no gubernatorial contest, and he was nearer the head of the ticket. Perry Conn wrote from Quincy on August 31 with this advice, "I trust you don't read a speech from now until November, and none over 30 minutes, rest of the time to handshaking, and having each person feel he had known you all your life, that was your father's big asset." The ghost of William Joseph Stratton still attended his son's campaigning.

A midsummer letter from Earl Madigan made it apparent that he and Stratton had discussed the campaign. While continuing to operate what was now the Lincoln Cab Company, Madigan was doing political work among ethnic groups, especially Belgians and French. Later he wrote again, "haven't heard from you," and asked if he was to travel with Stratton in the campaign. He felt that the results of the election would be similar to those of 1946. "The people are confused and discouraged and ... will again turn to the Republican Party," was his analysis. Early in September he wrote to ask, "How are the writer's cramps? I know that you are busy and that you have a good reason for not getting in touch with me. I am covered up with this darn cab business. I now have twice as many worries." He asked for Stratton stickers and match books to distribute and concluded, "I will be glad to do anything I can." Madigan had lost the party nomination for county sheriff in the April primary by a substantial margin, however, which did not speak well for his political appeal. By the fall it was clear that he had been relegated to a lesser role than he had hoped for and that he realized it.

In addition to the ethnics Madigan was recruiting, and those influenced by Andy Fasseas, Stratton had ethnic group support of his own. On September 7 Niccolo 'Lo Franco, publisher and editor of the "only Italian language newspaper ... in Chicago," *L'Italia,* wrote: "In all your campaigns [*L'Italia*] ... was for you and will be for you this time. The good Italians, held you always in high respect." A month later William G. Eovaldi of Benton, a longtime friend and supporter, urged Stratton to attend a meeting of the Americans of Italian Descent in Pekin. "This is an excellent bunch of boys," he wrote, "and they have always been for you."

Stratton and his fellow candidates Earle B. Searcy and Vernon Nickell headed a downstate caravan beginning just after Labor Day. Searcy was running again for clerk of the Illinois Supreme Court, and Nickell for state superintendent of public instruction. The record of the caravan details hour-by-hour schedules, persons to contact in each community, and those who accompanied the candidates. It was a well-organized, professional operation. They moved into Chicago for the campaign's finale.

The whole feeling of the campaign in 1950 was much different from what it had been two years earlier. The Republican party was free from the candidacy of Dwight Green, who had been a burden in 1948, and with Senator Brooks out of the picture it was a new start. By winning the nomination, Stratton had relieved the Republican party of relationships with the west side bloc and the Chicago Democrats. Those relationships had been troublesome to many Republicans. In 1950 and in 1952 Stratton ran as the downstate Republican candidate, independent of elements in Chicago that might have been an embarrassment to the party.

As the campaign neared its close there was a feeling of euphoria within Illinois Republican ranks and in the Stratton organization. Domestic problems and the so-called police action in Korea were weakening Democratic administrations in Washington and in state capitals, causing Republican fortunes to rise across the nation. The honeymoon was definitely over for Governor Stevenson of Illinois.

Stratton benefited from his experience of 1944 by appearing to many to be the courageous underdog who was battling the forces of evil in the shape of remnants of the Green organization. He was more relaxed in his candidacy than he had been in 1948. Everett Dirksen was proving to be a strong contender for the Senate. It was a new, fresh day for Illinois Republicans. Already, before the November election, there was much talk of winning the governor's chair in 1952.

Among other friends, Marion Keevers continued to keep in close touch with Stratton during the fall. She offered help during the evening hours, and was campaigning. She reported that she had "converted The Fair store and the 1000 block on Sheridan Road for you. Things look wonderful. Your publicity has been excellent." Late in October, as Stratton's chances to win seemed to be growing stronger, she asked about a job as secretary, administrative assistant, "or something. Being on the outside these last two years," she explained, "have [sic] been just awful. Particularly when you work with people who just aren't politically minded."

Stratton shared Keevers' optimism and from the La Salle Hotel, on October 28, after his downstate tour ended, he assured her she was "welcome to drop by at any hour. (I still keep odd hours)," he wrote. "On the other matter you mentioned [employment] nothing would please me better and we will make arrangements when I get back from a short vacation." He seemed to feel that victory was at hand. This letter closed with "Love and Kisses," a style quite unusual for Stratton in his correspondence with Keevers. His letter was initialed "skb" by his secretary. By this stage of the campaign, secretarial service, some of it loaned by corporations in Chicago and some volunteer, was available.[14]

During the primary campaign Stratton had become better acquainted with Shirley Breckenridge, whom he had known casually. His friend Andy Fasseas, working for the campaign in Chicago, had helped to bring him and Miss Breckenridge together. She was employed by an insurance firm in Chicago in a responsible secretarial position. She assisted Stratton as a volunteer with his correspondence during several evenings in the closing days of the campaign. The initials "skb" on Stratton's correspondence were hers. Perhaps there were romantic feelings on Stratton's part and the "love and kisses" of the closing of his letter to Marion Keevers was intended to suggest to his volunteer secretary that he was a dashing and sophisticated fellow.

Smokey Downey was working for Stratton as press secretary. His touch was evident in a late campaign news release in which Stratton raised the specter of the "criminally dominated" Cook County Democratic machine headed by "Boss [Jake] Arvey." He referred to "the alliance between the criminal syndicate and the Democratic party bosses," allegedly revealed by the Kefauver Committee's investigation of organized crime. Governor Stevenson was referred to as "the most spendthrift Governor in the history of Illinois." Speaking directly to Stevenson, Stratton himself stressed the former's "affinity for Alger Hiss, and how you went to the front for him and testified as to his 'good character.'" There was reference to a "personal attack" Stevenson had made on Stratton,[15] which may have been the start of the ill feeling between the two that persisted for many years. As a Republican candidate, it was reasonable for Stratton to be critical of a Democratic governor, even one who was not himself a candidate, but it was also probable that Stratton was already beginning his 1952 campaign for governor, anticipating that Stevenson again would be the Democratic standard-bearer.

As election day came near, Stratton predicted that there would be a favorable outcome, that he would carry "all but three" of the ninety-two counties he had visited during the campaign, and that he would gain a plurality of at least 135 thousand votes downstate. He spent election night awaiting returns at his home in Morris, as he had in earlier years. By this time, his mother was keeping house for him there, and she helped him entertain the friends who assembled. He did much better than he had anticipated, defeating Michael Howlett by 391 thousand votes. He won not only downstate, as he had predicted, but he also carried the Democratic stronghold Cook County. Dirksen won his contest for United States senator by a margin of 294 thousand. Incumbent Vernon Nickell led the ticket with a plurality of 490 thousand, and Searcy won, too. It was a strongly Republican year. Both domestic and foreign policies and events were hurting the Democrats badly at the national level, and the nationwide disaffection was reflected in state races.

On December 7, Stratton went again to Washington, D.C., for Charles Burgess' dinner party for Illinois winners and other prominent Republicans. His invitation read, "You are invited, urged and requested to be present. It is a MUST." It was the fourteenth such gathering that Burgess had hosted. A special railroad car was available on December 6, from Chicago, returning on the ninth. Nickell and Searcy were also present, as was Senator-elect Dirksen, George Perrine, Elmer Hoffman, who was Du Page County Republican chairman, Carlos Campbell, who was state Republican chairman, Judge Evan Howell, and several members of the Illinois congressional delegation. Senators Robert Taft and John W. Bricker also attended.[16] It was a gathering of the movers and shakers of the Republican party in Illinois—probably the most influential group to be found within the party at that time.

Election was not the only prize that Stratton won in the 1950 campaign. On December 27, shortly before he took office, he and Shirley Breckenridge were married. The new Mrs. Stratton was twenty-seven years old, dark haired, tall at five feet, eight inches, poised, and attractive. They soon moved into a new apartment building at 945 South Fourth Street in Springfield, an easy walk from Stratton's office in the capitol.

From left: the future governor; William J. Stratton, deputy state game warden;
Charles Kerwin Stratton; in 1918. As befits a game warden, the senior
Stratton is wearing hip boots.

William G. Stratton at twenty.

Campaigning in Lake County in 1940. *From left:* pictured on the wall, United States Senate candidate C. Wayland Brooks, Stratton, County Chairman William Marks, Richard J. Lyons, Richard Yates Rowe, and Dwight H. Green, candidate for governor.

Young Congressman Stratton, Sandra, Diana, and Marion, in Washington, D.C., in 1941.

Stratton on Okinawa in 1946.

Illinois congressmen who were leaving the House of Representatives after the 1947–48 term. *From left:* Stratton, Anton Johnson, Everett Dirksen, Evan Howell, and Roy Clippinger.

Stratton as state treasurer in 1951.

The house at 437 Vine Street in Morris, where Stratton kept his home
address and political headquarters for a quarter of a century, on the day he
announced his first campaign for governor, September 24, 1951.

Campaigning in Chicago in 1952. Presidential candidate Dwight Eisenhower
at the microphone. *To the right:* Congressman Richard Hoffman and Stratton,
who was running for governor.

Inauguration day in 1953.

"Open House" in 1953. Stratton with state Representative
George Brydia.

Sandra and Diana Stratton leaving the Executive Mansion for their walk to
Springfield High School, 1953.

Governor Stratton with two members of his cabinet who had been closely associated with his father. *From left:* Stillman Stanard, director of the Department of Agriculture; Stratton; and Glen Palmer, director of the Department of Conservation. At the state fairgrounds in 1953.

From left: the governor's mother, Mrs. William J. Stratton; Congresswoman Marguerite S. Church; and Mrs. Stratton's sister, Mrs. Blanche Ankley; during a visit to the governor's birthplace in Lake County in 1955.

A 1955 celebration of the approval by the voters of the reapportionment amendment in November 1954. *From left:* Robert Merriam, Ben Adamowski, Stratton, and Richard J. Daley. Adamowski and Daley were longtime political foes. Later in 1955 Merriam and Daley ran in the Chicago mayoral election. Daley won, the first of six times.

From left: Stratton, Adlai E. Stevenson, and Samuel W. Witwer in 1955. Witwer was a champion of constitutional change and Republican candidate for the United States Senate in 1960.

"An uneasy truce"—Stratton with state Auditor of Public Accounts Orville Hodge, *right.* Acting as peacemaker is state Senator Edward P. Saltiel.

"On the stump"—Stratton campaigning in 1956.

"The winner and still champion"—Stratton with former heavyweight boxing champion Jack Dempsey and Vice-President Richard Nixon, in 1956, after both Stratton and Nixon won.

"Opening day—the first ball" in 1957. Stratton with
Al Lopez, manager of the Chicago White Sox, *left,*
and Lou Boudreau, manager of the Kansas City
Athletics, *right.*

Governor and Mrs. Stratton (*right*) with the actor Clark Gable and Mrs.
Gable (*left*).

Stratton and state Representative Paul Powell at Hillsboro in 1957. Later
Stratton helped make Powell Speaker of the House.

The mature Stratton—official photograph, 1958.

Stratton sharing chewing gum in the Soviet Union
in 1959.

Stratton with Queen Elizabeth and Prince Philip (*behind the governor*) in
Chicago in 1959. Prime Minister John Diefenbaker of Canada is next to the
prince; and Mayor Daley on the right, foreground.

Stratton with President Eisenhower in 1960.

The helicopter campaign tour, 1960, at Cairo. Governor and Mrs. Stratton.

Shirley Stratton in 1960.

Stratton, Shirley, and their daughter Nancy, on vacation in Louisiana in 1964, shortly before his trial.

7

State Treasurer Again

From the start, Stratton's second term as state treasurer was a campaign for the governor's chair. He was familiar with the duties of the treasurer and placed trusted, old friends in key positions. Marion Keevers was his executive secretary, Earl Madigan his chief clerk, and Smokey Downey his press secretary. Stratton's office was on the first floor of the Capitol, where he was easily accessible. People came "by the hundreds" to see him.[1] It was a good base from which to campaign for promotion to the governor's office on the second floor.

It is Smokey Downey's opinion that Stratton was a potential candidate for governor from the day in 1950 that he won the nomination for treasurer. Downey, who continued as press secretary through Stratton's first term as governor, recalls that Stratton decided to run for governor the day after he took office as treasurer in 1951: "We had planned all along in the office of state treasurer to assemble a record for . . . good government." Toward that end, Stratton "set up his own [reduced] budget." Downey remembers that Stratton "wouldn't hire people that wouldn't work. And that was almost unheard of then."[2] Joseph Immel, a key Stratton supporter from Chicago, recalls that he "was oriented in the direction of trying to do a job for the state and also, of course, to further his own political image."

Immel was later to be the assistant manager for Stratton's Cook County campaign in 1952. He was a lawyer, educated at Georgetown University in the early 1930s, politically active in Chicago as early as 1936, and Republican precinct captain in the forty-first ward. He became an alderman and member of the City Council in 1947. As time went on, he learned that many Republicans in Cook County were trading votes with the Democrats rather than seeking statewide victories for their party. For that reason he opposed Republican County Board president

William Erickson for governor. He did not like the political company Erickson kept, even though he respected him as an individual. Stratton's age appealed to Immel. "I could talk to him as a peer," he remembers, "and we got along fine."[3] That Stratton had been divorced was a political problem, one on which Immel worked with the clergy and press in Chicago.

Stratton probably evaluated every move and policy in his role as treasurer with an eye toward its effect on his chances of becoming governor, which is not a standard of conduct for which one need apologize. The end of one marriage and the start of another represented a new beginning for him. His defeat in the race for secretary of state in 1948 seemed to free him from the compulsion to seek the office his father had held, and by 1951 he appeared to be more comfortable with himself than he had previously been.

When Stratton became treasurer in 1951, he "announced a policy of trying to expand the number of state interest-bearing accounts" as a public-relations move and in the interest of "fairness." Bankers tended to be influential in their communities, and for Stratton as treasurer to do business with an increasing number of them was in his political interest. He allowed every bank that wanted a deposit of interest-bearing funds to have one. The number of banks in which state funds were placed went from 382 to 504. In 1956 Stratton told representatives of the United States Senate Committee on Banking and Currency, when he appeared before it in regard to wrongdoing by the state auditor, that spreading the deposit of state funds more broadly "is one of the issues I felt gave us such strong support for governor."

Stratton as treasurer also avoided the practice of forcing employees to contribute a percentage of their salaries—often 2 percent—for political uses. He told the Senate committee that in 1951 and 1952 he never allowed any "assessment" or "advance contribution" to be levied on employees. "I had a strict rule," he said, "that I wouldn't accept any contribution of any kind, unless I am actually running for a specific office, so the contributor knows that he is making it to a campaign fund."[4] When he became a candidate for governor in 1951, Stratton took pride in having ended the 2-percent levy.

According to Joe Immel, Stratton never doubted his ability to be governor. He realls that "Bill thinks positively," and also that Shirley Stratton encouraged her husband to run. Her attitude "helped Bill tremendously." When he was asked why Stratton chose to run for governor in 1952, Immel replied, "I never asked Bill why. Do you ask a football player if he likes to kick a football? Stratton is a political animal, [and] he was greatly ambitious." He believes that Stratton was the logical

Republican candidate in 1952—he had substantial name recognition, good political background, and strength both in Chicago and downstate.[5]

Willard Ice recalls that Stratton "was well known in party circles on his own," in contrast to 1940, when he had been elected on his father's reputation and name.[6] He knew the Republican county chairmen on a first-name basis and was widely known about the state. Immel recalls that "he could walk into a drugstore or a gasoline station or a church or a pool hall and they'd all say, 'Hello Bill'" and that "no man . . . knew Illinois better than Bill Stratton."[7]

Stratton formally announced his candidacy for governor on September 24, 1951, at his home in Morris. But this time there was a difference—there was a "huge throng on hand," according to the *Morris Daily Herald.* The mayor had designated the day as "Stratton for Governor" day. The Morris Community High School band was there, as were state officials Nickell and Searcy. State Senator Victor McBroom of Kankakee presided and several other legislators were present. Stratton's announcement was lengthy, positive, and upbeat.[8]

In his primary campaign Stratton had to run once more without the support of a statewide Republican organization. He responded by going directly to the people. Edward P. Saltiel, who was then a state senator and candidate for the Republican nomination for attorney general, remembers that Stratton had scheduled a number of meetings and was willing to have other Republican candidates share the platform with him. Saltiel often traveled with Stratton and found him a pleasant companion. "He was always laughing," according to Saltiel. "In fact he didn't laugh, he cackled." That cackle was so distinctive that it allowed his friends to locate his presence even in a large crowd.[9]

Stratton had the help in his primary campaign of a trusted group of longtime friends, including Chester Todd, Andy Fasseas, and Richard Lyons. He also credits Shirley Stratton with being a significant new factor in this and future campaigns. Charles J. Fleck, Republican committeeman for the forty-fifth ward in Chicago, supported him from the start, as did Immel. Among committeemen in Chicago Fleck had at first stood alone for Stratton against the candidacy of William Erickson, who was president of the Cook County Board and had much patronage at his disposal. Stratton eventually backed Fleck for Republican chairman in Cook County, though not successfully.[10]

Erickson was a strong contender for the Republican nomination for governor in 1952. He had ties to the ill-reputed west side bloc, however, and even though he attempted to purge its members from the Republican organization in Cook County, he got into difficulty with the law and public opinion when it was discovered that there were "payrollers," persons doing no work, on the county's rolls, and that several of them were associates of the west side bloc.[11] Joe Immel recalls that the Cook County public "wanted a change. . . . [They] were getting sick and tired of politics as usual, and Bill [Stratton] seemed like a breath of fresh air in the Republican Party."[12]

Erickson was indicted and withdrew from the primary race, but too late to get his name removed from the ballot. For all practical purposes, however, his candidacy was ended. There was no agreed-upon organization candidate for the nomination for governor.[13] Most of the ward committeemen came over to Stratton's side. Remaining opponents were Park Livingston, a political unknown, even though he was chairman of the University of Illinois Board of Trustees, and the perennial candidate Richard Yates Rowe. Against that competition, Stratton ran strongly. Even so, it was not an easy contest everywhere in the state.

Among Chicago's newspapers, Stratton had the *Tribune* and the *Herald-American* on his side; but the *Sun-Times* and the *Daily News* were opposed. In postprimary editorials the *Sun-Times* called him "Billy the Kid," "a political spoilsman," the "least able" of the three leading Republican candidates for the nomination, and a "political hack." That was the Democratic line on Stratton.[14] The "Billy the Kid" tag hurt; it implied that he still stood in his father's shadow and that he was in a sense an "outlaw." Such strong criticism of Stratton by the Democrats and by the *Sun-Times* probably indicates that they realized that, of the Republican aspirants, he would be the strongest in the general election in November.[15]

G. A. Robichaux, who thought well of Governor Stevenson, wrote in the *New Republic* of Stratton:

> Stratton's entire approach to politics is perhaps best illustrated by his attitude toward the handshake. "You grab first," says Stratton, "otherwise you may get your hand broken." His success in Illinois cannot be attributed solely to the practical application of that policy, but it has certainly helped. . . . Stratton's nature is such that he likes to run a one-man show. He is unwilling to delegate authority or to allow patronage matters to get out of his own hands. Throughout his political career he had been a lone-wolf.

Robichaux further suggested that, as state treasurer in 1943 and 1944, Stratton staffed his office with "undeserving politicians." The second time around as treasurer he "was able to run his office without scandal."[16] The implication was that there *had* been scandal during the earlier term.

In the primary Stratton won decisively, finishing far ahead of Rowe and Livingston, even though the latter won in the Cook County suburbs. For Rowe this defeat marked the end of his career as an office-seeker, and he went into the insurance business in Jacksonville. His son Harris Rowe, who was active in Morgan County politics during the 1950s, remembers that his father and Stratton enjoyed an amicable relationship, even though they had often been rivals, and that the elder Rowe hosted a reception for Stratton during the 1952 campaign and supported him in 1956 and 1960.[17]

Stratton ran strongly in the primary in Chicago, and had built "a tremendous following downstate," according to the *Daily News.* Even though he was still a young man, Stratton was far ahead of his rivals in political experience. He used television in his primary campaign—unusual for the time—even though he did not like the medium. He felt that it did not enhance his appearance, and disliked the makeup which was necessary.[18] Johnson Kanady, who was a reporter for the *Tribune* in 1952 and Stratton's press secretary during his second term as governor, recalls that Stratton "was young in years but very wise in politics," and that Warren Wood, who was the Republican Speaker of the House, once said that Stratton "knows Illinois like the palm of his hand."[19] That familiarity was soon to be put to use as Stratton turned to the general election campaign against the incumbent governor, Adlai E. Stevenson.

Stevenson had come to the office of governor after having worked in Washington, D.C. and as a lawyer in Chicago, but he had had little experience in Illinois government. His father had been active in Illinois politics and had served a portion of a term as secretary of state after having been appointed to fill a vacancy. His grandfather had been vice-president of the United States. So Stevenson, like Stratton, had been born into a political family. There the resemblence ended. Stevenson's strongest interest had been in international relations in the years before he became governor. In 1948, when he was elected, his preference had been to run for the United States Senate.[20] The Chicago politicians who controlled his party preferred, however, to send Paul Douglas to the Senate and thus out of the state and so slated Douglas and Stevenson as they did. As a result Stevenson came to an office that had not been his first choice with little knowledge about how to conduct himself there.

In Stevenson's defence it was a difficult time to be governor of Illinois. Almost twenty years of depression and war had left the physical plant of the state in a tattered condition. The highway system was obsolete. There had been little building of schools for many years, and the "baby boomers," children of the generation that had fought World War II, were rapidly coming to school age. The veterans' "G.I. Bill" had raised the level of consciousness within the state as far as attending college was concerned, but facilities for higher education were greatly lacking. Even so, one more experienced in Illinois government than Stevenson would probably have fared better as governor.

Republican political activists, such as Immel and Downey, viewed Governor Stevenson as ineffective in getting legislation through the General Assembly—which is not surprising. They recognized his wit and the speaking ability for which he became noted but felt that, at the start of his tenure, he knew few persons outside Chicago and that he would have been more at home in the State Department or in the United States Senate. Republican Elbert Smith of Decatur, who was in the Illinois Senate during Stevenson's term as governor and later served as state auditor, recalls that Stevenson blamed lack of progress in road building under Governor Green on Green's shortcomings and excessive patronage. Those were not the problems, according to Smith; instead it was simply a lack of funds. Stevenson was slow to recognize that lack and would not take the initiative in seeking a higher tax on gasoline in 1949. Nor would the General Assembly, and the result was stalemate and inaction. Stevenson supported a five cent per gallon increase in 1951, and the General Assembly concurred, but progress in road building was then two years behind where it might have been.[21]

Even those who were politically neutral or who were of Stevenson's party found few concrete accomplishments with which to credit him as governor of Illinois. The historian Richard J. Jensen states that

> Stevenson was an ineffective governor. Temperamentally he could not cooperate with local or legislative leaders; his real interest was in international affairs. His major achievement was use of state law enforcement officials to destroy syndicated gambling–prostitution–loan shark rings in Rock Island, Peoria, Joliet, Decatur, Springfield, and even in the notorious East Saint Louis region. Except in the last area, organized vice remained suppressed, and local politics took a quantum leap away from the corrupt linkage between the underworld and politicians.[22]

Democratic legislators who were in the General Assembly while Stevenson was governor generally did not feel that there was much legislative accomplishment during that time. John Fribley, who was the Democrats' downstate leader in the Senate, was of that opinion.[23] Leland Kennedy of Alton, who was in the House of Representatives during Stevenson's term, respected the governor's intellect and believed he "grew" in office, but about the legislation he supported, Kennedy remembered best the Gateway Amendment, which eased the process of amending the constitution. He felt that Stevenson failed at attempts to improve mine safety.[24] Martin Lohman of Pekin, a veteran lawmaker in the Senate, praised Stevenson as a "diplomat," principally on the basis of his later role as United States ambassador to the United Nations. Years later he recalled that the party organization did not favor Stevenson in 1952, and was glad to have him run for president rather than for a second term as governor.[25]

Donald J. O'Brien, a Chicago attorney who was elected to the state Senate in 1950 and became Democratic minority leader in 1958, knew Stevenson well. He opposed Stevenson's use of the state police in raiding Elks Clubs and American Legion halls for illegal slot machines, contending that such action should be left to sheriffs and state's attorneys and that it was not good politics. When Stevenson replied that he had been elected by a plurality of 425 thousand votes, which suggested that he could withstand the political heat, O'Brien countered by saying that it was the Democratic party organization that had elected him. "You couldn't stand at the corner of State and Madison [in 1948]," O'Brien told Stevenson, "and call one hundred people by their first name." O'Brien suggests that the party organization abandoned Stevenson before he lost to Eisenhower in Illinois by 443 thousand votes in 1952.[26]

Clyde Lee, a Mt. Vernon Democrat in the House of Representatives during Stevenson's term, recalls that the governor told him he did not want to run for president, that he would have preferred a second term. Lee believes he was "popular," "had a good record," and would have been reelected if he had run again. In this account Lee did not go into detail about the content of the Stevenson record.[27] Leland Rayson, a Democrat who served in the House from 1965 to 1977, credits Stevenson with attracting him to politics. "Stevenson could inspire the best in you," he recalls. Even so he thought him a "loser," who brooded about the 1960 presidential nomination while others were working hard to get it, with the inevitable result.[28]

Maurice Scott, longtime executive director of the Illinois Taxpayers' Federation, admired Stevenson's wit and felt that he gave education strong support and improved the state police. He credits Stevenson with bringing some good young people onto his staff and into state government.[29] Willard Ice, a career bureaucrat who knew and worked for several governors, recalls of Stevenson that "you would get that impression that he did really care [about people] but somehow he didn't know how to put that across" and "he didn't entirely convey what ... he felt." Even though Stevenson was criticized for being indecisive, Ice never found him so in the limited contact he had with the governor, which was in regard to the problem of missing cigarette tax machines, late in his term.[30]

While Bernice Van Der Vries, a Republican who served in the Illinois House of Representatives from 1935 to 1957, feels that Stevenson should

have gone for another term as governor and "could have had another
... I'm sure," she also damns him with faint praise. "Although a lot of
people said he was weak ... I didn't find him weak. He was deliberate."[31]
It should be noted that in her lengthy memoir, Van Der Vries has little
to say about Stratton, good or bad, even though her service in the
General Assembly spanned most of his political career.

Difficulties in the General Assembly and in funding and accomplishing road building were not the only problems that Governor Stevenson
faced. His testimony in the Alger Hiss case, the "horse meat scandal" (in
which, despite state inspection, horse meat was sold to the public in
butcher shops as hamburger), the West Frankfort mine disaster, the
cigarette tax fraud scandal, the sins of his appointees (as in cases involving race track stock), and rioting at Menard Penitentiary all worked to
his disadvantage. It is ironic that, just as Governor Green experienced
the mine accident at Centralia and suffered at Stevenson's hands at the
polls for it, the latter in turn was charged with allowing one of similar
dimension to occur at West Frankfort.

The cigarette tax fraud incident was an especially unsavory matter.
According to Joe Immel, who could be expected to put the worst
possible face on it, Stevenson "gave the west side politicians control of
cigarette tax collection in Chicago. When [Richard J.] Lyons became
director of Revenue he was looking for the meters. And he and [Assistant
Director] Fasseas made a search and found a lot of the meters in west
side garages." Immel has stated that, even though Stevenson relinquished
his candidacy to run for president, his party in Illinois had to run on his
record—which was a "disaster."[32]

While one must bear in mind the natural biases of partisans, such
as Immel and Downey, the fact is that Governor Stevenson's record in
office was not strong. Because 1952 was a Republican year, Stevenson
probably would have lost the election to Stratton if he had remained on
the ballot. That Stevenson did not carry Illinois in the contest for president, losing to Eisenhower by 443 thousand votes, suggests how much
his political standing had suffered.

During a luncheon at the Illinois Athletic Club in Chicago in mid-
June, Governor Stevenson challenged Stratton to a debate. There was
already ill-feeling between them, and a debate would have been interesting, but even as he made the challenge Stevenson was the "hottest thing
in American politics," according to the *Chicago Sun-Times.* Soon he was
chosen to be the Democratic presidential candidate at that party's national convention. Some believed that Stevenson was drafted against his
will, but there is much evidence to the contrary.

Stratton, as the highest-ranking Republican state official and the
nominee for governor, had welcomed his own party's national conven-

tion to Chicago and Illinois on July 7. It was a bland presentation, in which he invoked the memory of Abraham Lincoln, condemned the New Deal, expressed fear of the results of Democratic foreign policy, and hoped for victory in November, nationally and in Illinois. He was steering a middle course between the rival candidacies of Eisenhower and Taft for the Republican nomination for president.

When Stevenson took his name out of contention for governor, he insisted that his party replace it with that of Lieutenant Governor Sherwood Dixon, probably not the strongest candidate the party could have chosen—one thinks of Secretary of State Edward J. Barrett, who had beaten Stratton decisively in 1948—and again the element of luck seemed to be on Stratton's side. But he took nothing for granted and went campaigning as vigorously as he had in earlier contests.

His campaign style was well matured by 1952. Johnson Kanady remembers that "Stratton was a street campaigner. He loved to go into a town and talk to people around the square." He loved campaigning and the people it brought him into touch with.[33] According to Ed Pree, "He was a very good candidate. . . . He was pleasant, people liked him, he laughed and he smiled; he was genuine and he loved people. He got along with people . . . and he was very inoffensive."[34] Joe Immel recalls that while Stratton came to Chicago regularly during his campaign, he "was more at ease . . . going into the communities . . . and being Bill rather than being on a platform and being a candidate for governor."[35]

During the campaign Stratton "had a standing bet with newsmen that before he walked a block in any town someone would greet him with 'Hi, Bill.' He never lost a bet. Said he, 'My father used to say he knew 250 thousand people in Illinois. I think I know more than that.'"[36] Smokey Downey recalls that Stratton "was a good campaigner. He loved to campaign. He'd go house to house, and he'd go farmer to farmer. . . . He traveled the state so many times. He knew people."[37]

In Stratton's own thinking, as he went into the 1952 campaign, his strengths were substantial. He had a good formal education in political science, public finance, and administration. His family background added to his understanding of politics; and his earlier offices had given him much practical experience. He had proven his electibility. His Navy service helped, as did his civic (Lions Club) and fraternal (Delta Chi, Masons, Shriners) ties.

As his campaign got under way, his manager in Cook County, Charles Fleck, opened an office for him in Chicago. Joe Immel remembers that other like-minded Republican candidates, such as Charles Carpentier, who was running for secretary of state, clustered around, and "Stratton built a team so that when he went into office he had something." The candidate for state auditor of public accounts, Orville Hodge, from downstate in Granite City, was also expected to defer to Stratton's leadership.

Even though the *Chicago Sun-Times* implied during the campaign that Stratton, as "Billy the Kid," had already enriched himself through the sale of patronage, nothing could have been farther from the truth. He was almost totally without personal funds and other assets in 1950 and little better off two years later. Campaign funds were at first in short supply. Joe Immel recalls that "when Bill started [in 1952] he had very, very little money.... I used to go out and buy things in the stationery store for the headquarters and paid it [*sic*] out of my pocket.... Bill was never a man of affluence. He was a middle-class young man with a nice background, but he didn't come from wealth." By mid-1952 money began to come into the campaign in significant quantity. After Stevenson left the Democratic ticket as candidate for governor, the Republican movers and shakers decided that Stratton could win and contributed generously, which was encouraging. Immel, speaking about the campaign, said that we all "worked our heads off."[38]

Had Stevenson continued to be the Democratic candidate for governor he might have conducted a more personal campaign against Stratton than did Sherwood Dixon. Even though Stevenson and Stratton had worked well together as public officials, by 1952 there was substantial friction between them. Dixon, however, chose primarily to campaign against former Governor Dwight Green. In speaking to the Democratic state convention in Chicago on September 12, he said "this is not the time ... to change back to the kind of Republican administration we had in Illinois for eight years.... the days of favoritism for political cronies, padded payrolls, contract kick backs, coddling of gamblers."[39] Dixon was suggesting, of course, that to elect Stratton would be to invite a return to those conditions.

As election day approached there was much confidence in the Republican party of a decisive win. The Strattons spent election night at their house in Morris and a large crowd gathered there. Joe Immel sensed from the early Chicago returns that a solid win was in the making and called Stratton to congratulate him. When Stratton said, "Why don't you come on down and join me?" Immel went. Andy Fasseas was there, with others of the campaign team.

It was a happy group that chalked up the returns through the night, for when they were all in Stratton had defeated Dixon by 228 thousand votes. Other Republican candidates fared better. John W. Chapman, a relative unknown who had been Governor Green's executive secretary, was elected lieutenant governor by 249 thousand votes. Charles Carpentier accomplished the unusual in Illinois politics by beating an incumbent secretary of state—Edward J. Barrett—by 9 thousand votes. Orville

Hodge won the office of state auditor of public accounts by 335 thousand. Republicans Elmer Hoffman and Latham Castle were elected treasurer and attorney general, respectively.

Stratton clearly ran behind his party, yet he carried ninety-three counties. Only in Cook, Christian, Franklin, Gallatin, Macon, Macoupin, Madison, St. Clair, and Union did the Democratic candidate win. Stratton prevailed everywhere except in the most urban Democratic strongholds, in places where the influence of the United Mine Workers was strong, and in a few rural Democratic bastions.

With victory in hand, Governor-elect and Mrs. Stratton soon left for Tucson, Arizona, for a vacation. Shirley was not yet thirty years old and had been married to the man who was soon to be governor for not quite two years. They had much to think about as they planned their move into the executive mansion. It was only a few blocks down the street from their modest apartment but a world away in the style of life they were soon to know. One of their decisions at this time was to have Stratton's two daughters share the mansion with them as a part of their family. His mother was to continue to live in the house in Morris.

By coincidence, Adlai Stevenson also vacationed near Tucson, following his loss of the presidency to General Eisenhower. Stratton had campaigned against him and his record as governor, which was appropriate since Stevenson had headed his party's ticket and was thus fair game. From Arizona, Stevenson rejected Stratton's campaign charges that his administration had been on a "spending spree." Only in road building and education had appropriations been higher than before, he pointed out, and those only in the last two years of his term. He claimed to have legislation for road modernization—the first since 1929—"already passed." He may have been attempting to blunt any claim Stratton might later make to such an accomplishment. Stevenson told newsmen that the presidential campaign of three months' duration was less strenuous than his ten-month campaign for governor in 1948.[40]

After losing the presidential election, Stevenson continued to take an interest in Illinois politics. His biographer, John Bartlow Martin, who served him as a speech writer in 1952, reported that he wrote "to his cousin Bud Merwin: 'I was bitterly disappointed about the State ticket in Illinois and the people will have cause to regret it.' The election of Stratton as governor was painful to Stevenson," Martin felt, for "he thought William G. Stratton epitomized the worst in the Illinois Republican party." If that feeling on Stevenson's part was correctly reported by Martin, it illustrates clearly the lack of understanding that Stevenson had of Illinois politics. For one as little experienced in state government as Stevenson was, in comparison to Stratton, his judgment of his successor seems shallow.

Martin also reported that "in 1953 ... several young men who had worked for Stevenson.... were forming the Committee for Illinois Government ... to keep watch on Governor Stratton. Stevenson encouraged them: he was bitter toward Stratton." He had opposed Stratton the first time he ran for Congress, in 1940. He thought then that Stratton was too young and too inexperienced, and regretted his isolationism. Stevenson himself had taken a courageous stand against isolationism at a time when it was difficult for him to do so.[41] Stevenson's feelings toward Stratton in 1952 and 1953, and those of the "several young men" to whom Martin refers, seem both arrogant and vindictive.

In that simpler time, there was little effort spent in any formal transition from one administration to the next. Almost the whole of the transition from Stevenson to Stratton was accomplished in a single evening in December 1952, when Carl McGowan, Stevenson's legislative aide, spent two or three hours talking with Ed Pree, who was to be Stratton's administrative assistant.[42]

For many years a report, perhaps apocryphal, circulated in Springfield, of an exchange late in 1952 between the retiring governor and the governor-elect. It went as follows: "Stevenson: 'What can I do for you?' Stratton: 'There are only two things I want from you, governor, the key to the office and the key to the mansion!'"

8

First-Term Governor:
First Biennium

The Illinois that Stratton was to serve as governor during the 1950s was a giant among the forty-eight states. It ranked fourth in population, first in the production of farm machinery and steel and in meat packing, and third in manufacturing. In 1950 it yielded fifty-seven million tons of coal and sixty-two million barrels of oil. In the following year it ranked first in the production of both corn and soybeans. It was the transportation hub of the nation and a center for business, banking, finance, and communications. With twenty-five congressional districts it was a potent force in Congress and in the election of the president of the United States.

The age of television was just arriving. The national conventions of the two major political parties were rated as the best public affairs programs of 1952, the first year for them to be on television, and *Look* magazine reported that the "networks spent more than $10,000,000 to take politics out of smoke-filled rooms and into the parlor." As a participant in the Republican convention, Stratton had his moment on the flickering tube. The first television showing of the annual awards of the Academy of Motion Picture Arts and Sciences—the Academy Awards—came in 1953. Rights to the show cost the networks $100,000, and it ran to what was then a lengthy one and one-half hours. Magazines such as *Life* and *Look* were still the most graphic illustrators and advertisers of the times.

After the brief vacation in Arizona, following his election in November, Stratton set out to accomplish the complicated task of choosing a personal staff and of forming a cabinet. At the core of his staff were his longtime associates Marion Keevers and Smokey Downey. Keevers, who served Stratton as executive secretary, was believed to be the first woman to fill that role for an Illinois governor. Downey was press secretary, legislative liaison, agent for patronage, and adviser in general. Another staff member who quickly became important to Stratton was Edward Pree, who at first handled the details of patronage and soon became a general administrative assistant.

Pree's personal and professional qualifications allowed him to become a key figure during Stratton's first term. He was born in Springfield in 1919. His father, a lawyer who was an assistant state's attorney for Sangamon County in the early 1920s, helped prosecute Governor Small in the case that served to advance William Joseph Stratton, the governor's father, to political prominence. The younger Pree was very much a part of the Springfield establishment. Herb Georg, the premier photographer and portraitist of decades of politicians and other citizens of Springfield, was his uncle. Pree went to Colgate University for his freshman year, then to Northwestern University, where he was active in Republican politics as an undergraduate. He became acquainted with Stratton in 1941 at a Young Republican convention. Stratton was in Congress then, and Pree was impressed by his anti-interventionism. "I was immediately attracted to him," Pree recalls, "because he was a young man," and "kind of a boy wonder."

Pree joined the Stratton administration before inauguration day, hoping to continue a law practice with his father on a part-time basis. That task proved impossible, as his personnel, legal, legislative, and other work for Stratton took all his time.[1] Photographs show that Pree was an attractive person—tall, handsome, balding, well-dressed, with a broad smile and a level gaze—obviously an asset to the Stratton team.[2]

In forming only a small personal staff, Stratton was in the tradition of governors' offices generally, at that time, and within the budgetary limitation established during Stevenson's term, a total of only $197,010 for the 1951–53 biennium.[3] According to John Parkhurst, who was a member of the General Assembly, Stratton "stood right at the crossroads of the old system [of staffing] versus the new." He had only a small staff and no budget office, employed a "vest pocket" style, and "was the last of the . . . [Illinois] governors who was able to manage it all by himself."[4]

Before inauguration day Stratton's selection of his cabinet was nearly complete. His choices comprised a mix of persons who had been associated with his father and subsequently with the governor-elect himself, others who had been political associates of his, other active Republicans, and still others who were well-qualified careerists. On the whole it was a mature group, which may explain in part the reason he turned to younger persons for personal staff. Ed Pree remembers that Stratton "wanted some young people around him. So many of his directors were older men."[5]

It is interesting to speculate about Stratton's choice of persons who had been associated with his father for cabinet posts; they may have represented a continuation of his compulsion to equal his father's political accomplishments, which had been evident in earlier years. Perhaps he was attempting to repay political debts, which he felt the Stratton family still owed, in his choice of some cabinet members.

Stratton accomplished two notable firsts in appointing a woman and a black to his cabinet. Circuit Judge Vera M. Binks, of Henry County, was named director of the Department of Registration and Education. She had supported him in earlier campaigns, and had demonstrated her own political strength by winning election as judge, not an ordinary accomplishment for a woman at that time. Joseph D. Bibb was chosen to be director of the Department of Public Safety. He was believed to be the highest ranking black to serve in any state since Reconstruction. Blacks still had difficulty in 1953 finding hotels and restaurants that would admit them in Springfield, "Mr. Lincoln's home town." It could not have been an easy thing for Stratton to have named a black to the cabinet. He felt that "if Bibb makes a success of his job, as I'm convinced he will, it's bound to contribute to better understanding between the races and to have a good effect all around."[6]

Fred Selcke of Petersburg, who worked in Stratton's campaigns when allies often were few, feels that he "was way ahead of his time . . . regarding women and . . . blacks." The latter "were all locked in with the Democrats," so Bibb's appointment would not make them Republicans, Selcke believes. "Bibb was a competent guy and I think it was a move to let the blacks realize that . . . they had some spokesmen of their race in the state administration."[7]

Bibb was well qualified. He was a lawyer who had attended Harvard, Yale, and Columbia universities. With a long record of Republican activism, he had been a journalist with the *Chicago Sun,* and was managing editor of the Chicago edition of the *Pittsburgh Courier* when he was named to the cabinet. Corneal Davis, a black man who served in the General Assembly from 1942 to 1978 and as a leader in civil rights, recalls that "the highest job any black had . . . was Joe Bibb. . . . I am a Democrat but I want to be honest, no other black ever had that title."[8]

Conspicous among Stratton's cabinet officers who had known his father were Richard J. Lyons, Glen Palmer, and Stillman Stanard. Lyons, of Lake County, who had unsuccessfully sought several high state offices, was appointed director of the Department of Revenue. Palmer was named to head the Department of Conservation. He had worked in the department in the 1920s, under the governor's father. From the start of Stratton's political career Palmer had been a faithful ally. Smokey Downey remembers that "Glen kind of fathered him," calling him "Willy," often in the presence of others. Ed Pree recalls reports that Palmer "used to hold little Billy on his lap." In any case, Palmer had access to the governor, an important commodity. Stanard had been director of the Department of Agriculture in the 1920s, when the governor's father headed one of its divisions. Appointed to his earlier post, he was well qualified by education and experience.

Cabinet choices having strong political backgrounds were Morton H. Hollingsworth and Edwin A. Rosenstone. Hollingsworth, named director of the Department of Finance, had been a Boy Scout executive and had later gone into business. He was chairman of the Republican State Central Committee, a member of the party's National Committee, and clearly a political powerhouse. Rosenstone had earned a degree in political science at the University of Illinois and put his learning to work during four terms as county clerk of Henry County. He had served for nine years on the Illinois Commerce Commission, and was assistant treasurer when Stratton was treasurer the second time. He was appointed director of the politically sensitive Department of Public Works and Buildings. In these two men, Stratton obviously had mature, experienced, competent cabinet members with much political sophistication.

Stratton chose to retain three cabinet-level administrators who been appointed by earlier governors. Roland R. Cross, M.D., had been director of the Department of Public Health since 1940. Joseph K. McLaughlin, a lawyer from Decatur who had served in the Navy, had been director of the Department of Aeronautics since 1949. The third was Major General Leo M. Boyle, the adjutant general and head of the Illinois National Guard since 1940. He was a career soldier.

To head the Department of Public Health, Stratton chose Otto L. Bettag, M.D. He had been politically active, with experience in working in state tuberculosis sanitaria. Roy Cummins, of Joe Immel's ward in Chicago, became director of the Department of Labor. Cummins had no political experience, hence his selection was not purely political. He had been a labor leader. Ben H. Shull was appointed head of the Department of Mines and Minerals, which was a sensitive post—recall the problems Governors Green and Stevenson had with mine disasters. Shull was the oldest member of the cabinet, nearly seventy, and had long experience in mine management.

Robert E. Barrett was appointed director of the Department of Insurance. His chief qualification was that he was the brother of George F. Barrett, who had been attorney general when Green was governor. (Barrett and Green had usually been at odds.) Robert Barrett had a law degree from the University of Chicago and some experience in insurance. A veteran Springfield newsman told me in 1985 that one of the understandings of the Barrett appointment was that Mrs. Barrett, a lady of some sophistication, would offer Shirley Stratton schooling in the gracious performance of her social duties as first lady.

Stratton's longtime political supporter George R. Perrine, of Kane County, was appointed head of the Illinois Commerce Commission. An attorney, he had served on the commission when Green was governor. Major General Robert R. Woodward was named director of civil defense. He was a career soldier and lawyer who had served six terms in the Illinois House of Representatives.

Not every person whom Stratton approached accepted a position in the cabinet. Joe Immel turned one down to remain in Chicago as an alderman. He told Stratton that one day he would like to be a judge. In some cases Stratton had a long memory for those who served him well, and six years later appointed Immel to the Superior Court of Cook County. Immel recalls that "I found him to be a man I could trust." Stratton directed considerable patronage toward Immel's ward, including drawing from it the director of the Department of Labor, Roy Cummins.[9]

It was unfortunate that one of Stratton's staunchest supporters, Rupert Bippus, did not have the opportunity to serve in his cabinet or to sit as a judge as he would have preferred. Bippus had run unsuccessfully for Cook County assessor in 1950 and then had become a judge, but he died of a heart attack before presiding over a courtroom or enjoying seeing Stratton become governor.[10] Standing alone, his correspondence with Stratton would comprise an interesting political history of the period. Stratton lost his best adviser when Bippus died.

Even though Stratton appointed a number of old friends to cabinet posts, he was discriminating about ability and qualifications. Several longtime supporters never made it to the inner circle. Examples are Earl Madigan and Fred Selcke. While both were advantageously employed in state government during the time Stratton was governor, neither ever held cabinet rank. Nor did John Graham return to a significant post under Stratton's control. Stratton had the ability to judge human talents, and the strength of will to place people accordingly.

On the whole, Stratton's first cabinet was a good one. It was remarkably durable, with only two changes during his first term of office. McLaughlin resigned as director of the Department of Aeronautics in 1954 to seek higher income and was replaced by Arthur E. Abney, who had been assistant director of the Department since 1950. Abney was a Navy veteran, a pilot, and a lawyer. Barrett died in 1954 and was replaced as director of the Department of Insurance by Justin T. McCarthy, who had experience in real estate and investments and had worked for two state attorneys general, one a Republican and one a Democrat, as chief appraiser for inheritance tax matters.

Ed Pree recalls that Stratton "had ... very good relationships with all the members of his cabinet. So many of them had been old time friends of his." "There was a real sense of purpose, a zeal that permeated the administration," and "the whole administration ... was imbued with a spirit of wanting ... to make a great record." Stratton was ambitious for higher office, and that spirit was transmitted to his associates. Pree feels that he inspired people at all levels to good performance.[11] As experienced an observer as Smokey Downey judged the cabinet to be quite capable. The directors were politically astute; Stratton kept the "engineers" in the field, where Downey feels they belonged.[12] Stratton seemed to be fully aware of the importance of serving the political need, while insisting on capable and honest people. He might be criticized for appointing a number of longtime associates to his cabinet; however, his choices were good, and few governors of Illinois in this century, at least, have had the breadth of political experience to provide them with such a large pool of trusted associates that could be drawn on.

Stratton was inaugurated on January 12, 1953, before an estimated crowd of six thousand, in the state armory in Springfield. The motorcade from the mansion to the armory was led by the Morris High School band. Stratton had promised it that place in the inaugural parade when he made his announcement for governor.

Governor Stevenson moved out of the mansion the day before the inauguration. Governor-elect and Mrs. Stratton, Sandra and Diana, both now in their teens, moved in that afternoon. As the governor and his successor posed for pictures at the mansion, before the inauguration, Stratton remarked, "Your family ran to boys, and ours to girls." Never one to pass up an opportunity for a quip, Stevenson replied, "Neither of us is very well balanced."[13] He left by train for Chicago soon after the inaugural ceremony.

In his inaugural address Stratton stressed his legislative and executive experience. The goals that he considered most important were highway improvements and safety, reapportionment of the General Assembly, judicial reform, establishment of a state crime commission, construction of a state office building, and improvements in public health and education. He hoped that the primary election date might be set later in the year and that the treasurer's term could be lengthened to four years. The Republican platform upon which he ran had identified other goals, such as the consolidation of state agencies and improved mine safety.[14]

Stratton held a cabinet meeting on his second day in office. It was a "get acquainted and guidelines session." A few days later in an interview he mentioned the "open house" that he planned to hold one day each week. He believed that "the people of Illinois have a right to come in

110

and talk to him." "As for the executive mansion," Stratton said that we "intend to make that a home for [our]selves and the girls. It will be a middle Illinois country home if [we] can make it so."[15]

Shirley Stratton was intent on being much more than simply the keeper of the official residence. She was the first full-time hostess in the executive mansion for more than twenty-five years. She had the vigor of youth, as earlier governors' wives often had not. Adlai Stevenson had been separated from his wife early in his term as governor, then divorced, so there had been no active first lady during his time, although his sister, Elizabeth Ives, filled a portion of that vacuum. Shirley was determined to become a full-time partner in the business of governing the state: she accepted the political life and all that went with it.[16] She went to work immediately. Stratton, unlike Stevenson, who had located his principal office in the mansion, had set up his base as governor in the capitol. He and Shirley often worked together in the mansion office upon matters that were not basically governmental or political.

The "mansion file" reveals that from the start Shirley was active in correspondence and as official hostess. She was attentive to small courtesies. Her letters reveal a clear, strong mind, concern for others, and attention to detail. Photographs of the time show her well dressed, attractive, confident and regal in carriage, yet sometimes a bit overwhelmed. In all forms of expression—correspondence, news articles and photographs—she came through as a strong and positive personality. In 1951 and 1952 she had become active in Springfield community affairs and in the First Methodist Church, and that sort of participation was expanded. In addition to other concerns, the mansion was badly run down and in need of much redecoration and repair.[17]

Immediately after becoming governor, Stratton had to deal with the matter of patronage in all its many forms. There was the expectation on the part of many Republicans that all Democratic jobholders would be discharged. If simply being a Democrat were not sufficient grounds, surely being politically active was. An April 30 memo to Ed Pree from Director Stanard of the Department of Agriculture illustrates that feeling. "We have an employee," Stanard wrote, "who was a candidate on the Democratic ticket in the recent election. Maude Myers [president of the Civil Service Commission] suggests . . . there is some question regarding the discharge of a Civil Service employee for this reason. What do you have to do to justify a discharge under Civil Service? Is a conviction and sentence for murder necessary?"[18] Apparently on Stanard's scale of depravity, running as a Democrat ranked just above homicide.

Stratton was fully aware of the significance of patronage to his party, to the quality of service provided the public, and to his political future. He intended from the start to handle all patronage personally, as he had done when he was treasurer. In doing so he was assisted by Smokey Downey and Ed Pree, especially the latter. Pree recalls that "for the first three months Governor Stratton was personally handling all the appointments." Downey remembers being deeply involved, and that "there was nobody appointed that Stratton didn't know about."[19] Through February Stratton and Pree worked together on patronage matters during many nights and Sunday afternoons, as well as during more routine hours. By April the details of all but the major appointments had been turned over to Pree, but Stratton still controlled the decisions.

Pree recalls that "the amazing thing about [Stratton] was that he knew so many people personally.... He had been through so many political campaigns up and down the state so many times, that he knew people by the thousands." He knew not only the people, but the communities and counties in which they lived. He knew where a particular person could function well, and he used that knowledge in deciding appointments. According to Pree, "it was understood by the department heads that the governor made the major appointments and that he was in charge of the personnel in the state government." It was a process that involved the Republican county chairmen, ward and township committeemen in Cook County, and other party leaders who made recommendations; members of the General Assembly; and persons in the governor's office, including Pree and Downey. Discussions of appointments with Stratton were full and detailed—of the local setting, the personalities, the position, everything. "He was on top of it all the time and he wanted to be kept informed." Pree remembers that "we had constant activity; it never lets up; it never ceases."[20]

The Stratton papers contain many references to his keen personal interest in the distribution of patronage. There are a great many notes in his hand pertaining to such matters, and no position was too obscure to escape his attention.[21] Stratton appeared to respect the civil service system, but he felt that employees who were not covered by it—not "certified"—should be discharged if they were Democrats or politically neutral. There were clear understandings between Stratton and the department heads about how the personnel system was to work. The department was to inform the governor's office of open positions. A "directive" would then go from the governor's office to the department, asking that a specified person be interviewed, or in some cases, appointed, retained, or terminated. The department was asked in the directive to inform the governor's office of the result. If no name could be referred to the department, it would ask for a "release" to recruit on its own initiative. When positions were filled in that fashion, the governor's office was informed. The file of directives was carefully kept, with associated correspondence.[22]

Department heads were expected to conform to the directives in all cases where it was possible to do so. The sole exception to that general rule was Ross Randolph, the warden at Menard Penitentiary, where a riot during the 1952 election campaign had embarrassed Governor Stevenson. Randolph could say no to personnel directives from the governor's office. Even though Randolph had been appointed by a Democratic governor, Stratton was sensitive to the importance of having a well-run prison and allowed him some discretion in hiring.[23]

Fred Selcke, who was in a responsible supervisory position in the Department of Registration and Education, remembers that "we didn't fire a lot of people [when Stratton's term began]. The people that did the work ... we didn't get rid of." He also recalls that "Stratton made it very clear ... he didn't want any payroll jobs.... You had to work.... There were no ghost payrollers around that I knew of."[24] Ed Pree has the same recollection. "One thing [Stratton] insisted upon from the beginning was that there'd be no so-called political jobs where they didn't work.... He said, 'if they don't want to work, we don't want them.' ... He didn't want these so-called, payroll jobs that former administrations had had—I guess in both parties—where they put somebody on the payroll and he'd show up to collect his check."[25]

Stratton initiated the practice of holding "open house" in his capitol office soon after becoming governor. On some of the "public days" the line would stretch for two blocks. It was intended at first to be a once-a-week affair, but as time went on it was more likely to be once a month. Many years later he recalled with pleasure those public days.[26]

Life magazine reported upon one of the first of the open houses, held in February, 1953. The callers on the day of *Life*'s visit, according to its reporter,

> were patronage hunters, truckers, farmers, well-wishers, favor-seekers and plain time wasters. Stratton, who launched the "public days" because he wanted "to know what's going on," is pleased with the way it has been going. Thursday open house is now a fixture.... "It's worth the time," he feels. "Look at all the things we take care of this way. And in the summer," he adds hopefully, "there'll probably be large groups of children—and not as many job seekers."

Life's pictures show the crowd in line at the office door, ordinary-looking citizens, and a youthful governor, his dark hair slicked back, intent on conversation with Mrs. Stella Davis, who confided to Stratton "only that she is 'in very bad with the politicians.'"[27]

Before he had been in office for many weeks Stratton displayed a clearly defined administrative style. Willard Ice recalls that he "had an entirely different style than Stevenson. He was more down to earth and friendly.... He could make you feel like you were just an old buddy."[28] While a somewhat critical article published in 1953 held that Stratton delegated little authority[29]—and undoubtedly he did retain personal control of patronage matters—others felt that he delegated extensively.

Fred Selcke remembers that he had easy access to the governor, and that Stratton said, " 'All I want you to do is to run it right.' And he delegated, he wasn't sticking his nose in every five minutes."[30] Ed Pree, too, recalls that Stratton had enough confidence in himself and in the persons he had chosen as directors to delegate authority freely to them. "Governor Stratton was a strong executive. He had such force of personality and ... knowledge of government that they all respected him.... He knew as much about their departments as they did."

Pree remembers that "everybody ... worked. His directors were all hard working. He was the example himself . . . of what a state servant should be. He worked all the time and he loved it.... He used to comment ... 'we like our job ... we enjoy our work.' " Pree mentions Directors Lyons and Stanard as being especially hard working. Lyons died in office and Pree feels that Stanard shortened his life by working too hard and staying on too long.[31]

Ronald Michaelson, who was a member of Governor Ogilvie's (1969–73) staff and later the executive director of the State Board of Elections, feels that Stratton acted as his own chief of staff, and believes that he maintained

> an exceedingly loose formal organizational structure.... Staffers were allowed and even expected to roam freely into many areas. This was in part due to the fact that the demands on the small staff were increasing steadily ... while the size of the staff remained relatively constant.... One of the Governor's assistants acquired the reputation as a very strong and influential figure who emerged as the Governor's "top" aide.

Michaelson did not identify this person, but it was undoubtedly Downey.

When Stratton submitted his budget request to the General Assembly for money for staff for the fiscal years 1954 and 1955, he asked for almost exactly the same amount that had been appropriated for the preceding biennium. In doing so, according to Michaelson, he "chose not to heed the recommendations of the Commission to Study State

Government (Schaefer Commission) that Illinois governors needed more staff." In Michaelson's view, staffing of the governor's office throughout Stratton's two terms "was grossly inadequate,"[32] but increased staff would have violated Stratton's intent to reduce costs. A larger staff would also have reduced the degree of Stratton's personal management of all that went on in state government, an end he would not have willingly sought. However, understaffing probably reduced his effectiveness.

It is evident that Stratton's style of management was direct and personal, face-to-face or by telephone, rather than by correspondence. Neither the Stratton papers nor the archives contain much correspondence with the heads of departments and other agencies. The formalities were put on paper, but most of the management, it appears, was by conference between the governor and his subordinates rather than by written directive. What emerges is a picture of an energetic and well-informed administrator guiding the business of state government through cabinet meetings—which were not frequent—and individual conferences and telephone conversations, in addition to the usual delegation of authority in routine matters.

Stratton did commit to paper, early in 1953, his feeling about the 2-percent funds, the assessments upon state employees for political purposes. In an undated, handwritten note to his administrative assistant, Ed Pree, he ordered that "no state employee [is] to be assessed."[33] On March 19 he issued a directive to agency heads, which read "I am unalterably opposed to political assessment.... from employees.... [They] are entitled to every penny they earn. If anyone approaches an employee in your department ... seeking an assessment, I want that person to report immediately to you."[34] I have found no evidence in the Stratton papers or archives, nor the recollections of persons involved, that the governor's rule regarding such assessments was violated to any significant degree.

It was necessary for Stratton in his first term to become involved quickly with the General Assembly. It met only biennially then, and to miss the opportunity for accomplishing a legislative program in 1953 would have been to let it go by for two years. *Time* magazine noted that not much was expected of a "39-year-old politician with a pompadour and an adolescent voice" whom liberals regarded as a reactionary and old-guard Republicans as an upstart.[35] Stratton understood the importance of good relationships with legislators and their leaders and of working with Democrats as well as Republicans, even though he had the advantage of having a majority of his party in both houses, as Stevenson had not. Legislators of both parties had access to the governor. Although he preferred to fill positions with Republicans, he used patronage to benefit Democrats as well, when a clear-cut need to win votes was shown. Ed Pree recalls that many Democrats in the General Assembly liked Stratton better than they had Stevenson, a fellow Democrat, and that with Stratton there were "closer contacts and maybe a stronger friendship."[36] Fred Selcke remembers that Stratton "took the [Democratic] minority into his confidence . . . too" and names John Lewis, Pete Granata, Paul Powell, Arthur Bidwell, and George Drach as the legislative leaders with whom he most often dealt. "He'd call in five or six . . . on both sides . . . and they would tell the rest of the members how it was going to be."[37]

Smokey Downey feels that "Stratton was a good in-fighter in dealing with legislative matters. He knew what he wanted," and was flexible.[38] Paul Randolph, a Republican who was a member of the state House of Representatives from 1945 to 1977, remembers that during legislative sessions Stratton often held open house for legislators at 8 A.M. on Wednesdays. A light breakfast— juice, coffee, and rolls—was served, and the atmosphere was mainly social, with a little business thrown in. Such occasions must have given the governor much opportunity for making his case for particular legislative proposals and counting votes. Randolph also recalls that "you could walk into his office any time. He . . . had a great grasp of all legislation. . . . He was easy to see."[39]

The Strattons entertained all the members of the General Assembly and their wives at a series of dinners in the executive mansion during the 1953 legislative session. Downey recalls that "Mrs. Stratton was a little bit up-tight about some legislators bringing their wives over and she knew they weren't their wives."[40] In spite of such minor embarrassments, this entertainment contributed to the friendly relationship that Stratton enjoyed with members of the General Assembly.

Stratton sensed that a primary objective in 1953 had to be redistricting of the General Assembly, if his policy goals in highways, education, and mental health were to be realized. In spite of the fact that the Illinois constitution called for redistricting every ten years, none had been accomplished since 1901. The urban areas of the state were the most underrepresented. The rural regions were consistently overrepresented; and thus they strongly opposed any redrawing of district lines. After Stratton left office he wrote that "without . . . [redistricting] we would have been unable to meet the problems of the state."[41] Redistricting allowed a greater compatability between the General Assembly and the governor by better aligning their political bases.[42]

A complete redistricting of both House and Senate on the basis of population, as the constitution directed, was not politically attainable in 1953. Rural legislators, who had been most advantaged by the General Assembly's failure to redistrict for over forty years, were strong enough to prevent it. Thus it was necessary to put redistricting within the context of an amendment to the constitution—a more practicable step after passage in 1950 of the Gateway Amendment, which had made later amendments easier to obtain. Governor Stevenson had strongly supported Gateway, opening the door to Stratton's reapportionment efforts in 1953.

Stratton realized that the expanding suburbs of Cook County and its ring of collar counties were primarily Republican. Redistricting the General Assembly on the basis of population would give the suburban Republicans greater representation. At the same time Chicago Democrats also would be strengthened. Thus Stratton sought support in both parties for redistricting. Years later he recalled that he "buttonholed legislative members on both sides of the aisle."[43] Rural downstate leaders of both parties—notably Speaker Warren Wood and House minority leader Paul Powell—were opposed;[44] however the opposition was reduced by an agreement to increase the size of the Senate from fifty-one to fifty-eight members, and the House from 153 to 177. Those increases would save the seats of legislators from even the most overrepresented districts, and would also provide new seats for aspiring politicians, a fact calculated to increase the acceptability of the plan.

The proposed redistricting followed the "congressional model" of one house based on population, the other not. The House of Representatives was to be structured on districts of equal population. Rural downstate would continue to have a powerful voice in the Senate. With these provisions, to the amazement of many, the General Assembly passed a resolution referring the proposed amendment to the voters in 1954. It was one of Stratton's chief accomplishments of the 1953 legislative session and led to redistricting two years later.

While he fared well with redistricting, he did not succeed with judicial reform. In 1953, Stratton had to choose between the two. He was committed both to legislative redistricting and to change in the judicial article, but realized that only a limited amount of significant constitutional change could be gained during his first term in office. Any amendment proposed in 1953 would have to submitted to the voters in the following year. If approved, it would require legislative implementation in 1955. To attempt legislative redistricting and judicial reform at the same time would have been a greater political load than their supporters could carry. Sensing the importance of redistricting to his other political goals, Stratton opted in its favor.

Change in the judicial article of the constitution, however, had long been sought. There was little articulation of the separate judicial circuits and no central administrative direction of the courts of the state. Minor judgships—those filled by justices of the peace and police magistrates—

required no legal or other educational qualifications. Those persons benefiting from the status quo in the judicial branch for the most part opposed any change. On the other side were law school deans and professors, other members of the bar, and citizens in general who realized the defects of the system in use.

Stratton was keenly aware of the importance of the judiciary and enjoyed a cordial relationship with judges, especially those of the Illinois Supreme Court. Every month that the Court was in session it invited the governor and Ed Pree to dinner in its living quarters on the top floor of the Supreme Court building. Pree feels that Stratton had an outstanding personal relationship with members of the Court.[45]

In like manner, the Strattons entertained the Supreme Court judges and their wives at an annual dinner in the executive mansion. Following the dinner in 1953, Chief Justice Walter Schaefer challenged the governor to a table tennis game. The table was ready in the room that Governor Stevenson had used as an office and in which Schaefer had worked as one of Stevenson's staff members. Stratton beat him easily; even after the judge removed his shoes to have better footing, he was no match for the governor.[46]

Another legislative matter of prime concern to Stratton in 1953 was the treatment of his budget proposal. There was no Bureau of the Budget. The Department of Finance and the Legislative Budgetary Commission together made recommendations to the governor. He then personally worked out the proposed appropriation for each agency and university.[47] Stratton recalls that he went without sleep for whatever amount of time—and black coffee—it took. He believes he was the first governor since Frank Lowden (1917–21) to give such detailed personal attention to spending proposals. Almost certainly he was the last to do so. Stratton would confer, usually by telephone, with agency heads and university presidents as his work on the budget went forward.[48] He personally penciled his budget messages to the General Assembly on long, unlined white sheets.

In his 1953 budget message, Stratton emphasized economy. He did, however, recommend an increase for highways and a raise in school aid from $160 to $173 per pupil. The mental health facility at Galesburg needed expansion, and the Psychiatric Division at Menard Penitentiary needed better funding. Little attention was given to public aid; and no tax increase was recommended.[49]

In his first press conference on the budget, Stratton declined to have questions submitted in advance, as had been the custom with earlier governors. He wished to take every question without opportunity for advance preparation. To one query, Stratton replied: "Faust, look on page 212 and you'll see what it costs." Smokey Downey recalls that

Harold Faust did so, "and he just shook his head. He said, 'Thank you, Governor.' And sat down. And then he said, 'The smart son-of-a-bitch.' I can hear him yet." Stratton knew the budget in 1953 "through and through," and "he was a no nonsense guy. That changed a lot of people's thinking about him."[50]

The state was in good financial condition when Stratton took office. When all appropriations for 1953–55 had been made, and gubernatorial action on them completed, the total was 1.59 billion dollars for the two-year period. (For comparison, more than 22 billion dollars was appropriated in 1988—for a single year.) Spending for welfare and public assistance was to be at about the same level in 1953–55 as in the preceding biennium. Highway expenditures were substantially up as a result of tax increases in 1951 for that purpose. Aid to elementary and secondary schools was increased; for higher education it was about the same.[51] Altogether it was a frugal spending program that reflects Stratton's values as they interacted with those of the General Assembly.

Stratton was fortunate in 1953 that he had additional revenues for highway building that had been provided by the gasoline and vehicle license tax increases of 1951, for he was a "highway oriented" person. During his political campaigning he logged many thousands of miles on Illinois roads. Smokey Downey recalls that Stratton was "scared to fly," and in fact he traveled little by air until well into his second term as governor. To Downey he said of flying, "You can't get any votes up there in the air." Stratton appreciated the need for improved highways and knew where the work should be done.[52] He told a newsman in 1953 that "I know Chicago [streets] like the back of my hand. That goes for the whole state, too. There isn't a road or a bridge you can name ... that I haven't been over."

Stratton had promised in his inaugural address that Route 66 would be four-laned from Springfield to Lincoln in time for the State Fair. The chief highway engineer said it could not be done because of federal restrictions. Stratton's reply was, "If you can't get that highway built, then I'll get somebody in that job of yours that can do it." By October the project had been completed. Stratton was proud of that accomplishment and remarked to a reporter, "My predecessor did nothing about it in four years."[53]

Stratton also wanted to expand Route 66 between St. Louis and Chicago into a four-lane highway and to provide toll roads for Cook County. When a bill to authorize a Toll Highway Commission was introduced in the Senate, Stratton promised full support, and the measure passed. It specified a commission of three persons to be appointed by the governor that would have the power of eminent domain in acquiring property, have bonding authority, and have freedom from civil service rules and procedures in hiring. The arrangement was a "patronage dream" for a patronage-oriented governor. At the same time, improved highways were vital to the growth of Chicago, Cook County, and all of northeastern Illinois. Right-of-way was still at reasonable cost levels. If toll roads were not built in Cook County during the 1950s, they probably never would be. Establishment of a Toll Highway Commission served public and party purposes; and it opened the doors to political difficulties and major accomplishments during the years that followed.

There were other acts of the General Assembly in 1953 for which Stratton claimed credit. Construction of a new state office building was authorized and 12.5 million dollars appropriated for it. A stronger mine safety law was passed. A legislative Commission to Study State Government Personnel Administration was established. *Time* reported when the legislature adjourned that even those who had initially been critical of Stratton viewed the session with "amazed admiration," and observed that his "record made slow-starting Adlai Stevenson's first six months look like a political-science class picnic." *Time* viewed the redistricting and the mine safety code as the outstanding accomplishments. However, the magazine was critical of Stratton for reducing truck license fees and holding the purse strings too tightly on education and welfare;[54] others were critical because a fair employment practices bill had been lost.

Stratton surprised and pleased his liberal critics by vetoing Senate Bill 102—the Broyles bill—which would have required a loyalty oath of all public officials. Its sponsor, Senator Paul Broyles of Mt. Vernon, was called by some "a bush league Joe McCarthy," after the red-baiting senator from Wisconsin. In his veto message Stratton wrote that such a loyalty oath requirement "would place upon all governmental units in the State a burden of administration which I feel is completely disproportionate to the dangers that may be involved."[55] Some critics felt that he vetoed the Broyles bill for the "wrong reasons."[56]

On the whole, the 1953 legislative session was much to the credit of the General Assembly and the governor. The verdict on Stratton was still out, but some felt that he had made a good start. Albert Votaw, an observer who was inclined to favor the Democrats, wrote that the Republican majorities in the General Assembly had become the "reform party." He stated that Richard J. Daley, newly elected Democratic Cook County chairman, had as yet "done nothing to revitalize the party," that "corruption in Chicago is Democratic," and that liberal Democrats might have to turn to the Republicans in 1954.[57] The Chicago newspapers that had opposed Stratton in 1952 and earlier expressed some respect by mid-1953. A *Sun-Times* editorial of July 16 was headed "Stratton is Showing Courage and Leadership."

When the legislative session ended, the Strattons had time for a vacation and business trip to the Governors Conference in the state of Washington in late July and early August; it was one of only three trips he made acrosss the state's boundaries during the year. With attendance at the Governors Conference he began an association with other governors that was to be important to him during the next seven years.

The Strattons were back in Springfield well before the State Fair, which was an important social and political event for them. On August 19, the eve of Governor's Day at the fair, they entertained former Governor Dwight and Mrs. Green at the executive mansion at a dinner for 230 persons. This hospitality makes an interesting footnote to the friction between Green and Stratton in 1944 and subsequent years. Stratton never was one to hold political grudges.

Stratton's administrative style was maturing as he completed three-quarters of his first year as governor. A complete legislative session was behind him, one that was deeply satisfying in many ways. In speaking at the State Fair he challenged "anyone to show me where a comparable [legislative] program was ever devised and placed into operation in a like period." His budget for the biennium was in place. He had begun an association with other state leaders through the Governors Conference. A highlight of the Springfield year, the annual State Fair, and come and gone. Stratton was keenly aware of the potential for good and for harm to his reputation which the fair presented. He had banned the sale of beer at the fair in 1953, and after it ended he studied reports on it carefully. The manager of the fair, James E. Tays, was discharged on December 1; apparently his stewardship had not come up to Stratton's standard. It is typical of the governor's kindness to subordinates, however, that Tays was allowed to continue to live in the manager's house on the fairgrounds while awaiting another Stratton-promised job.

When a reporter, Wesley Hartzell of the *Chicago American,* asked Stratton in October "if he liked his job" he replied: "Very much . . . [It is] an opportunity to improve the state's services to the people. I have no other hobby. . . . Being able to look personally into the state's affairs to see they're being run with efficiency and enthusiasm is like meat and potatoes to me."[58] At thirty-nine, Stratton was still youthful in appearance and manner. A picture taken at Boys State shows him trim and slender, with dark hair combed back, a white double-breasted suit and two-toned shoes—still "Billy the Kid" in many ways.[59]

Cabinet members could meet with the governor when that was necessary. That was a part of his basic style. Ed Pree recalls of agency heads "that whenever they had to get to the governor on something of vital importance . . . they could see him. They all had access . . . and the governor knew what they were doing and was in touch with them, and on a matter of policy making . . . the governor was a part."[60] Willard Ice attended meetings on tax policy matters where Stratton presided, and recalls that the governor "took a very quiet approach . . . and let people have their say. . . . He didn't try to dominate any meeting I was ever in."[61]

The General Assembly met in regular session only in odd-numbered years in the 1950s, so 1954 was not a legislative year. Still, matters set in motion by the legislature in 1953 were going forward, such as the work of the Commission to Study State Government Personnel Administration. While Stratton was publicly committed to improving personnel practices, he continued to be as deeply involved in the distribution of patronage as the civil service system allowed him to be. Like a later governor, Richard Ogilvie, he probably felt that "the only trouble with patronage is there's not enough of it." Demands for patronage appointments upon Stratton's administration were insatiable, and the performance of some of those who were appointed failed to come up to a reasonable standard.

There were marks of progress in 1954 as well. Ground was broken for the new state office building on February 15, less than one year after its authorization. The governor's open houses, held each week when his schedule permitted, allowed him to talk individually to 2,872 persons during his first year in office. From an initial attendance of 164, the number dropped off to the forties.[62]

In anticipation of rising demands upon the state's colleges and universities, Stratton by executive order formed a Higher Education Commission of distinguished educators "for the purpose of making a thorough investigation, study and survey of existing facilities and resources." He hoped that greater use of private institutions might lessen the pressure upon public ones. Handwritten notes show that Stratton gave personal attention to the appointment of commission members.[63] Legislator Paul Randolph feels that it was this commission that led to the establishment of the Scholarship Commission, which aided many students in gaining college educations. Walter Reum, a member of the State House of Representatives during a portion of Stratton's tenure as governor and a member of the General Assembly's School Problems Commission, recalls that "on many matters we consulted with Governor Stratton. And . . . it was amazing the grasp that the governor had on some of the problems."[64]

The Strattons continued a busy official social schedule in 1954. Among many other events they attended the White House Conference of Governors in Washington, D.C., in April; the Lions Clubs State Convention in Springfield in May; and in midsummer the Governors Conference, this time traveling by train to New York, accompanied by Sandra and Diana. President Eisenhower addressed the conference. The Strattons also had the pleasure of entertaining the president at the State Fair in August, where he spoke on Governor's Day. This suggests Stratton's standing in the national Republican party, and the president's awareness of the political importance of Illinois. Stratton, as the state's highest ranking Republican officeholder, had been conspicuous at the 1952 Republican National Convention, which nominated Eisenhower. He had gone there leaning toward Senator Taft for the nomination, but had swung over to Eisenhower as the tide of opinion and votes flowed his way.

Though Stratton was in midterm and not himself a candidate, 1954 was an election year, and he was deeply involved. Nationally the McCarthy frenzy was nearing its climax, but Stratton kept himself removed from it. He had vetoed the Broyles bill, but for reasons other than objection on principle. Perhaps his performance in that case was more astute than was generally recognized. When in January he received a resolution from an American Legion post supporting Senator McCarthy, he replied noncommittally. Stratton seemed to sense that a moderate stance was best for him. He never appeared to be a McCarthyite and was never caught up in the anti-Communist fervor of the time. He took few positions in regard to foreign policy.

Stratton's support for open primary elections, developed during the days when he was often running without official endorsement from Republican leaders, may have hurt his party in 1954. The contest for the Republican nomination for the United States Senate attracted ten candidates who, without official endorsement, fought it out in ways that created hard feelings and factionalism. State Senator Edward Saltiel, a Republican who was up for reelection, feels that Stratton erred. He remembers that he said, "Bill, you're the titular head of the party, you have to see that we have a strong candidate for the U.S. Senate." Stratton answered, "I want to be neutral. I don't want to take sides." Saltiel argued with him for an hour, fruitlessly.[65] He feared that the candidate would be Joseph Meek, whom he regarded as philosophically a throwback to the eighteenth century, likely to weaken the whole ticket in the fall. Meek, a well-known Springfield lobbyist for small retail business, won the April 13 primary with 284 thousand votes out of a total of 957 thousand. Warren Wright was another unendorsed minority winner, with 330 thousand votes for the nomination for state treasurer. Saltiel's fears were eventually realized, and he was one of the casualties.

Even without a candidacy of his own to advance, Stratton became active in the final campaigning. He was interested in the public referendum upon the legislative redistricting plan that the General Assembly had approved, with his support, in 1953. Since it represented constitutional change, it could not become effective without voter approval, and by an extraordinary majority. In mid-September Stratton made a lengthy speech on behalf of the proposed amendment to a gathering of newspaper editors.[66] He continued to be a leader in support of the proposal.

He also ventured briefly into Cook County politics, attacking Joseph D. Lohman, the Democratic candidate for sheriff, for remarks Lohman had allegedly made while head of the Pardon and Parole Board under Governor Stevenson. Stratton was in possession of a recording of a speech in which Lohman said that "policeman [sic] have a disproportionate number of wives that were prostitutes." Lohman claimed that an alteration had been made to the recording, and that he had been taken out of context. He then called Stratton an "ignoramus." Angry words followed, and Stratton demanded an apology.[67] Stevenson then got into it, saying, "Evidently no political knavery is too high a price for political influence for this Republican governor,"[68] who "has intervened with unspeakable tactics to try to influence a campaign for sheriff."[69] The matter was short-lived; perhaps Stratton realized it was counterproductive. Lohman was elected. He was a potential Stratton opponent in the 1956 race for the governor's chair, as was Stevenson.

In the general election on November 2 Senator Paul Douglas defeated Joe Meek by 241 thousand votes. Republican Warren Wright won by 9 thousand; and Vernon Nickell retained his position as state superintendent of public instruction by a 38-thousand vote margin. On the whole, there seemed to be almost equal balance between the two parties. The Republicans retained control of both houses of the General Assembly. To the surprise of many, the redistricting amendment was approved, with strong support even in rural areas, and the approval of 80 percent of those who voted upon it. Stratton must have felt that the election represented a victory for him, even though growing Democratic strength suggested future problems.

Late in December 1954 President Eisenhower hosted a dinner for Vice-President Nixon, national Republican party Chairman Leonard Hall, Attorney General Herbert Brownell, Postmaster General Arthur Summerfield, presidential assistant Sherman Adams, General Lucius Clay, Herbert Hoover, Jr., Edward L. Ryerson of Illinois and the Inland Steel Company, and others. It was a select group. The subject of discussion was "how to remake the Republican Party along 'progressive-moderate' lines." The group agreed the party should attempt to recruit attractive, young politicians, while retaining conservative support. While it was assumed that the president and vice-president both would run again in 1956, Eisenhower stressed the need to develop prospective candidates for later campaigns.

According to a *Newsweek* report, "among the younger men specifically talked about as 'comers' were Governor William G. Stratton of

Illinois," Robert Anderson of Texas, Governor George N. Craig of Indiana, and William P. Rogers of New York. "It was the concensus" [*sic*] of the group around the White House dinner table, according to the *Newsweek* account, "that all these men, while especially promising, were not well enough known beyond their own states ... and that steps should be taken to advertise them."[70]

With that recognition Stratton was marked as a potential leader of his party and the nation. As his first two years as governor came to an end, he could feel that he was becoming a national figure, that the presidency was within his grasp, and that his boyhood dreams of such an office might eventually come true.

First-Term Governor:
Second Biennium

One of Stratton's first official duties in 1955 was to deliver the "state of the state" address before the General Assembly on January 5. He urged continued prudence in spending but hoped to see an expanded highway program, where he was expecting more federal aid as the interstate system was initiated. While the Illinois Toll Highway Commission was making progress, he reported, he was concerned with highway safety and recommended a speed limit and an increase in the number of state policemen.

The governor told the General Assembly that among constitutional matters, reform of the judicial system was still a pressing need. Annual sessions of the General Assembly should be authorized, and House terms lengthened from two to four years. Enrollments were growing in the public schools; and expanded facilities for higher education would soon be needed, including a full campus of the University of Illinois in Chicago. He again stressed the need for a state crime commission.[1] It was clear that he expected a busy legislative session.

Stratton's schedule was a busy one as he began his third year as governor. In one week in January he talked face-to-face with more than 175 individuals, including twenty-six legislators during a single day, and took part in at least thirty telephone conversations. The line to the mansion was open twenty-four hours a day and there was a phone in the governor's car. He made one formal speech, several welcoming talks, sent a detailed legislative program to General Assembly leaders, and worked on the budget.[2]

Stratton's budget message to the General Assembly in 1955 was a frugal spending plan that recognized urgent needs in education, highways, and welfare in the face of limited revenue. He pointed out that more than half of all state agencies would spend less than in 1953–55. What few increases there were would be for welfare, education, conservation, the Youth Commission, and the Department of Agriculture. Capital spending was recommended for schools, state hospitals, prisons, and highways and funds were requested to increase the number of state troopers from five hundred to six hundred. To meet those expenditures he recommended an increase in the sales tax from 2 to 3 percent, for one year.[3]

The tax increase that Stratton sought was crucial if the spending needs of the state were to be met. A year later he told the United States Senate Committee on Banking and Currency, during its hearing on the Hodge embezzlement, that in 1955 "we had to get an additional half-cent increase in the sales tax to take care of our school problems."[4] Perhaps he asked for the full cent hoping in the end to obtain the half. In any case the margin of difference allowed him vital room for maneuver.

Editors around the state were for the most part emphatically opposed to the proposed tax increase. Newspapers in the larger cities— such as Decatur, Peoria, and Champaign—tended to be more favorable. Some urged a use tax, or broadened sales tax base, as an alternative.[5] Bear in mind that the state did not employ an income tax at that time— it was believed that the consitution did not permit it.

Soon after Stratton recommended a tax increase the Chicago mayoral election took place. Winner of a first term was Richard J. Daley, chairman of the Cook County Democratic Central Committee. He had served in the General Assembly, in both the House and the Senate, and was director of the Department of Revenue under Governor Stevenson. He had a good reputation personally, as a student of public finance, and as an administrator. Willard Ice thought well of Daley, saying, he "took an interest in people," was intelligent, "an excellent administrator," and "a high-type politician."[6] Journalist Johnson Kanady recalls that Stratton enjoyed a good relationship with Daley, that there was "never any enmity" between them and in fact "considerable mutual admiration" and exchanges of favors.[7] In 1955 the two were already acquainted, at least from the time of Stratton's first term as treasurer.

Soon after Daley became mayor, he and Stratton conferred upon the proposed tax increase. Daley controlled the Democratic votes that the governor needed. With a Republican majority in both houses, obviously Stratton could do much to give Daley and Chicago some of the things the mayor wanted. Smokey Downey recalls Daley's saying to Stratton, "Here's what I want. Let's work this out."[8] Daley needed more money—thirty-four million dollars—to run the city properly, and he and Stratton agreed on a one-cent (on the dollar) sales tax increase, with the state to get one-half cent and the cities that chose to to get the other half. If a city did not want the half-cent, it would not be collected within its boundaries. If it wished to have it, the state would collect and rebate it. In that way the state received the revenue it needed, Chicago did too, and any other municipality could similarly benefit.

The Stratton-Daley program was agreed to in a series of conferences that were completed by May 18. Smokey Downey recalls that after the conclusive meeting between the governor and the mayor, Stratton said, "I had no trouble at all with him, Smoke . . . [I got] everything that I asked him for." Apparently Stratton obtained Daley's help in implementing the redistricting amendment that had been approved in 1954, especially in the arrangement for Senate districts.[9] There was also agreement upon a new convention center for Chicago (which became McCormick Place), a revised revenue article for the constitution, to be voted upon by the public in 1956 (it was defeated), a 5 percent utility tax for municipalities, and the need for a judicial reform amendment. Whether the latter was to be approved by the General Assembly in 1955 or 1957 was not clear. It turned out to be the latter. Clearly the interaction between Stratton and Daley was a productive one.

The tax plan agreed upon by Stratton and Daley was opposed by the Illinois Federation of Retail Associations, headed by Joe Meek. His group did not wish to see an optional city sales tax, for it would put merchants in cities that chose to have it at a disadvantage. It favored a one-cent increase levied everywhere by the state, with the half-cent collected within cities rebated to them. That arrangement would avoid differential taxation between cities choosing to participate and all other areas. Stratton saw through that arrangement at once. Veteran legislator Charles Clabaugh remembers him saying, "'No soap. I will help pass . . . a bill to give . . . your city council, the authority to raise a sales tax. And will collect it. . . . But I'm not going to ask the legislature to take the monkey off the back of the city council and put it on their back.' . . . That was how Stratton was," according to Clabaugh. "And he was talking to a realist, two of them got together when Stratton and Daley got together."[10] In a conference with Meek's group, Stratton held out for the plan he and Daley had agreed to,[11] which took considerable political courage.

Bills to implement the Stratton-Daley tax agreement were introduced in the General Assembly late in the session. Eventually they were passed, and a strong link between the two men had been forged. It was to be of great importance in other votes in 1955, and in significant political matters in the following year.

Years later, in looking back upon the sales tax compromise of

1955, Stratton expressed satisfaction with it in a speech to the Illinois Municipal League. It was philosophically pleasing to him, because the decision about whether each municipal corporation would share in the additional revenue could be made locally. It had the result of keeping the pain of taxation together with the pleasure of spending.[12] That the additional revenue yielded by the compromise for the state and Chicago was essential to both is beyond doubt.

Not everything in 1955 went well for Stratton. Democrats in the General Assembly were unhappy with the way the toll highway program was being developed. Not only was it a Republican patronage bonanza, it also had excited complaints over the routes and the taking of property. Democrats saw a chance to fish in troubled waters and were also concerned with getting the program off to a good start.

Late in April it was alleged that Stratton's old friend and one-time colleague in Congress, Evan Howell, chairman of the Toll Highway Commission by the governor's appointment, had engaged in "drunken abuse" of Democratic legislators who wished to investigate the commission. It was said that he had threatened certain persons, including Representative Paul Powell, with political reprisals, in the dining room of Springfield's St. Nicholas Hotel. Powell was not one to take such actions lightly, and a formal investigation was launched in the House. Of special concern was the National Turnpike Association, which Howell had organized and of which he was president. It solicited membership fees of one thousand dollars from public officials and from bankers and contractors who might wish to do business with the commission.

The House investigation also looked into the matter of Howell's expense account. He had kept his home and family in Washington, D.C., where he had been a federal judge and had been charging the cost of travel and the cost of an apartment in Chicago to the commission. In eighteen months he had spent eleven thousand dollars for those purposes. That amount may seem modest, but it should be noted that new, three-bedroom, brick-veneer houses, with gas heat and automatic washers and dryers, in Canterbury Gardens in Cook County at Kedzie and 159th Street were selling for $14,950. They were advertised as being only one-half hour from Chicago's Loop and available to qualified veterans for $750 down. In such a market Howell's expenditures were substantial.

Howell admitted to the investigating committee that he had tried to silence critics of the toll road program by going to their employers—General Motors and Illinois Bell. The committee also learned of a loan by the Continental Bank to a consulting engineer who was employed by the Toll Highway Commission, suspected of having been made for the purpose of obtaining trusteeship of the forthcoming four hundred million dollar plus bond issue for toll road construction. By mid-June the bipartisan committee severely censured Howell, and agreed to ban him from further membership dues solicitation in the National Turnpike Association, which was generally regarded as a shake-down mechanism for the benefit of Howell and certain of his associates. The committee did not call for his resignation, but Howell seemed to be politically dead even though he claimed that the governor had "indicated his continued support."[13] He soon resigned.

The toll highway program went forward under new leadership, with the commission's bonds going up for sale in October 1955; however, the Evan Howell matter must have caused Stratton considerable embarrassment and political difficulty. While his cabinet choices were generally good ones, he erred in several other appointments, as he did in this case, in placing an old friend in a position of trust for which he was not suited. When such mistakes were made, Stratton was capable of calling for a resignation, as he probably did privately in the Howell affair. Even so, his initial choice of Howell was a mistake and one he should have learned from to a greater extent than it later appeared he did.

As a footnote to the Howell matter and its investigation, the General Assembly authorized, before it adjourned in 1955, a $245 million Cook County revenue bond issue for expressway construction, to be retired out of gasoline tax proceeds. The Cook County superintendent of highways, William J. Mortimer, wanted to build expressways rather than toll roads. Democrats in the General Assembly felt that if a Republican administration was to have nearly one-half billion dollars for building toll roads, with all that that construction meant in patronage and in public benefit, then a Cook County Democratic highway department should also have funds for major road building.

Stratton facilitated the Cook County bond issue authorization and both political parties concurred. It went through the General Assembly quietly, and when the governor signed the bill he said to Mortimer, who was present, "I assume . . . that you will be too busy building expressways to be troublesome about my toll road." This agreement was another instance of cooperation between Governor Stratton and Mayor Daley. The bond issue allowed expressway building in Cook County to go forward smoothly. The federal program to fund interstate highways was begun in 1956, and when federal aid lagged, bond issue funds were used and then repaid from federal grants.[14] The progress of both toll roads and expressways, so vital to northeastern Illinois, moved at a good pace during the decade of the 1950s.

Another significant enactment of the General Assembly in 1955 was the Personnel Code, which created a Department of Personnel. The three-member bipartisan Civil Service Commission, which had been in existence for more than fifty years, was to be part of the personnel system. Legislators, and no doubt the governor, were wary of the effect that the new Personnel Code would have on politics, especially upon the use of state employees as political foot soldiers, which explains why the effective date of the code was put more than two years in the future. With that schedule there would be no impact upon the coming 1956 election.

Maurice Scott, longtime executive director of the Illinois Taxpayers' Federation, recalls that creation of the Personnel Code was "a highlight" of his experience with state government, and that Representatives Warren Wood, Paul Powell, and Reed Cutler were especially instrumental in getting it passed.[15] According to then-state Senator Elbert Smith, the Personnel Code "was hard to put through. And it finally got through in a conference committee.... It was quite a radical idea, the change of personnel practices in ... Illinois" or in any of the states.[16]

Ed Pree had taken a keen interest in the establishment of a personnel code. He talked to and corresponded with interested groups and persons about the roles of civil service and patronage, and viewed the new system as a means of finding a balance between the two. He had good reason to desire a more orderly procedure for filling state positions. The demand for patronage appointments was insatiable. In most cases, once filled, jobs could not be offered again for some time or not for a period of time equal to the governor's tenure, so there was a continually decreasing pool of positions for a continually growing body of applicants. Neither in Stratton's time nor in that of other governors has the supply of patronage positions ever been equal to the demand.

Stratton maintained an interest in patronage in 1955 and 1956, and the Toll Highway Commission provided a patronage carnival. By the end of June 1956, it had 821 positions—engineers, appraisers, attorneys, and central office personnel—all exempt from civil service status. Stratton and Pree were involved in filling them all.[17] Another source of considerable patronage was the state-regulated horse-racing industry. State Racing Board jobs at the tracks were exempt from civil service and were much sought after. They were seasonal and could often be fitted in with other positions. Not only were jobs distributed but also passes to the track grandstands, which were valued as marks of political favor and prestige. Stratton felt that he should take a personal hand in distributing race track jobs and passes and regularly did so. The files contain many notes in his hand regarding such matters. He maintained his insistence upon "a day's work for a day's pay," to the extent that during the primary campaign in 1956 two Republican county chairmen who were employed by the state—as most of them were—were fired for not working.[18] One can imagine the salutary effect upon their peers.

Stratton and Pree were also active in distributing summer jobs, which were usually civil service exempt. The governor was on friendly terms with the university presidents and attempted to provide summer jobs for athletes. The State Fair continued to be an annual patronage heaven for summer positions, and in 1955 the *Chicago Tribune* found that the twelve hundred employees at the fair were hired under the "tight patronage reins" of the Stratton administration. Pree was quoted as saying that "every personnel appointment at the fair stems from the governor's office." Stratton acknowledged that he personally selected the several superintendents—such as of beef cattle and swine, saying "that's what the people elected me for." Recommendations for fair jobs were solicited from the Republican county chairmen, and a county outline map was kept, showing the distribution of those appointed. When Pree was asked what happened if he and Director Stanard, who was responsible for the fair's operation, disagreed about an appointment, he replied, "I don't think we've ever had a situation where the director and I have not seen eye to eye." The system sometimes had odd results. For example, in 1955 the two "Curry boys" were properly recommended by their county chairman, approved, and assigned to the swine department as assistant superintendents. When they reported for "work" the "boys" turned out to be seventy-six and eighty years old.[19]

As the 1955 session of the General Assembly came to a close late in June, Stratton had reason to feel pleased, for a number of his legislative goals had been met. When he was interviewed by Godfrey Sperling, Jr., for the *Christian Science Monitor,* Sperling reported that he found Stratton to have a "friendly, calm disposition," "a very, very firm handshake," and "the reputation for being the hardest working governor since Horner. He works a 14 hour day." Sperling contrasted Stratton favorably with his predecessor, Adlai Stevenson. The latter had leaned too much on his advisers and subordinates and in that way had gotten into trouble. Stratton was "shaping up as a premeditated opposite," Sperling wrote. If he erred, it was in assuming too much responsibility, not in delegating too much. He had become the "undisputed head" of state government in Illinois, with "wide acceptance." He ran against the Stevenson record in 1952 and continued to do so. One observer whom Sperling interviewed saw Stevenson as an idealist of lofty principles who paid little attention to the record he was compiling, and Stratton as a pragmatic politician concerned with accomplishments.

Sperling found Stratton sensitive to the danger of scandal. He took special pains to guard the purchasing process and required a monthly report from each department on expenditures. "Knowledgeable observers," Sperling had found, considered Stratton "to be the real chief highway engineer for the state," and that he "has hopes of being remembered as 'Stratton the builder.'" He also observed that "Governor Stratton takes care of patronage personally, and it is a powerful weapon in his hands"—half of all state positions were in the patronage realm—and that he insisted on a day's work for a day's pay. On the debit side Sperling pointed out that still no judicial reform resolution had passed the General Assembly, nor had the Governor achieved the highway speed limits he sought.[20]

Stratton had the pleasure of hosting the 1955 Governors Conference in Chicago. It was the first time it had been held in Illinois, a distinct political plus for him. He arranged a full program of social and recreational activities, including big-league baseball, the all-star football game that matched the best of the collegians with the professional champions, horse racing at Washington Park, fishing, golf, boating, and horseback riding.[21] These activities suggest Stratton's own interests. Shirley Stratton led a group of the governors' wives to Springfield for a day of sightseeing and lunch in the executive mansion.

The Strattons allowed themselves more vacation time in 1955 than in earlier years. He was beginning to pursue interests of his own, aside from those that were governmental and political, and continued his work in the Masonic Lodge, gaining the thirty-third degree of the Scottish Rite Freemasons. The Strattons were studying log-cabin plans, with the intention of building a "lodge" on their farm on the nearby Sangamon River. They were also boarding two riding horses—Royal Man and Flicka—at the fairgrounds.[22] In September the Strattons and his mother visited the modest house in Ingleside where Stratton was born.

Late 1955 brought additional satisfactions of a public sort to the governor. The new state office building, which had been authorized only two years earlier, was ready to be used by October 15. On December 5 an open house attended by ten thousand persons marked its official opening. The speed and economy of its construction were unusual: ground had been broken for the structure, of almost one-half million square feet on nine floors, in February 1954. With $12.5 million appropriated, it was built for 1 million less.[23]

Stratton formally announced at Morris on January 6, 1956, that he would run again for governor. A rally at the Center School attracted fifteen hundred persons. He stressed the accomplishments of his first three years in office, and while he promised no new programs, he did express a continued interest in judicial reform, which had so far eluded him. It was clear that he was proud of his record.[24]

All of the incumbent state executive officials who could legally run for reelection did so in the 1956 primary. The treasurer, Warren Wright, who could not succeed himself, sought the nomination for secretary of state against incumbent Charles Carpentier. When Stratton refused to approve that arrangement, coming close to reversing his earlier stands for open primaries, Wright became piqued and entered the primary for governor. He and Stratton had been in competition for the top political posts in Illinois since 1942.[25] No one expected the contest to be close.

The governor continued to be attentive to even the smallest details of administration.[26] His interest and influence was also directed toward the governance of the state's universities, and to the management of his political party.[27] Upon the eve of his renomination in the April 1956 primary, Stratton stood close to the peak of his popularity and influence. With a president of his party likely to be renominated and to win decisively in November, and with his own electoral fortunes riding high, he could look forward with confidence to another term. State Representative Paul Simon, who later became lieutenant governor, a congressman, a United States senator, and a candidate in Democratic presidential primaries in 1988, described Stratton at this time as the most powerful man in Springfield. He could get what he wanted from the Senate, Simon felt, and with Mayor Daley's help could do so as well in the House. His veto authority was almost above challenge.[28] Even the *Bloomington Pantagraph,* owned in part by the Stevenson family, supported him and admitted that "he has made a much better Governor than we thought he would." The *Pantagraph* identified redistricting of the General Assembly, improvement of mental hospitals, the half-cent municipal sales tax, and highway building and repair as the chief accomplishments of Stratton's first term. It was critical of the toll highway program, and ended with what was probably an attempt to keep peace in the family by expressing regret that Stratton continued to be critical of Stevenson, who seemed likely again to be the Democratic candidate for president.[29]

One of Warren Wright's practices was brought to Stratton's attention during the primary campaign by a letter from H. E. Emerson, a banker in Cairo, to Elmer Hoffman, who was the leading Republican candidate for treasurer, the office Wright then held. Emerson wrote that he had "received a telephone call from a gentleman who ... said the 'going' was a little rough, that they needed some money for Mr. Wright's campaign, and they thought it only fair that the bankers who had benefited from deposits of State money, be asked to contribute." Emerson had declined on the ground that he was committed to helping Stratton, against whom Wright was running, and he feared that "the next thing that will happen to me is that he will call our state deposit."[30]

On primary election day on April 10, Stratton beat Wright 557 thousand to 188 thousand. The Democrats nominated Cook County treasurer Herbert C. Paschen, who was not well known downstate, for governor. The other Republican incumbents were all unopposed. With the primary over, Stratton could turn his attention to what he felt would be his next big political opportunity, the Republican National Convention. Late in 1955 *Newsweek* magazine had published a piece on "dark horses" in presidential politics, pointing out that President Eisenhower might choose not to run again, since he had suffered a heart attack in 1955. Noted personalities were suggested as possible replacements for Eisenhower, or for Nixon if he were nominated for president or dropped from the ticket. Only three Republican governors were mentioned—Craig of Indiana, Herter of Massachusetts, and Stratton. His greatest asset would be his control of the Illinois delegation at the San Francisco convention. The most negative factor would be "his background as an isolationist," *Newsweek* believed. It reported that in 1955 Stratton "describes himself as a down-the-line Eisenhower Republican."[31] Such notice strengthened Stratton's hope that he might be the Republican candidate for vice-president.[32]

It was hard from an Illinois base—or from any base for that matter— to campaign for the nomination for vice-president. Stratton had at least one good opportunity, when he spoke to the National Republican Club in New York City on March 8. That the speech was especially important to him is indicated by his having composed it personally in longhand, something he did only when his interest was deeply engaged. He began by praising President Eisenhower, then turned to criticizing Adlai Stevenson, who probably again would be Eisenhower's opponent. He felt that his predecessor had left much undone in Illinois and that "we are perplexed as to how . . . Stevenson, can be seriously considered for chief executive . . . when his . . . record as governor showed such obvious deficiencies." Stratton then reviewed his own record. He derided Stevenson's "self- appointed role of authority on any and all subjects, domestic and foreign."[33] Stratton took pleasure in attacking Stevenson on any occasion and felt fully justified in doing so in 1956 when the latter was again seeking the Democratic nomination for president.

Shirley Stratton also was finding satisfaction with the way their lives were going during the first few months of 1956 and was having a busy and exciting time. Study of the mansion file makes it apparent that she was very much a partner in the business of being governor and worked hard at it; she was efficient, well liked, and a good hostess and correspondent. Her pace had not slowed. She had worked diligently at making the executive mansion into a home and felt that she had succeeded, for the old building had been substantially redecorated. She was busy with committees and other groups and entertaining in the mansion. Sandra was a sophomore at the University of Arizona, but Diana, a senior at Springfield High School, was still at home.

Governor and Mrs. Stratton found time to visit their farm occasionally, and to walk or ride horseback there. They often traveled together.[34] As they began their fourth summer in the executive mansion, they were content. They had the State Fair to look forward to, and the Republican National Convention at San Francisco, where Stratton might, they could imagine, be tapped to run for vice-president. Lacking that good fortune, the governor was still safely nominated for a second term in a good Republican year, and with strong state and national tickets and an opponent little known outside Cook County, reelection seemed assured.

10

The Case of the Errant Auditor

The summer of 1956 was not to be as peaceful as the Strattons had hoped. Disquieting rumors about State Auditor of Public Accounts Orville Hodge appeared in print early in June.[1] Since the appropriation for his office was being drawn down too rapidly, reporters were looking over the record of warrants (checks) written against it. The auditor issued all warrants in payment of state expenditures, including those for the expenses of his own office.

Before he was elected auditor in 1952, Hodge had been a member of the state House of Representatives. He had also been in the insurance and real estate business in Granite City and in Republican politics since 1936. He and Stratton had been acquainted at least since Stratton's first term as treasurer. Hodge was considered a wealthy man; he owned two airplanes, four automobiles, including a Lincoln and a Cadillac, an expensive home on Lake Springfield, and kept a suite in the Drake Hotel in Chicago.

At forty-eight, Hodge was thought to be a potential candidate for governor in 1960 and had even considered challeng ing Stratton for the nomination in 1956. He had been well regarded while he was in the General Assembly. His colleague Corneal Davis remembers that "Everybody thought [he] was a millionaire ... the way he spent money.... I thought he was a fine man. I think everybody in the House had a high opinion of Hodge." Davis feels that if all had gone well he "would have been governor."[2] Maurice Scott, who is well qualified to judge, thinks that "Hodge was a good legislator. He knew how to get a bill passed."[3]

Hodge's reputation in his home town was good—he was its "man of the year" in 1954. Stratton attended a testimonial dinner for him at that time. Such activities as Community Chest, Little League, Red Cross, and fraternal orders and clubs had claimed much of Hodge's time. Early

137

in his term he gained favorable publicity by locating surplus state property and by having it sold at auction.[4] He took pride in improving the business methods of the auditor's office, and like Stratton, in June he was looking forward to attending the Republican National Convention as a member of the Illinois delegation and was a candidate for reelection.

Stratton's assistant Ed Pree remembers that the first warnings about Hodge came from Secretary of State Carpentier in June.[5] No doubt Pree told the governor of Carpentier's suspicions. State Treasurer Warren Wright had definite knowledge of some of Hodge's problems even earlier. In October 1956 he told a committee of the United States Senate Committee on Banking and Currency which was investigating banking practices in the Hodge matter, that he had "first realize[d] the improper dealings of Mr. Hodge . . . in March or so." That Wright was then Stratton's opponent in the primary may have caused him to withhold such information from the governor, although one wonders why he did not use it in the primary campaign.

When Senator Fulbright, chairman of the committee, asked Wright, "It was about June 11 that you were asked [by Hodge] to refrain from letting the newspapers see the warrants?" the reply was "That's what the Auditor asked me. . . . He said I was his friend and should protect him. He didn't say what I should protect him from." Wright testified that Hodge "told me that if he went down, the whole team would go down, toll roads and all." Wright refused Hodge's pleas, and made the record of warrants available to reporters. Then on June 19 Hodge asked Wright for help in covering up his embezzlement. Knowing of the friction between Wright and Stratton and knowing they had contested the Republican nomination for governor in the April primary, it is conceivable that Wright did not tell the governor of his suspicions in March, nor of Hodge's entreaties in June. There is nothing in the record to suggest that he did.

On July 5 Wright laid photographs of forged state checks on the governor's desk. Later he reported that Stratton said to him, "Warren, it looks like someone is going to the penitentiary." On the same day the *Chicago Tribune* reported that Stratton had requested that the General Assembly's Budgetary Commission investigate Hodge.[6] The commission was a bipartisan body whose chief duty was—with the governor, who was an ex officio member—to prepare the biennial budget. It was a logical place for Stratton to go with his concerns. "The Illinois Budgetary Commission is charged by law with the duty of making a thorough study and investigation of all State expenditures," he wrote in his request to the commission. He wished the commission to make such a study and to offer a report and recommendations "at the earliest date possible."[7]

Stratton also placed a security guard on Hodge's office and warehouse on July 6, while allowing reporters to have access to all records. Hodge, who on July 5 had welcomed an investigation and promised full cooperation, said on the following day that he feared some records might already be missing, and that "an investigation was started a month ago by the Sangamon County state's attorney," George Coutrakon. On July 9 Coutrakon, a Republican and then a candidate for the General Assembly, petitioned the circuit court to investigate "reported irregularities" in the auditor's office. A grand jury was called for that purpose. Coutrakon said that "several hundred" warrants were missing from Hodge's files. Apparently he had been at the investigation for some time, as Hodge had said.[8] Stratton and Coutrakon had been acquainted since at least 1948, when the latter was elected state's attorney. He had earned a reputation for being tough on gambling, including church bingo games and barbecue raffles. It is hard to believe that Coutrakon had not informed the governor that an investigation was under way.

Events were moving rapidly, and on July 10 Stratton and Attorney General Castle met with Hodge. Smokey Downey remembers "Hodge going in to see the Governor and Attorney General. 'Hey, Smoke, how are you buddy?'" Hodge said. "I said, 'Fine, Orville. They're waiting for you.'" Hodge said " 'I'll be out in a minute.' He came out about half an hour later and he looked like the wrath of God had hit him. . . . He said 'I can't trust those people. Neither one of them are any good.' "[9] Stratton had demanded that Hodge give up his candidacy for reelection. The auditor told newsmen "indignantly that he had no intention of withdrawing."

Democrats wasted no time before fishing in the troubled waters of Hodge's affairs. They criticized Stratton for not requiring semiannual reports from the auditor, as the constitution permitted. Stratton had been careful to safeguard spending by agency heads whom he appointed, but apparently had not taken the precautions available to him so far as the elected executive officers were concerned. The release of funds from appropriations for the other elected state officials was under the governor's control,[10] but it was a routine authorization on Stratton's part. If used with care, that procedure might have prevented or reduced Hodge's embezzlement. Herbert Paschen, the Democratic candidate for governor, refused to endorse Stratton's efforts to get Hodge off the ballot and out of office.[11] Clearly, Democrats would benefit by keeping him in both positions for as long as possible before the November election.

On July 11, Stratton tightened the screws on Hodge by taking advantage of an old law that authorized him to require the auditor to double his personal bond of fifty thousand dollars, or be replaced within twenty days.[12] The governor said, "In my estimation, it is obvious that public and party confidence in the officer and his official operations no longer exists." Stratton had moved quickly from wanting Hodge off the ballot to wanting him out of office. It was hardly likely that Hodge could obtain increased bonding from any responsible surety company. When asked if he would resign, Hodge was emphatic. "No, sir. Not at this time." Would he run in November, even if there was a Republican-backed independent candidate? "I believe I would," he answered.

On July 16 Hodge met again with Stratton and Castle, and after some persuasion submitted his resignation. Stratton recalls that "The Auditor was upset and highly emotional. He wept. . . . I finally had coffee served. Once he made up his mind to resign he seemed to get better control of himself." Arrangements were made by telephone with the state's attorney for Hodge to "get the story off his chest" the next day. "We gave him another cup of coffee," Stratton remembers. "He made up his mind to face the music and face the press."[13] Hodge's letter of resignation was to the point—"I hereby resign." It was notarized by Marion Keevers and formally acknowledged by Stratton on the same day.[14] Ed Pree recalls that Stratton told him "that when he forced Hodge's resignation . . . he had never talked that way to any man in his life, the way he had to talk to Hodge." It was a clean sweep on Hodge's part—resignation from office, from candidacy, and from his position as delegate to the Republican National Convention.[15]

As he emerged from Stratton's office, Hodge declared, "I'm beat, but I feel better. At least I haven't killed anyone."[16] He must have had twinges of conscience, however, when on July 31 one of his administrative assistants drowned himself in Lake Springfield. He had defended Hodge's innocence until it became evident that he was mistaken. A week before his death, he told his wife that "Hodge broke my heart," and just a day before he died that he had discovered he had been a messenger in one of the fraudulent check transactions.

On July 17 Hodge declared that he would plead guilty and expected a quick trial. He promised to reveal all aspects of his embezzlement and denied that racketeers in St. Clair and Madison counties—the "mob"—had forced him to steal to pay campaign debts, and any other underworld connections.[17] Smokey Downey has another view of that matter, however. He recalls that Hodge had promised to get the East St. Louis area opened up for illegal slot machines and had said he could control Stratton in preventing state police action against the "slots." When the governor said no, Hodge went in to see him about it. "As he walked out . . . he said, 'He's a lying son of a bitch, Smoke. You can't trust him.'" Downey suggests that Hodge wanted to go to the penitentiary quickly, because he feared for his life at the hands of the mob.[18]

With Hodge out of office Stratton moved quickly to replace him.

On July 17 he appointed Lloyd Morey, president emeritus of the University of Illinois, to the position of auditor to complete the balance of Hodge's unexpired term. The name of state Senator Elbert Smith surfaced as a possible replacement for Hodge as a candidate for the position. Stratton made it known that Smith was his preference, although the final decision was in the hands of the Republican State Central Committee. Both of these selections were pluses for Stratton. Morey had been president of the university for two years, after serving as controller and professor of accounting. He was an authority on university management and finance and a member of Stratton's Commission on Higher Education. Elbert Smith was a Decatur lawyer and a decorated Navy veteran, had been in the Senate since 1948, had a good reputation as a legislator, and in 1955 was given an award by the Independent Voters of Illinois.[19]

Smith recalls that when Hodge resigned, he was at a regional meeting of the Council of State Governments. He received a telephone call from Stratton, asking him to replace Hodge on the ballot. Learning that Morey had already been named to complete Hodge's term, Smith was impressed with the speed at which Stratton was moving. He accepted the offer, feeling that he "probably wouldn't win, that it looked like the Republicans had forfeited it [the auditor's office] and maybe the whole ticket." But it was a good cause, Smith felt, and would be a short campaign during a nice time of the year. He was ready to leave the Senate in any case. There, "I'd had enough," he recalls.[20]

Dr. Morey moved quickly to strengthen his hold on the auditor's office. During his first few hours there he fired the custodian of the auditor's warehouses and one of Hodge's assistants. He also ended all relationships between his office and Edward A. Epping, an aide to Hodge who had fallen under suspicion. By August 1 he had cut seventy-nine persons from the auditor's employ—apparently "payrolling" was rife.

On July 21 a federal grand jury in Chicago indicted Epping, Hodge, and a Cook County banker named Edward A. Hintz. The matter must have been under consideration for some time. Hintz was the former president of the Southmoor Bank and Trust Company. When Hodge resigned and admitted guilt, Hintz did the same. He had been a key accomplice of Hodge. The three were arrested on state charges the same day.[21]

Hintz was widely known in banking and political circles in Illinois. He was a judge of amateur boxing matches, and a duck hunter. Earlier in the year Stratton had considered appointing him chairman of the Illinois Athletic Commission, and may have gone to the point of offering him the post, but Hintz took himself out of contention because his bank was under investigation by the Federal Deposit Insurance Corporation.

He was a friend of Hodge and had gone with former Governor Dwight
Green to Granite City in 1954 when Hodge was honored as man of the
year.

Green had been involved with Hodge in the Bank of Elmwood Park,
which Hodge as auditor had closed for "alleged irregularities." Then
Hodge had bought stock in the bank, and it was reorganized by Green
and reopened with him as chairman of the board. Lumping Hodge, Hintz,
and Green together, Stratton referred to the whole matter as a "mess,"
and said "I am disgusted that any of the people involved would do this
sort of thing."

Hintz seemed eager to talk about his wrongdoing. He discussed his
friendship with Hodge, their visits and hunting parties with major league
ball players—identified by Hodge as Stan Musial and "Red" Schoendienst
of the St. Louis Cardinals and Warren Hacker of the Chicago Cubs—"of
how 'Orv' gave him a bolt of Italian silk [so he could have a suit like
Orv's, no doubt], and how he let the warrant cashing deal begin and
grow just to be friendly with Hodge." He called himself "stupid but
honest"—a judgment that was at least partially correct.[22] His role in
Hodge's wrongdoing was to cash the fraudulent warrents, that were
brought to him from Hodge's office, usually by messenger, and credit
the amount to an account called the "brown envelope" account. Hodge
then withdrew money from the account at his pleasure, sometimes in
cash but usually by check, with special handling by Hintz. The record
of the account was carefully kept. An eventual audit of it showed that
the first deposit was made in December 1953, when Hodge had been
in office less than one year, and the last entry was on May 10, 1956. A
total of $1,296,029.72 passed through the account.[23] The magnitude of
Hodge's embezzlement might be put in perspective by noting that in
1956 a three-bedroom home in suburban Cook County could be purchased for little down and seventy-five dollars a month, principal and
interest. Chicago policemen were then paid an average of five thousand
dollars a year, and the police commissioner eighteen thousand. Hodge's
theft of hundreds of thousands of dollars was no minor wrongdoing.

Hodge was indicted in Sangamon County on state charges on July
24, on 276 counts of confidence game, embezzzlement, and forgery.
State's Attorney Coutrakon said of the case "it's colossal" and hinted that
other persons were involved.[24] Stratton made an "official report" to the
public on August 1, by radio and television. His great concern over the
Hodge case is evidenced by the many notes he made as he prepared
this speech. One can picture him laboring at this task night after night
at his desk in the mansion, where the papers were filed. It is obvious
that he gave it extraordinary attention.

The August 1 speech was Stratton's chief public attempt to defend his handling of the Hodge affair. He stressed the independence of the elected executive officers from control by the governor. He had been prompt, he pointed out, to refer the matter to the Legislative Budgetary Commission and to ask it for a full investigation and report. He then put a police guard on the records, while allowing reporters access to them. He asked Hodge to resign, and when he did not, doubled his bond to compel him to vacate his office. Then he persuaded Hodge to resign, temporarily closed the offices of the treasurer and auditor, and appointed Lloyd Morey. He was proud, he stated, of his prompt, innovative action in behalf of the public interest.

In his peroration Stratton declared that "my opponents tried to pussy foot the issue. They were hesitant to attack Hodge. They wanted to wait and see. They wouldn't have had the courage to act."[25] This speech was Stratton's major effort, before the Republican National Convention, to defend his actions in the face of scandal during his administration, perpetrated by an elected Republican official. It reveals clearly the steps that he took and that he felt were worthy of credit. It was his attempt to salvage all possible standing before he led a delegation of Illinois Republicans to San Francisco, where for many months he had dreamed he might become a national figure.

There is no doubt that Stratton acted quickly and decisively once the Hodge scandal became public knowledge. He knew it would hurt his party in Illinois in November, and hoped by the speed with which he moved to reduce the harm. Both Ed Pree and Fred Selcke believe that if Stratton had not acted quickly he would have been defeated for a second term.[26]

On August 13, Hodge pleaded guilty in state circuit court. Sentencing was delayed for a week at the state's attorney's request. Hodge went into the Sangamon County jail at noon, and made his entrance there by introducing himself and shaking hands all around among the seven prisoners in the dayroom. (The vote-getting habit dies hard!) At 7:00 P.M. he was certified ill and taken to St. John's Hospital with a stomach ailment. On August 15 he was sentenced in federal court to twenty years in prison. With restitution of the amounts stolen, the sentence would be reduced to ten. His attorney said all of his holdings would be liquidated to begin restitution. The judge expressed the desire that the sentence be served concurrently with any that might come out of the state court.

Hodge was sentenced in state court on August 20 to twelve to fifteen years and was taken that day to Menard Penitentiary at Chester where he was issued a blue denim coverall with the number 25303 on the back. He wept as he entered the prison. He would be eligible for parole in seven years and three months.[27] There seemed to be great haste in sentencing and imprisoning him, perhaps to have it done before the Republican National Convention got under way. Circuit Judge Clem Smith of Carrollton, who sentenced Hodge, was a political supporter of Stratton's. The Judge told Ed Pree "that he gave Hodge the maximum sentence not only because of what he had done but [also because] he wanted to protect Governor Stratton."[28] So, on August 21, instead of being at San Francisco with other delegates to the Republican National Convention, Hodge was serving his first full day at Menard, a day that began at 6:00 A.M. with sweeping out his cell, receiving a crew cut, and being tested for work aptitude.

Hodge's legislative colleague Charles Clabaugh says of him, "It was just a case of a dishonest man. He was always a strutter, a four-flusher." He feels that "some shady characters" were involved in Hodge's background.[29] In making those judgments Clabaugh had the advantage of hindsight, of course. Fred Selcke takes a different view. "I think [Hodge] was just a victim of circumstance. I don't think he stole that money. I think some people around him stole it . . . he took the rap for whoever it was."[30] Selcke does not say who the culprits might have been.

While Hodge was settling in at Menard, Stratton was at the Republican Convention. Eisenhower was nominated; and Nixon was again given second place on the ticket. Stratton's hopes had been in vain, but it is probable that the ticket would have been the same even if the Hodge scandal had not occurred. Its principal harm to Stratton's political career lay in the future.

Meanwhile the widening circles of the Hodge investigation had reached the Democratic candidate for governor, Herbert Paschen, who was the Cook County treasurer. Cook County funds had been deposited in both the Southmoor Bank, which Hintz had headed, and the Bank of Elmwood Park, in which Hodge had owned stock. On August 2, Paschen asked for and received the resignation of his chief deputy and campaign treasurer, John E. "Big Ed" Sullivan. Sullivan had been the first president of the Bank of Elmwood Park after it was reorganized in 1953 by Hodge and former Governor Green. The next day John W. F. Smith, Paschen's chief personnel officer, resigned. He had worked for several state auditors, including Hodge, for twenty years, until mid-August 1953, when he had fallen under a cloud regarding his handling of trust funds and left state service.

That Sullivan and Smith had charge of an "employees' welfare fund" in Paschen's office had been discovered. The fund was sustained by "shakedowns" of banks in which county funds were deposited—at the rate of one-tenth of one percent of each deposit. Paschen defended the fund, explaining it was used to benefit "hardship cases," for flowers for funerals, and for burial costs in some cases. There was no pressure on banks to contribute, he claimed. The fund had contained only modest sums, perhaps because bank contributions intended for it were sometimes channeled into other pockets. Books of the fund showed that most payouts went to Democratic party affairs and personages; for example, the Democratic party of Cook County, $600.00; Chicago's Morrison Hotel, $1196.00; Springfield's St. Nicholas Hotel, $152.00; Herbert C. Paschen, $547.00; and various "golf days" (golf outings for the benefit of political parties or candidates, for which tickets are sold) for public officials. Other payments were identified as "miscellaneous." The nature of the fund was clear. On August 13 Paschen announced he was dissolving it, and returning its balance of $14,307 to contributors. Bankers had admitted contributions to the fund, stating that they thought it was only for benevolent, not political, purposes.

By mid-August the Democratic National Convention, meeting in Chicago, had crowded the Paschen matter off the front page. Still he was in deep trouble. With leading Illinois Democrats all in Chicago for the convention, conferences upon the Paschen problem were easy to convene.[31] Presidential candidate Adlai Stevenson favored his friend Stephen Mitchell as a substitute for Paschen. In 1952 he had been able to dictate his own replacement; now he found little concurrence among party leaders with his preference. Mitchell had alienated many of them during his tenure, as Stevenson's choice, as national party chairman.[32] They were in no mood to see him become the candidate for governor.

Mayor Daley was at first noncommittal about Paschen withdrawing, then began to hint that perhaps he should. Time was short if a new name was to go on the ballot. On August 29, Paschen withdrew after a series of statements by Daley had made his position untenable. The choice of his successor was to be made by the State Central Committee, by weighted vote, determined by primary election results, in which Cook County had a 6.24 to 3.38 advantage over the rest of the state.[33]

On August 31, Stevenson, Daley, and Democratic party leaders from five states met for most of the day. Daley was publicly deferring to the State Central Committee while exercising considerable power behind the scenes. Finally, on September 4, the committee unanimously selected Judge Richard B. Austin to be the party's candidate for governor. His name was not exactly a household word. When it was offered to the committee, downstate members were heard asking "Who's he?" They must have been fast learners, for half-an-hour later the judge was the committee's unanimous choice.

Judge Austin had spent his adult life either in Cook County politics or on the bench. A native of Chicago, he graduated from the University of Chicago Law School in 1926. For sixteen years he was an assistant state's attorney and made a reputation as a prosecutor at a time in

Chicago when there was much to prosecute. When Dwight Green, also a former Cook County prosecutor, left the governor's chair in 1949, he announced the opening of law offices with Austin.[34] In partnership, the two could successfully walk both sides of the partisan street. Austin campaigned for Cook County Democratic State's Attorney John Gutknecht in 1952, became a circuit judge early in the following year, and ended his association with Green in the practice of law. He had a good reputation as a judge when he was chosen to run for governor.[35]

With only two months remaining before election day, Judge Austin faced a difficult campaign. He had little political standing in Chicago and Cook County, and none at all downstate. In selecting him to be its candidate for governor, the Democratic State Central Committee passed over a number of persons who would have run stronger. Some of them, such as Illinois Supreme Court Judge Walter Schaefer and Senator Paul Douglas, obviously had good reasons to decline. Others, like Cook County Clerk Edward Barrett and Sheriff Joseph Lohman, would have jumped at the chance.

Mayor Daley had good reason to hope that a Democrat would not be elected governor in 1956. To have a rival for power of his party in the governor's chair would have been disturbing to him. Daley and Stratton had worked remarkably well together in 1955 and had plans for further cooperation. Daley had eased Paschen, who himself was not a strong candidate, off the ballot and held the political cards which would have allowed him to dictate the choice of Paschen's successor, if he chose to play them. He probably did. It seems not implausible that Daley put up a candidate in 1956 who was likely to lose, and one who would work well with Daley should he win. Democrat John Stelle, who as lieutenant governor in 1939 had become governor when Henry Horner died, looked upon Judge Austin as Daley's " 'Charlie McCarthy.' That's what all of us Downstaters thought Austin was when he ran for governor," Stelle said.[36]

Stratton faced severe political problems in the 1956 campaign. From an almost certain winner in June, he had been so harmed politically by the Hodge affair that he knew he would have to make a tremendous effort to win. Publicly Stratton insisted the Hodge matter would cost him few votes. Even though Hodge's associates had been sentenced and had gone to prison—Hintz to Joliet on August 26 and Epping to Menard, where he joined his former employer on September 12—the whole matter would not die. It continued to be a political embarrassment to Stratton throughout the 1956 campaign and for as long as he remained in politics.

Stratton hoped to persuade both President Eisenhower and Vice-President Nixon to campaign in Illinois in 1956. What he received from

Washington, instead, was an investigation by the United States Senate's Committee on Banking and Currency, headed by Democratic Senator J. William Fulbright of Arkansas. It was a thinly disguised effort to keep the Hodge case fresh in the voters' minds. Illinois Senator Paul Douglas, who had not forgotten his wife's defeat by Stratton in the 1946 congressional election, had called for a federal investigation of the Hodge case soon after it came to light.

Hodge himself was one of the first witnesses to appear before Senator Fulbright, who was virtually a one-man committee. Hintz and Epping were there with him, all three out of the penitentiary for the day, manacled and under guard. Such drama was hardly necessary for an investigation of banking practices, but it made good election propaganda for the Democratic cause, even though Hodge successfully protested the presence of a television camera.

Hodge, who appeared "repentant . . . and some 25 pounds slimmer after seven weeks in prison, blamed 'temporary insanity' for his theft." He said he had not needed the money, had no political debts, and owed no one. He "insisted that he had stolen only $600,000 and if the newspapers would print 'the right amount' he would not 'look so asinine to my friends and the people.' His voice broke and he was near tears as he said newspaper stories about him were 'hard on me and my family.'" Almost four hours of questioning produced no new information. Hodge was vague about many things but insisted that he was "not covering up for anyone." At one point he told Senator Fulbright, "You're not as fair as I thought you would be, Senator," and Fulbright answered, "I'm sorry that I am a disappointment to you."

Stratton appeared voluntarily before the Fulbright committee on October 19, for more than three hours. As he and the senator fenced verbally, the political nature of the whole proceeding was clear. Some of Stratton's feeling about Hodge was evidenced when he said that the auditor "was politically active against me, and started an abortive campaign for governor against me [and] . . . caused me political difficulty for several months before he was found out as a common thief." In response to a question from Fulbright, the governor stated that "He [Hodge] didn't associate with me. I didn't know what his personal habits were. Politically he was unreliable. Mr. Hodge had a tendency to make abusive remarks at many state officers."

Stratton missed no opportunity to turn the questioning to partisan advantage. When Fulbright called a certain piece of corruption "small potatoes" compared to the Hodge matter, Stratton observed: "You talk of small potatoes, Senator. Under a former administration the state lost 13 million dollars in cigaret stamp revenue. Apparently when there are scandals in Illinois they are on a large scale." When Fulbright asked if there was a deal to whisk Hodge off to prison to silence him, Stratton denied it emphatically, saying "I thoroughly resent any implication that any political deal was made." Earlier State's Attorney Coutrakon had denied that there was any pressure by state officials to get Hodge quickly and safely in prison. "He said that 'never did anyone' in the state administration urge him to make a deal that would send the Hodge principals off to prison 'where they would keep their mouths shut.' "

The partisan nature of much of the hearing was clear. At one point Fulbright asked: "Governor, you have said this investigation was political. You don't really believe that, do you?" Stratton hedged a bit in answering, pointing to the "coincidence" in timing. He did not believe Senator Fulbright personally would "make political capital" out of the hearing.[37] No one in the room doubted that a spirited partisan exchange was taking place. Smokey Downey recalls that there were four hundred thousand persons viewing the hearing on television and that the exposure helped Stratton "tremendously."[38]

In spite of the demands made upon him by the Hodge case, Stratton campaigned in 1956 much as he had in earlier years. He began with the fair circuit during the summer, toured downstate counties in September and early October, and ended with three weeks in Chicago. Pictures taken at the State Fair show him apparently enjoying the festive atmosphere. One of his fair costumes was a double-breasted white suit, worn with two-tone shoes. He was still dark-haired and youthful.[39] As the autumn went on, however, and he realized how close the election was to be, he seemed to age noticeably almost overnight. His hair grayed, a suggestion that the Hodge episode was a stressful one for him.

In addition to Hodge, Stratton's chief political problems were the toll highway project and commission, and state regulation of gambling, or its lack. Highway improvements and better mental hospitals were political pluses.[40] One of Stratton's favorite campaign subjects was Adlai Stevenson's record. As the Democratic candidate for president, Stevenson was again fair game. Bad feeling between the two had persisted since the 1952 campaign. That sentiment had not been lessened in May 1956, when Stevenson's sister, Mrs. Ernest Ives, volunteered criticism of Stratton in reviewing her book *My Brother Adlai.*

> Mrs. Ives said she saw Adlai's growth, his complete concentration on his job as a working governor.... "He worked until midnight. He worked all the time." Apropos of this Buffie [Mrs. Ives] was quite frank about "Adlai not having any more money when he finished his term ... than when he went in." ... Speaking about the present governor, she said, "They're very rich

indeed. . . . And we happen to know what their status was when they went in."[41]

It was a classic case of the arrogance of "old money" toward new, and not an accurate portrayal of the Stratton finances. While the Strattons were somewhat better off than in 1952, when they had very little, they were far from being "very rich indeed."

During the campaign Stratton stressed the accomplishments of his first term. In a speech prepared for delivery over the University of Illinois radio station WILL on October 11, he pointed first to his accessibility. Next he claimed credit for advances in education and highway improvements; better welfare services, labor benefits, food inspection, and mine safety completed his list.[42]

In spite of Stratton's campaign efforts, a *Chicago Sun-Times* poll taken three weeks before the November 6 election had him trailing. Intensive campaigning produced some improvement in his standing,[43] and by October 29 the *Chicago Tribune* reported that Stratton would win by a larger margin than he had in 1952! That was whistling in the dark, and the candidate, if not the newspaper, surely knew better.

Stratton employed a theme that had served him well since his first campaign, and his father before him, that of wicked Chicago versus virtuous downstate. He claimed that Judge Austin, if elected, would be the "puppet of that crowd in Chicago's city hall." On October 31, Austin, in his last paid television appearance, responded to Stratton's allegation that he was handpicked by the Daley organization with charges that in fact the mayor was ordering his aides to deliver votes to Stratton.[44]

As the campaign came to a close, Stratton struck again at Stevenson, while other Republicans were urging the voters "to pull the lever for Ike." They hoped in that way to get straight-ticket votes for the rest of their candidates. The Strattons went to their home in Morris to vote and wait out the returns. On election night it was clear that Eisenhower was a landslide winner, but Stratton was trailing. It must have been a sleepless night for him.

It was not until after sunrise on Wednesday, November 7, with remote downstate returns coming in that Stratton appeared to be the winner. He claimed victory at 9:00 A.M. when Morris High School students came to his home to serenade him. When the votes were all counted his margin over Judge Austin was only 36,877. The candidate who was "picked to lose" had almost won. Stratton's vote was strong in the black wards in Chicago, a result in part of the presence of Joseph Bibb in his cabinet.

It was definitely a Republican year in Illinois. Eisenhower carried ninety-seven counties while beating Stevenson by 848 thousand votes.

Senator Dirksen won reelection by 357 thousand. Secretary of State Carpentier bested his opponent by 600 thousand; and Lieutenant Governor Chapman and Attorney General Castle enjoyed margins of 276 thousand and 406 thousand, respectively. Elbert Smith, who had expected defeat when he went on the ticket in August, beat Michael Howlett for auditor by 225 thousand votes. Stratton feels that "it was a miracle that we were able to retain the auditor's office," and that it was the quality of the Republican candidate which allowed that to happen.

The election returns from Chicago suggest strongly that Mayor Daley did his best to elect Judge Austin. Daley may have chosen Austin because he thought he could not win, but once the judge was on the ballot, Daley was too much the professional to let him down. The Democratic machine simply could not overcome the tremendous strength that President Eisenhower brought to the ticket.[45]

Later, Elbert Smith said that the reason he won was that "Hodge didn't rub-off" on him. Stratton won, Smith believes, because Judge Austin "was very inept. He just didn't know much of anything about the state of Illinois or politics ... and then the newspaper fellows began tricking him." They would ask such questions as "Judge Austin have you been down to Van Buren County," knowing there was no such county in the state, as Austin did not. The opportunities for error in his responses were broad. "And by contrast, Stratton—hell, he knew where every highway was and every bridge.... He knew the difference between the city of Hardin in Calhoun County and Hardin County." Smith credits Eisenhower with helping the whole Republican ticket in the state, as it was clear he did, and Stevenson with being a burden on his.[46]

It is clear from the election returns that the Hodge case hurt Stratton badly. When a Republican candidate for president could win with a margin over 800 thousand votes greater than Stratton's, and other Republican incumbents win comfortably, it is apparent that Stratton carried a heavy burden of discredit in the eyes of the voters. No amount of disclaimer of responsibility on his part could overcome the voters' view that he was at least partially responsible for Hodge's misbehavior. It is true that he acted decisively when Hodge's misdeeds came to public attention. It is almost certainly equally true that he had known for some time that there was something wrong in the auditor's office and had done nothing about it. He had not compelled Hodge to submit semiannual reports, as the constitution authorized him to do. Nor had he reviewed carefully the routine requests for spending approval that Hodge and the other elected executives submitted to him. While he did act quickly and wisely once the newspapers revealed Hodge's misdeeds, forcing his resignation, choosing Lloyd Morey to serve as auditor, and favoring Elbert Smith to run for that office, he must be given a share of

150

the responsibility for allowing the whole unsavory matter to occur. The voters sensed that and reacted accordingly on election day.

In contrast to earlier postelection periods, the Strattons did not leave Springfield to celebrate the victory in 1956. "Shirley and I didn't get away after the election, just stayed around the mansion for a week or ten days and went out to the farm for a little relaxation each day,"[47] the governor reported to a friend. As 1956 came to a close, Stratton went about preparing a second inaugural address and reforming his cabinet and staff as he awaited the beginning of his second term.

11

Second-Term Governor: Third Biennium

Stratton was sworn in as governor for the second time on January 14, 1957. His inaugural address outlined the goals he sought. Again he was eager to improve education and highways, including highway safety. A 236 million dollar bond issue for higher education and mental health was recommended. A tax increase, he declared, would be acceptable only for the benefit of education and welfare. He sought constitutional changes for annual legislative sessions, budgets, and appropriations, and judicial and fiscal reform. He hoped that the public would be allowed by the General Assembly to vote on the question of calling a constitutional convention.[1]

Stratton's budget message was delivered on April 9. For operations, aids, and grants he sought 1.5 billion dollars, up only slightly from the last biennium. Increases were mainly in the fields of education, mental health, and highway safety. He recommended a capital outlay of 581 million dollars, mostly in federal highway grants. He asked for no new taxes. Funds were sought for six hundred new state policemen—an enhancement of Republican patronage as well as of highway safety. In education, he stressed capital needs and teachers' salaries. Money was also requested for two new mental hospitals. Hunting and fishing license fee increases were requested, to fund greater spending for conservation and parks, including seven million dollars for capital expenditures. He felt his budget was balanced, prudent, and sensitive to state needs.[2]

Stratton made few changes in his cabinet and staff in 1957. All directors of code departments were reappointed except Justin McCarthy, who was replaced by Joseph S. Gerber as head of the Department of Insurance. The cabinet continued to be remarkably stable throughout Stratton's second term. His old Lake County friend Richard Lyons died

152

and was replaced as director of revenue by the assistant director, Andrew Fasseas, who was Stratton's longtime associate. Willard Ice recalls that as director Lyons had "bent over backwards" not to be "political." Fasseas filled the position in a different fashion, spending most of his time in Chicago. To Ice he seemed to be "a politician filling a political job."[3] Fred Selcke remembers Fasseas as a "go-getter," a fixer. "You'd go to see Andy ... if it could be done, he'd get the job done for you."[4] In 1958 Conrad Becker was appointed to head the new Department of Financial Institutions. He had succeeded Stratton as treasurer in 1945, and the two were friends of long standing.

The record of Stratton's cabinet for longevity in office is explainable by the care he used in choosing agency heads, their maturity and previous experience, and in most cases, their solid attachment to the Republican party. The governor was a good judge of character and of where each one who came to his attention could best serve him and the public. Remarkably little scandal touched any of his agency heads. Strong bonds of loyalty held him and his cabinet together; three of them literally died in his service, and two others soon after they left office. A quarter of a century later, Stratton spoke with fondness of several members of his cabinet who were then still living. He knew their whereabouts, and recalled names of their wives and children.[5] He combined loyalty to subordinates who served him well with discernment in their selection, and he had the ability, sometimes lacking in executives, to remove summarily those who did not perform well or who became political burdens.

Nineteen fifty-seven brought change to Stratton's personal staff. Obviously Smokey Downey was stretched thin. The governor relieved him of the press secretary's duties, and selected Johnson Kanady for that post. To do so he had to supplement Kanady's salary by more than eleven thousand dollars over four years, from his campaign treasury, to equal the sum he had been paid as a reporter for the *Chicago Tribune.*

Kanady was born in Shawneetown, Illinois, grew up in Springfield, and attended Illinois College in Jacksonville. He was a political reporter for the *Tribune* from the early 1940s until 1957. As a reporter he covered Stratton's activities as treasurer and governor. Kanady recalls that Stratton "never equivocated; any answers I got I knew were straight."

Obviously Kanady had the opportunity to know Stratton well, as a reporter knows politicians, and to know Downey well, as a reporter knows a governor's press secretary. Of Downey, Kanady remembers that "every newspaperman I ever knew liked him. [He was] ... an Irishman and full of stories and blarney, but he never lied that I know of."[6] Of others who found it necessary to do business with Downey, Fred Selcke recalls that "Smokey was a political operator.... [The politicians] hate him or love him." In his job in the Department of Registration and Education, Selcke feels that he was never asked by Downey to do anything irregular.[7] Maurice Scott, who had opportunity to know, thinks Downey was very good at his liaison work with the General Assembly and well informed about state government.[8]

By employing Kanady as press secretary Stratton gained a better speech writer and had better speeches to deliver. He preferred to speak, even on radio and television, not from a prepared text, but with his message clearly in mind.[9] Downey recalls that Stratton "never went for the writing of speeches. He didn't like to have a prepared speech. He liked to get up and talk."[10] Radio and television, however, and formal occasions, made some speech writing necessary. One suspects that Stratton may have relied little on prepared texts while Downey was press secretary because Downey did not like, or did not have time, to write speeches. All of that changed when Kanady came on the scene. He maintained a well-organized file of Stratton's speeches for each of the years 1957 to 1961. Each portion of a year was indexed, and the speeches were filed accordingly. They make an invaluable and highly accessible record of Stratton's thoughts, positions, and public utterances during his second term.[11]

In Ed Pree's judgment Stratton, from an indifferent start, "developed as a speaker ... his speeches were filled with good sound content and substance as well as logic, and he developed a good speaking style."[12] Kanady recalls that it was not difficult to write a speech for Stratton. He would discuss the subject with the governor and work up a general outline. To Kanady, Stratton was "an easy man to work with."[13]

As the General Assembly got under way in 1957, following Stratton's budget message, he realized that it was a critical session for his program. A number of recommendations had come to the General Assembly from the Legislative Budgetary Commission regarding changes that might prevent a recurrence of the Hodge embezzlements.[14] Alterations in technical accounting and auditing procedures were proposed, as were changes designed to give the governor greater control, such as allowing him to appoint the treasurer. This would have required an amendment to the constitution. Stratton felt that his political future depended on the adoption of at least some of these proposals. A substantial number of statutory changes recommended by the commission were eventually enacted, but none of the constitutional sort.

Another matter of concern to the governor and the General Assembly was the final polishing of the Personnel Code before it went into effect on July 1. It created a Department of Personnel and a nine-member Personnel Advisory Board and linked them with the Civil Service Commission, then more than one-half century old, into a single personnel system. Job classification, better salaries, employment on merit, and protection from discharge for patronage purposes were principal goals of the new system.[15]

As one who knew the importance of patronage to his political style and also of the necessity of having competent employees, Stratton had a deep interest in the Personnel Code and the new department. The Personnel Advisory Board, which was composed of persons from the private sector, met for the first time in February 1956. Stratton called it to order and addressed it briefly. He noted the problems of personnel administration then in existence and the significance of the board in interviewing candidates for director of the new department and consulting with the governor about his selection of the director. It is evident that Stratton relied heavily on the board to help get the Personnel Department off to a good start.[16]

By June 1956 the Personnel Advisory Board had found Donald McAdamis to be the best-qualified person for director. Then employed by General Motors, he was described by a member of the advisory board, Ward Castle, a friend and political ally of Stratton's, in a letter to the governor on July 7, as

> by all odds the best we have been able to dig up—in fact he is [the] only one of the dozens we have screened who appears to be fully qualified. I am very much afraid the General Motors people will walk out on us on their very generous offer. Maybe if we take this man, his first assistant could have the necessary political qualifications and could take over after a year or eighteen months. Please give these ideas your serious consideration.

Stratton discussed this matter with Castle two days later and apparently did give it serious consideration, for McAdamis was eventually appointed.

During Stratton's time as governor patronage was of great importance to him and to his party. It had been equally significant to Democrats during Stevenson's term and was to be so again during Kerner's administration in the 1960s. The several governors brought differing views and styles to the matter, but to their party organizations it was life's blood. There was a continuing contradiction between the need of the political parties to reward loyal workers with state jobs and other favors, and the need of the public for a system that would be fair and nonpartisan in its assignment of jobs, and would provide efficient and nonpartisan service. Establishment of a Personnel Code and a Department of Personnel in the 1950s was simply an aspect of that contradiction. Governor, legislators, party leaders, and the general public were all caught up in it. Most state jobs were still in the patronage domain.

Key persons in the patronage structure of the Republican party felt much concern early in 1957 about the impact that the Personnel Code, soon to go into effect, would have on the patronage system. A number of them met in March with Director McAdamis. Of those who took part in the discussion the most forceful were Edward R. Moore, Cook County chairman, and Elmer Hoffman, state treasurer and DuPage County chairman. Moore declared that the code, as it then stood, meant "goodbye to your political organization." He was concerned about restrictions on the political activity of employees under the code, saying

> as I read the regulations ... I am surprised that they say a person [employed by the state] can vote. ... When we have rules and regulations like this, then Mr. County Chairman, you should be ready to do all of the work yourselves. There will be very little help. We should be allowed to maintain our organization in the interest of good government. ... It takes a lot of work to go out and get the people to register, to go from house to house, and change their addresses, and to go out and get votes. Who is going to do it all? The county chairman can't do it alone.
>
> We appreciate the effort and hard work and the intent of [the Personnel Code], but we better stop and think how far it is going.

Hoffman fully agreed. He was critical of civil service and suggested that it was "to some extent ... unconstitutional. It bars a man from promoting the people he thinks best for the government. ... If we do what this personnel code calls for it is goodbye political parties. It means the end of your two party system, the end of the kind of government that you and I like. All of us should ... do a little work on this proposal."[17] As a result of these views and others like them, changes in the Personnel Code were made by the General Assembly. So altered, the code went into effect on July 1.

Stratton's interest in patronage matters continued to be keen. Notes in the governor's hand regarding patronage appear frequently in his papers until the end of his second term.[18] In 1955 he appointed Robert Perz, who had been principal of Springfield High School, to assist Ed Pree with personnel matters. Pree thought highly of Perz, who was an educator with a doctoral degree, not a common accomplishment for a high school principal in that day, and found that he could work easily with both politicians and professionals.[19] Perz became the chief personnel assistant to Stratton when Pree departed in 1957. When Donald McAdamis left the position of director of the Personnel Department in 1958, to return to General Motors, as had been his intention, Stratton wished to name Perz to that post.[20] The Personnel Advisory Board had recommended several other persons, including Maud Myers, who was chairman of the Civil Service Commission. The board reported to Stratton that it found in Perz "many admirable qualities," but also a lack of "practical working experience."[21]

In spite of the recommendations of the board, Stratton named Perz to be the director. Ward Castle's suggestion two years earlier—that a professional be named to head the department, to be succeeded by a more political assistant—had been fulfilled. Thereafter, Perz functioned in a dual and sometimes contradictory capacity; he handled patronage matters for the governor and directed the work of the Personnel Department. There is much evidence of that arrangement scattered through the Stratton papers.[22] The governor's continued deep interest in patronage and his employment of it as a tool in legislation and party leadership are evident in the files of his correspondence with the Department of Personnel in 1958 and 1959.[23] In one sense he had the best of both worlds—he could claim support of a reform measure and continue to use most state positions for patronage purposes.

As a result of the legal requirements of the Personnel Code and new record-keeping technology, attention given to personnel and patronage matters became more sophisticated and detailed in the late 1950s. The patronage system continued unabated. That Stratton was very much a patronage governor throughout both his terms is undeniable. After the Personnel Code became effective, it was a matter of fusing two systems—and perhaps Perz, with his experience in the governor's office, was well qualified for that task. He could carry out the legal requirements of the code while attending as best he could to Stratton's desire to continue to head a viable patronage system. To meld political expectations and the mandates of the law must have been a difficult task.

There is evidence that there were Republican efforts in 1958 to be rid of Maud Myers as chairman of the Civil Service Commission. If so Stratton must have been a party to them. Recall that the Personnel Advisory Board had recommended her, among others, to be director of the Department of Personnel when McAdamis left, in preference to Stratton's choice, Bob Perz. Myers had begun her career with the Civil Service Commission in 1931 as a clerk. Later she was appointed to the necessarily bipartisan three-member commission as a Republican, was named its president by Governor Stevenson, and was retained in that position by Stratton. In 1957 the title was changed by the General Assembly to chairman.

In August 1958 Myers was asked by the federal Civil Service Commission to accept a position in Washington, D.C. She demurred; the commission persisted. She went to Washington, then was asked to take a job in the Department of Labor instead of one in the commission. She refused; then was told the position she had originally been offered would go to another. She returned to her position in Springfield. The *Chicago Sun-Times* reported that Stratton had wished to appoint Illinois Civil Service Commissioner Saul Epton as chairman in place of Myers.[24] She chose to continue in that position and later was appointed by Stratton's successor, Otto Kerner, as director of the Department of Personnel. She was a remarkable survivor.

In addition to improving fiscal management and "perfecting" the Personnel Code in the legislative session of 1957, Stratton continued to push for a change in the judicial article of the state constitution, which had been on his agenda since 1953. He knew how important the judiciary was to political dominance and took a personal interest in judicial politics. In 1953 and 1955 proposals in the General Assembly of a revised judicial article were defeated, in the main because they provided for nonpartisan selection of judges. Partisan legislators were opposed. In 1957 Stratton and Daley agreed on a judicial reform proposal that did not specify nonpartisan selection.[25] Late in the legislative session Stratton employed the unusual device of a special message to the General Assembly in which he urged it to approve the resolution that would offer a revised judicial article to the voters in 1958. He stressed its bipartisan support and offered suggestions for content changes.[26] The modified resolution was approved before the session ended.

Another resolution that Stratton successfully backed in 1957 was one that would allow the voters to decide the fate of a proposed bond issue for university and mental health buildings. The flood of "baby boomers" into the elementary schools was rolling on toward the high-school level, and implications for the colleges and universities were clear. Even though "Stratton was a pay-as-you-go man," according to legislator Charles Clabaugh,[27] he realized the need to borrow, through the sale of bonds, for capital investment in university and hospital buildings. He was also pleased that in 1957 the General Assembly authorized a ten-million-dollar revolving fund for school-building construction, an increase of thirty-three million dollars in aid to the common schools, and a new scholarship fund for higher education.[28]

Representative Clabaugh, whose home was in Champaign, making him sensitive to education issues, credits Stratton with supporting the state scholarship and aid to gifted children programs. Clabaugh recalls that for increases in state aid to local school districts "Bill Stratton could get Democratic votes. They always knew that ... Stratton was the man to talk to. Paul Powell, the ranking Democrat in the legislature ... knew he and Bill Stratton could sit down and talk turkey and usually come out together."[29] Smokey Downey felt that Stratton was supportive of increased funding for education because he "was a student. And he didn't come from any wealthy family. He didn't have any money."[30] Presumably for those reasons Stratton could appreciate the need for good educational facilities and services at reasonable cost.

Other legislative accomplishments in 1957 with which Stratton was pleased included highway safety matters. He was the immediate past chairman of the Governors Conference Committee on Highway Safety. The General Assembly approved a highway speed limit, the first in the state's history, a substantial road improvement program, aid for driver training in the schools, and funds for five hundred additional state policemen (more patronage positions as well as a boost for highway safety). Stratton was proud that these and other accomplishments had been gained without a tax increase.[31]

When state Senator Arthur J. Bidwell, a Republican from River Forest and president pro tempore of the Senate, was asked late in 1957 how he felt about Stratton's interactions with the General Assembly, he replied: "Pretty well.... He is better than any other governor in my time [which dated from 1935]. The man is always available ... and he is completely aware of the importance of the legislature. He's astute politically ... and he knows how to get things done." When Senator William J. Lynch, Democrat from Chicago and minority leader in the Senate, was asked by the same reporter for his evaluation, he "praised Stratton with faint damns." He was critical of the Hodge matter, funding for schools and mental health, and toll road progress.[32] While the Hodge scandal still hurt, on neither of the other issues was Stratton vulnerable.

When the 1957 legislative session ended in August, Ed Pree left his position as administrative assistant to Stratton to return to the family law practice. He had enjoyed his association with the governor and regretted leaving.[33] Pree had been Stratton's principal aid in patronage matters, and from his carefully kept files, one can determine the extent of the patronage system during the first term and the first six months of the second.[34] It was everywhere in state government—wherever a job, a board or commission appointment, a contract, a fee or any other favor could be provided.

Ed Pree was much more than simply a patronage agent. He was assigned and assumed a wide range of duties, as an administrative assistant on a limited staff might expect. He made many speeches and was attentive to small courtesies. A cheerful, pleasant personality emerges from study of his papers. Photographs show him to have been a tall, strongly built, attractive person. It is obvious that he was a significant member of the administration. The politically sophisticated Fred Selcke thought well of Pree and recalls that he was "a peach of a guy," that "he was real good for Stratton," and had good "rapport with politicians and legislators." As a practicing politician himself, Selcke appreciated that Pree "would break his back to try to help you," that he would say yes or no without long delay.[35]

Pree worked closely with Stratton, but he was not a social intimate of the governor and his family. They had been friends on a "Bill" and "Ed" basis, but Pree recalls that he always addressed Stratton as "Governor" after his inauguration. Pree also remembers that Stratton "all during my association with him was always very kind to me. He never attempted to reprimand me or ever bawled me out or ... lifted his voice.... He'd be very emphatic.... He was never in any way unkind to me. I really couldn't ask for a finer person to work with."

Pree lived through the trauma of the Hodge scandal with Stratton and believes that politically it did "terrific damage" to the governor. Stratton, in Pree's view, "was badly shaken" by it and by his narrow margin of victory in 1956. "I detected a change in his attitude after that," Pree recalls. In 1957 there "did seem to be a different atmosphere" in the Stratton administration.[36] Certainly after Ed Pree left it was different. He was a valuable member of the team, and the void he left after mid-1957 was a disadvantage to Stratton's second term. Assistants of his caliber often are the little-credited heroes of the administrations they serve.

Although Stratton was deeply involved in the 1957 legislative session, he took time before it ended to make his annual trip to the Governors Conference, this time to Williamsburg, Virginia. Its program was mainly concerned with highways, education, natural resources, and government operations. Apparently most of the states had similar problems.[37] Stratton was chosen to chair the conference during the coming year, the first Illinois governor so honored. He also served then as president of the Council of State Governments, which was the secretariat and research arm of the conference. Many years later he recalled with much pride his filling of those two positions, and in the latter had taken the lead in revising the council's bylaws, doing most of the work himself.[38] The Governors Conference over which Stratton presided in 1958 was its fiftieth annual meeting.

As usual the Strattons enjoyed the State Fair in August. When the fall came they went boating on the Sangamon and Illinois rivers, often overnight. A group of friends had given them a thirty-foot houseboat that they named the Sandiana after Stratton's two daughters. They were grieved when Major, their Great Dane, died ("the Saturday before Thanksgiving. He was such a good dog," Shirley wrote.)[39]

At this time the governor's mother was living alone in the ten-room house at 437 Vine Street in Morris. She maintained a political headquarters there where Stratton could make announcements of candidacy and await election returns, and where friends and political associates could drop in at any time to visit. It was a continuous open house for the congenial Mrs. Stratton, but her son and his family could not often be there. There were many public and private claims on their time, of course, and after 1953 they had a farm on the Sangamon River near Springfield where they could go for relaxation.

They had purchased this farm in partnership with their friend and one-time landlord Robert Patton, whom Stratton appointed head of the Illinois Youth Commission in 1954. The governor paid ten thousand dollars for his share of the farm of 326 acres. By mid-1954 they were stocking it with cattle, and Glen Palmer gave Stratton a bull. "Dear Governor," he wrote, "I feel it to be a great pleasure to present you with the first herd bull 'Supreme Commander of Bobbill Farm.' I cannot predict how good his offsprings will be."[40] Soon the Strattons were planning to build a "lodge" on the farm. At one time they considered a log structure but finally decided on more conventional limestone and redwood. After the 1956 election when a second term was assured, they went ahead with building plans. Stratton made a cardboard model of the kind of structure they wanted, and in 1957 the chosen site was cleared of brush and trees and construction was started.

By the end of 1958 the lodge was completed. Standing on high, wooded ground overlooking the Sangamon River, it measured forty by seventy feet and was reported to have cost forty thousand dollars to build, a substantial sum for the time. The open-beamed ceilings, the stone fireplace, and its redwood and stone exterior fitted easily into its rustic setting. Inside, it was of less than conventional design with a forty-by-thirty-foot "great hall," and only one bedroom.[41] Clearly, it was something other than an ordinary home.

By the time the lodge was finished, the surrounding farm had grown to 527 acres and was in production. Two hundred twenty-five acres were suitable for row crops and 120 were in alfalfa. Late in 1958 two thousand bushels of milo grain were in storage as livestock feed. There were eighty Aberdeen Angus cattle and fifteen brood sows on hand, and calves and pigs had been marketed in the spring. There were six ponds for livestock and fishing and ice skating in season. Four saddle horses and a flock of sheep completed the pastoral picture. "Farmer Bill" Stratton, as the *Chicago Daily News* called him, and his partner Bob Patton were well started in the livestock business.[42]

The Strattons took up a new hobby in January 1958, when during a two-week vacation they went to Sun Valley, Idaho, for ten days of skiing. "It's a grand sport," Shirley reported. It was apparent that with their boat, lodge, and skiing trips, the second term offered more varied recreation and a somewhat different life-style. Stratton now wore tailored suits made for him in Chicago for a thrifty two hundred dollars; enjoyed an expense account for travel that was charged $487.43 in May 1957, for example; rode the Illinois Central Railroad at no charge, as one of its directors ex officio; and had free admission to Springfield's motion picture theatres and tickets to University of Illinois football games. Other than the farm, he did not have many investments. His salary was twenty-five thousand dollars a year, he had two daughters in college, and he maintained the house in Morris where his mother lived.[43]

Shirley Stratton continued, in 1957 and 1958, to be deeply involved in the pattern of activity she established during the first term. A portion of her time for four years had been spent in overseeing the redecoration of the twenty-eight-room executive mansion, inside and out. In it she played the role of hostess at luncheons, teas, and dinners. An estimated twenty-five thousand guests were entertained in the mansion each year. At such social events Johnson Kanady recalls of Stratton that "always at cocktail hour he and Shirley would walk around with apparently a bourbon on the rocks. It was bouillon. They never touched a drop at that particular time."[44] Shirley planned the menus for all meals, and supervised the staff of thirteen persons—a housekeeper, butler, maids, and cooks.[45] A detailed diary-engagement calendar that she kept shows that she paid careful attention to her clothing and to selecting the proper costume for the occasion at hand. It also records many conventional social and family activities and an interest in motion pictures and gin rummy games.[46]

Stratton continued to be attentive in his second term to the details of state government and to the leadership of his party. The department heads made complete narrative reports to him. He kept tight control over spending through the approval of requisitions and authorizations, and each department was required to file a monthly financial report.[47] He wanted no repetition of the Hodge scandal.

As much as Stratton wished the Hodge matter to recede into the past and never again come to public attention, during his second term it simply would not go away. Shortly after Elbert Smith took office as auditor he disclosed that Hodge began embezzling unclaimed trust funds in his care "the day he took office."[48] The Southmoor Bank liability in the Hodge case of 425 thousand dollars was paid by Lloyd's of London, the bank's insurer, early in 1958.[49] Edward Epping, Hodge's collaborator who had gone to Menard Penitentiary soon after Hodge, was tried on additional charges in March 1958 and found guilty. He claimed it was for "political" reasons in an election year, although it is hard to understand why Republican administrations in Springfield or Washington would wish to renew the matter.[50] These events helped to keep the whole affair fresh in the public mind.

In the Republican primary on April 8 there was a damaging contest over the nomination for state treasurer. Stratton favored Louis E. Beckman, who was beaten decisively by Warren Wright—a signal that the governor's popularity was waning. There was a recession under way in Illinois, and later in April Stratton flew to Washington to testify before the House Committee on Banking and Currency—the one in which he had been a member. He told the committee that nonfarm employment in Illinois was down 4.7 percent in February from the year before, and that unemployment in March was 7.7 percent.[51] Those figures represented a new political problem for him, since it was the first time as governor that he had faced a recession. Later in 1958 he called a special session of the General Assembly to consider extending unemployment compensation and funding public aid increases. The necessity for him to do so was further evidence of political difficulty.

One of Stratton's proudest political accomplishments came to partial completion in August. The Northwest Tollway—76 miles from Chicago-O'Hare International Airport to South Beloit—was opened to traffic. It was the first leg of the 187-mile toll highway system that had been authorized in 1953. At a dedication dinner at Rockford on August 20, Stratton called the toll highway venture "the largest public works program in the history of the state," and he was pleased that not even two years had passed since ground for the northwest portion was broken. Completion of the whole system was anticipated before the end of the year. It had been funded by bond sales of 441 million dollars, and through its tolls, the bonds were to be self-liquidating.

Although construction of the federally funded interstate highway system was under way by the mid-1950s, the Illinois toll road program proceded much faster. Vital to the growth of northeastern Illinois, it was eventually linked to interstate highways 55, 57, 65, and 80 and helped shape the pattern of urban growth in northeastern Illinois.[52] The development of such communities as Park Forest, Western Springs, Hinsdale, Downers Grove, Naperville, Wheaton, Elmhurst, Park Ridge, Elk Grove Village, Schaumberg, Hoffman Estates, Rolling Meadows, and Streamwood was tied into the pattern of surface transportation that the toll highway plan largely determined.

By any measure the toll highway system in northeastern Illinois was a great political, financial, and technological accomplishment. Illinois and its governor had good reason to be proud of it. It had not been an unmixed blessing for Stratton, however. The problems that led to the resignation of Evan Howell, first chairman of the Toll Highway Commission (recounted in Chapter 8), had left permanent political scars, yet Stratton and Howell continued to be personal friends.

After Howell left the chairmanship of the Toll Highway Commission, Stratton took pains to see that it had good leadership. The competent Austin L. Wyman of Chicago succeeded Howell, and when he chose not to continue, he was followed in 1959 by Stratton's longtime associate and adviser, the respected businessman Charles M. Burgess. In 1955, Stratton took the lead in recruiting the capable Charles L. Dearing from a long career with the Brookings Institution in Washington, D.C., to become the commission's executive director.

After Stratton left the governor's chair in 1961, Dearing wrote to him about their 1955 discussion of the position of executive director.

> You gave me certain assurances with respect to the support that I could expect from you in my capacity as a professional administrator without reference to current political pressures or problems. I am happy to say that during the five years that I have been in this position there was never any occasion for me to call on you either personally or indirectly for special support in my major purpose; namely, to operate the Tollway as a business enterprise.[53]

In spite of good management by Wyman, Dearing, and Burgess and the rapid completion of the toll highway system, it had in some measure become a political liability to Stratton by 1958. Its patronage, the selection of routes, and the use of eminent domain in acquiring right-of-way earned it many enemies. Even so, the building of the system in less than six years from authorization to traffic flow was a major accomplishment.

An event of 1958 that Stratton recalls with pleasure was the parole of the convicted murderer Nathan F. Leopold, Jr.[54] He and Richard Loeb, as young men, had been found quilty in 1924 of the "thrill killing" of fourteen-year-old Bobby Franks. Loeb died in prison in 1936 at the hand of a fellow convict. Governor Stevenson commuted Leopold's life sentence to a term of eighty-five years, making him eligible for parole during Stratton's time as governor. Leopold's family submitted a mass of evidence to Stratton in support of executive clemency.[55] Leopold himself offered an earnest and well-written petition to the Parole and Pardon Board in 1957.[56]

Stratton could have extended clemency to Leopold, and thus shortened his sentence, but he chose to follow the recommendation of the board and declined to do so. He pointed out that the path to parole was still open.[57] Leopold gained release from prison through parole in 1958, by action of the board (though less than unanimously) and the governor.

He justified their confidence in him by leading an exemplary life until his death a few years later.

Stratton in 1958 still kept open house in his office from time to time. Photographs taken during such an afternoon show the same line at the door and the same mix of politicians, job seekers, and ordinary citizens as before. He was keeping his hand in politically. To help Republican fortunes in the state generally, President Eisenhower came to Chicago on October 22 for dinner and a speech at the Amphitheatre on South Halstead Street, where Stratton introduced him. The governor was not on the ballot, but he wished to join Eisenhower in helping other Republicans who were—and to build his own political capital for the future.

Stratton was concerned about two referenda that were on the state-wide ballot, one for the judicial reform amendment and the other for the bond issue for capital needs in education and mental health. Change in the judicial article continued to be necessary for the adequate professionalization of the judiciary and the better articulation of all parts of the state's judicial system. It was opposed by entrenched elements favoring the status quo. On September 29, the governor recorded two brief spots for WIND radio, urging voters "to vote 'yes' for the Blue Ballot" on which the proposed judicial amendment was printed.[58] That advice may have contributed to the proposal's defeat, for the only legal marking was an *X* in the proper box. The State Bar Association had urged the same faulty action. Enough voters—one-hundred thousand—actually wrote in "yes" to have carried the issue, in addition to those marking the ballot properly. But the "yes" votes could not be counted and the proposal for judicial reform failed in the November 4 general election. The bond issue proposal came equally close but in the end fared no better—it gained a majority of those voting on the question, but not of all those voting in the election, and thus it failed.

While Stratton regretted the loss of the two referenda, more serious for him were the other results of the election. In what was narrowly a Democratic year, Joseph D. Lohman won the office of treasurer by 140 thousand votes over Warren Wright, and George T. Wilkins was elected state superintendent of public instruction by 209 thousand votes. Only two years after the large Republican margins in 1956, the Democrats appeared to be resurgent in Illinois, and Stratton faced the last two years of his second term in greater political difficulty than at any time in the past.

12

Second-Term Governor: Fourth Biennium

The last regular legislative session of Stratton's second term came in 1959. In his state-of-the-state address he called for greater investments in health, welfare, safety, and in attracting industry. He recommended the construction of a new minimum security prison. To the surprise of many of his listeners, he urged the reorganization of the entire code department structure, calling his proposals "the most far-reaching recommendations which I have to make."[1] One as politically astute as Stratton knew that entrenched interests would resist such change strongly, and probably successfully.

With the state-of-the-state address behind him and the General Assembly not yet active, the Strattons went to Idaho for another skiing vacation. The *Illinois State Journal* carried a picture of a robust-looking governor on the ski lift.[2] Perhaps Illinoisans who were toughing out the winter at home were less than cheered by reading about the Strattons' vacationing in Sun Valley.

Nineteen fifty-nine brought a rift in the previously amiable relationship between Stratton and Mayor Daley of Chicago. The Democrats had gained a majority in the state House of Representatives in the 1958 election and had the opportunity to elect the Speaker. Daley favored Joseph DeLaCour of Chicago, but Stratton intervened on behalf of downstater Paul Powell, from Vienna in deep-south Johnson County, and Powell won.[3] Longtime Democratic legislator Corneal Davis recalls that Powell "went over to see Stratton. And he made a deal. . . . I don't know what he promised."[4] At a reception in the mansion early in January, Stratton told Republican members of the House, individually, "I'd like for you to vote for Powell on the second ballot." As a result of Powell's election as Speaker, Stratton's role as a leader in the General Assembly

166

was strengthened, and criticism that he was too close to Daley was quieted. Political columnist John Dreiske observed that "Stratton plunged the knife into Daley, then twisted it about a bit."[5] The stage was set for further conflict between the two.

Early in March Stratton spent two days at Vanderbilt University taking part in classroom discussions and addressing the student assembly. His statements there are revealing of the ideas that he considered important for such an audience. He expressed pride, as he often did, in having a degree in political science and in being a politician, which he defined as "one who is experienced in the science of government." He regarded two-party politics as superior to single- or multiparty systems, and felt that in the two-party system, internal compromise was necessary before policy positions could be established. The political parties must always seek new blood and new ideas, and government must always be willing to assume new functions and challenges. Stratton expressed the view that politicians should go to campuses, as he was doing, and that professors of political science should go into politics from time to time.[6] Given the setting, Stratton was probably stating his feelings as clearly and openly as he could.

The legislative pace quickened in April. On the twenty-second Stratton delivered his budget message. He must have felt that it was critical to his program, for he wrote it out in longhand. Much editing and laborious work is evident in the draft.[7] He proposed operations spending of 1.8 billion dollars (up 160 million), capital spending of 600 million (mostly for highways), and increased spending for mental health. On the revenue side, he proposed higher taxes on liquor and tobacco, closing sales tax loopholes, and a one-half-cent increase in the sales tax, specifically for education. He recommended that the bond issue referendum again go on the ballot in 1960, this time in two separable parts, 120 million dollars for higher education, including a new University of Illinois campus in Chicago, and 150 million for mental health capital needs.[8] For the sales tax increase, which was essential to the governor's budget, Speaker Powell delivered enough Democratic votes to bring it about.

Before the legislative session ended, Stratton made a trip to the Soviet Union with the Executive Committee of the Governors Conference. He was working hard to gain greater national stature to increase his chance for a place on the national ticket in 1960 and made the trip to the Soviet Union for that purpose. It was cut short to allow him to entertain Queen Elizabeth and Prince Philip on July 6, during their trip to Canada and the United States.[9] A week later Stratton was in Los Angeles to speak to the United States Conference of Mayors, and on July 23 he went to Detroit to address the National Association of County

Officials. Even so he found time in July to squeeze in a fishing trip to Minnesota with his nephew.

Amid all that bustle, an event took place in Illinois that was little noticed but of great significance. In 1956 the Commonwealth Edison Company had been given a permit to build the Dresden nuclear power station in Grundy County. A hearing was held by the Atomic Energy Commission in July 1959, and an operating permit was issued for the Dresden plant. It was the first commercial nuclear power plant in the United States.[10] Illinois had ushered in, for better or for worse, the age of nuclear power in the commercial generation of electricity.

The Strattons continued their interest in boating and other outdoor recreation in 1959. In August he attended the all-star football game in Chicago with Vice-President Nixon and Mayor Daley (apparently the disharmony between Stratton and Daley was put aside for the evening). The governor attended the World Series baseball games in Chicago, to watch the White Sox, in September.

Because of his participation in outdoor recreation and for political reasons Stratton was still deeply interested in the program of the Department of Conservation, which his father had once headed. Glen Palmer, its director, had ready access to him. For its services to the public and for the patronage it provided, the department under Palmer was politically important. By the time Stratton's second term ended, twenty-two precinct committeemen and two county chairmen were game wardens, and fourteen committeemen were among the top fifty-five park managerial personnel.

Stratton was carefully weighing his future political course at this time. The early Illinois primary date made it necessary for candidates to declare themselves by January. He wanted a place on the national ticket in 1960, but was realistic enough to know the odds were against him. While many knowledgeable Republicans advised against seeking a third term, at the same time a number of his friends and associates urged him to make the race.[11] He was encouraged to learn that the *St. Louis Post Dispatch* and the Lindsay-Schaub newspapers would support him in 1960 if he ran. He had to ponder not only his own candidacy for a third term but also the question of whom he should back for the United States Senate. Of course, Stratton might have chosen to seek the Senate nomination for himself—a natural progression and one that would have avoided the third-term controversy. However, he was no more inclined to take up a legislator's role in Washington than he had been in 1942 and 1948. Samuel W. Witwer was eventually Stratton's choice for the Senate nomination.

There was some newspaper speculation late in November over

Stratton's chances for the vice-presidential nomination in 1960. A United Press International story filed from Springfield reviewed the Stratton record. It saw the Hodge scandal still his greatest liability, even after three years. He was judged to be strong with labor and blacks, and his transformation from isolationist in 1941 to mild internationalist in 1947 was noted. His biggest change as governor, it was pointed out, was from an "economy line" in 1953 to "tax and spend" six years later. He was substantially more supportive of education in 1959 than he had been two years earlier. "The former boy wonder of Illinois politics," the report concluded, "is now 45, with grey hair and a paunch.... His wife is regarded as a great asset to his political career."[12]

Shirley Stratton continued the pace of earlier years. While she did not make political speeches, comment on political issues, or substitute for her husband at political functions, her schedule was full of official entertainment, travel with the governor, organizations to which she belonged, and correspondence with family and friends. Far more than her husband, she kept up relationships with the extended Stratton family, and her letters to them were warm and caring.[13]

Early in December Stratton reached the decision to run for a third term, to the surprise of some of his closest advisers. Morton Hollingsworth told an incredulous Smokey Downey that the governor was planning a third term bid. "I was over at the mansion last night," Hollingsworth reported, "and he said the stars are right. She told him the stars are right for him." Who "she" was was not made clear, but from the context of the discussion it seemed to be Shirley Stratton. When Downey then talked to Stratton about the matter, the governor "stalled," Downey recalls, and he knew it was true. With the benefit of hindsight, Downey remembers that he knew then that Stratton could not win. But "there is something about that water at the Mansion," Downey suggests, "they all want to stay in."[14] So, on December 17 Stratton announced from his home in Morris that he was going to seek a third term. "I like being governor," he said. "I believe in the things we are trying to do."[15]

The announcement reignited his difficulty with Mayor Daley. The two had bickered in October, when the governor had commented on what he called Daley's "one-man rule of Chicago's courts," to which the mayor countered by criticizing the progress the state was making in completing interstate highways into Cook County and Chicago. Neither had forgotten an earlier Stratton taunt that Daley might try running for governor. Now, at the mayor's press conference on December 18, he parried questions about his intentions. When informed that Stratton had announced, he answered "Stratton? Stratton? Who's he?" He turned each question back into one for his interrogator. When a reporter observed that "the politicians say a battle between you and Governor Stratton would be the biggest fight the state has ever seen," Daley, smiling, said "Could be, could be."

Both former Governor John Stelle and Speaker of the House Paul Powell urged Daley to run for governor. If not Daley, Stelle hoped for Cook County Clerk and former Secretary of State Edward J. Barrett. He felt Barrett would be popular downstate. Powell professed to see Stratton as being stronger in 1960 than he had been four years earlier, which at minimum would not require much strength.[16] The Speaker's feeling may have been affected by the help Stratton had given him in gaining his position in 1959.

After the holidays were over, the Strattons went again early in January to Sun Valley for ten days of skiing. Soon after their return Stratton was blasting Mayor Daley over problems in the Chicago Police Department. Commissioner Timothy J. O'Connor had resigned on January 23, after Chicago policemen had been found to be involved in burglary—both actively and in condoning it in others. Stratton called for Daley to get about "cleaning up" the department—"or else." In reply Daley raised the ghost of the Hodge scandal. He charged Stratton with "mismanagement and misrule" and was again critical of progress with expressways and mental hospitals. Told that Stratton had spoken of taking "drastic measures," Daley "flushed and stood up behind his desk. 'Cheap politics!' he exclaimed. 'Let them come in here. . . . No one from Morris . . . is going to tell the good people of Chicago what to do.'"[17]

Democrats were determined in 1960 not to let the Hodge matter be forgotten. The presence of much material on the issue in Stratton's files indicates his sensitivity to it.[18] On February 2, State Treasurer Joseph D. Lohman, who had cause to wish Stratton political misfortune and who was himself a candidate for the gubernatorial nomination in the Democratic primary, expressed doubt that the state had recovered fully the amount of Hodge's embezzlement.

Stratton had insisted on January 23 that "every penny [Hodge] stole has been recovered."[19] On February 9, a special assistant attorney general stated that in the Hodge case, of a "total embezzlement of . . . $1,571,364.69. . . . The state has recovered . . . $1,003,880.28. . . . A balance of $567,484.41 will be obtained from the [Margaret Hodge] trust liquidation as outlined in the trust petition."[20] Stratton was wrong in believing then that all losses had been recovered.

At this time Hodge got into the act, by calling himself, during an interview at Menard, a "scapegoat in the governorship election." The banner newspaper headline read "I'M POLITICAL PRISONER, WHIPPING BOY: HODGE." He feared that Democratic insistence on continuing to raise the issue for political reasons was harming his chance of parole.

He insisted, as he had before, that there were culprits other than himself, who were still unpunished. His statements were vague and lacked credibility, according to the reporter doing the interview.

Warden Ross Randolph reported that Hodge was "a model and hard working prisoner." He was the director of the internal broadcasting system at Menard and a motion picture operator for films shown the inmates.[21] Elbert Smith, who was elected auditor of public accounts in 1956, succeeding Hodge and short-term appointee Lloyd Morey, recalls that "our people went down [to Menard] to see him once in a while seeking information. They didn't get anything.... He was clammed up. He didn't embarrass anybody but himself."[22]

In addition to Democrats Daley and Lohman bringing up the Hodge matter, Stratton had problems in 1960 within his own party. As had been the case in 1956, he had an opponent in the primary. The difference was that he had been in full control in the earlier year and had lacked a formidable challenger. In 1960 his hold on the nomination was less sure and his opponent was a substantial one. Hayes Robertson, the chairman of the Cook County Republican Central Committee and a state senator, announced his candidacy late in December. He "charged Stratton with being a 'selfish' failure as a party leader," and cited two factors that would beat him in the fall if he were the candidate: popular sentiment against a third term and his failure to strengthen his party at the local level.

Robertson claimed to have been visiting about the state and "said he has encountered 'apprehension about the situation [at] every level of responsibility.'" Robertson had hoped that Secretary of State Charles Carpentier would oppose the governor in the primary. The anti-Stratton movement had been building since the end of the 1959 legislative session, with Robertson a leader of the Republican township committeemen in Cook County in the effort "to dissuade Stratton from seeking a third term."[23] Robertson was spokesman for a group of Republicans who feared Stratton could not win.[24]

The governor should have had firm control of the apparatus of the party—three-quarters of the Republican county chairmen held state jobs, as did more than a thousand of the precinct committeemen.[25] Seven years of earnest application of the patronage system could provide a substantial advantage. But still he sensed trouble among the rank and file of his party. One of his friends reported that at a cocktail party one highly paid executive "said noisily 'I wouldn't vote for Stratton again.'" When pressed "he could give me no reason ... even after another stout martini."[26] Perhaps that could be called the stout-martini poll.

Stratton took nothing for granted in the primary campaign. He was wise enough to know that, if he rested on his oars, Robertson could beat him. His effort was a strong and persistent one. More so than in previous years, the Strattons were a team. Much campaign correspondence came to the mansion and was handled there by them and the mansion staff.[27]

On March 3, Stratton was in Chicago to open his Cook County headquarters. A large crowd greeted him there, and he publicly took a lease through November 8, to show his confidence in winning the primary. The week that followed was busy: it took the Strattons south, down route 127 through Nashville and Pinckneyville to Jonesboro and Cairo. A March 10 blizzard caught them between Shawneetown and Lawrenceville, and at least once Stratton had to shovel snow in order to free their car from the drifts. By Saturday, March 12, they were back in Springfield to face a barrage of bad news.

Smokey Downey, Stratton's longtime friend, political associate, press secretary, legislative liaison, and trusted aide, was indicted on March 11 on four counts of income tax evasion. Downey had quietly left state employment on January 1. The governor denied any knowledge of the matter and emphasized that no public money was involved. The last thing he wanted and the last his primary campaign could afford was another scandal of the sort that Hodge had caused four years before. It is hardly likely that an associate of such long standing could have left the administration without Stratton's seeking an explanation. Hayes Robertson charged that Stratton either "knew or should have known about Downey." The governor responded by continuing his intensive campaign effort. Robertson went on television to label Stratton "a sure loser" in November should he gain the nomination.

Shirley Stratton took to the platform during the closing days of the primary campaign—evidence of the extent to which Robertson posed a threat. She did not speak directly upon political matters, but of the executive mansion and her social activities. Still, her appearances were intended to have political impact. She concentrated on areas in northeastern Illinois where Robertson was strong. Earlier in the campaign she had virtually been Stratton's staff while he was on the road, driving the car, reading the newspapers to him while he drove, and helping him plan speeches.[28] Now her role was a larger one.

As the day of the primary election neared, evidence of problems for Stratton continued to come in. He was suffering from the "what have you done for me lately" syndrome. He was very much a patronage governor, but a position once filled could not soon be filled again, in most cases, so that as time went on there was a steadily decreasing number of jobs to be distributed. Thus, the longer Stratton was in office, the more difficult it was for him to maintain strong local units in a patronage system.

Primary day, April 12, was clear and mild, and the turnout was good. Stratton beat Robertson decisively, but not in a runaway, 499 thousand votes to 345 thousand. Sam Witwer, whom Stratton had endorsed, won the Republican senatorial nomination in a field of six, with 250 thousand votes out of a total of 911 thousand. Warren Wright was a close second to him with 226 thousand. Otto Kerner won the Democratic nomination for governor. The strength of the Democratic organization in Cook County was evident in Kerner's win. Stratton was conspicuously weak in the university counties—except Jackson—which is surprising in view of his support in 1958 and 1960 for the university-building bond issue. His weakness in such urban centers as Peoria, Rock Island, and Rockford, and in DuPage and Will counties, both adjoining Cook, was significant.

As usual the governor waited out the primary election returns at his home in Morris. Robertson conceded at midnight, and a jubilant Stratton called for "unity in the ranks" of Republicans. At least one Republican, Warren Wright, beaten in the Senate primary by Stratton's choice Sam Witwer, was not willing to be unified. He said, "I am going to give him the same enthusiastic support he's always given me," which meant none at all, or even less. Many years later Stratton remembers Wright as the one political acquaintance for whom he still harbors some ill feeling. He thinks that Wright actively aided Democrat Otto Kerner in the 1960 gubernatorial election.[29]

In giving the graduation address at Southern Illinois University at Edwardsville on June 14, Stratton said he expected the 185 thousand college students in Illinois in 1959 to grow to 300 thousand within ten years. For that reason the expansion of campuses must continue. Thus the bond-issue referendum for university buildings, "a number one interest of mine," was quite important. He had appointed a "Committee of 100" to work for it. "We will be set back at least a generation ... if we don't get it."[30]

The governor also worked for passage of the bond-issue referendum for mental health facilities. Maurice Scott recalls that Stratton had lunch with members of the Illinois Taxpayers' Federation, "talked and then answered questions for ... an hour and a half" and turned the federation around on the issue.[31]

Stratton felt the loss when the director of the Department of Finance, Morton Hollingsworth, resigned on June 15. He was one of the original cabinet and, during Stratton's first term, was chairman of the Republican State Central Committee. Hollingsworth was to become head of the United Republican Fund.[32] To lose from the cabinet one so experienced in Republican politics, in an election year and on the eve of the Republican National Convention, was a blow.

Stratton still hoped in 1960 that he might win a place on the national ticket.[33] He remembers, without admitting that he wished to have the nomination, that President Eisenhower had identified him as a potential candidate.[34] It is probable that few others shared his optimism. Ed Pree recalls that in 1960 there was no talk of the national ticket so far as Stratton was concerned.[35]

During the July convention in Chicago, the Strattons hosted a reception, a breakfast, and a luncheon. In spite of having the convention on his home turf, Stratton did not gain consideration for nomination for vice-president. The lingering ghost of the Hodge scandal probably extinguished any chance he might have had. Stratton recalls that after Richard Nixon was nominated for president and had decided on Henry Cabot Lodge, Jr., as his running mate, a group of midwesterners met through much of the night with Nixon to try to persuade him to change his mind and name someone from the Midwest. They favored Senator Dirksen or Congressman Walter Judd (Stratton included himself in the list, even if few others did) and argued with Nixon that, since Lodge had little chance to carry his home state of Massachusetts against John Kennedy, in that sense he would be a "wasted" candidate. They also thought that he was a poor choice on other grounds, and Stratton feels that Lodge's weak campaigning proved that point. He recalls that he argued the case so long and earnestly that he literally lost his voice. As the evening went on his supporters dwindled away. Stratton points out that if Dirksen had been the vice-presidential candidate Nixon probably would have carried Illinois and might have won the presidency.[36] (He was inferring that the same might have been true if he had been the candidate, though given the weight of the Hodge scandal that alternative is less likely.)

Even though Stratton today denies that he had any interest in getting on the national ticket in 1960, all evidence is to the contrary. One with his political sophistication had to know that he would have great trouble again being elected governor, and he would have welcomed a national nomination. He was not the only Illinoisan who was disappointed with the results of the convention. Senator Dirksen also hoped that 1960 might be his year. From their correspondence it is evident that the relationship between the two was a cordial one, with mutual respect.[37]

Only days after the convention ended, Stratton's electoral fortunes took another blow when Smokey Downey pleaded guilty to one charge of income tax evasion and nolo contendere (I do not wish to contend) on three others. After Stratton had directed Downey in 1953 to end his connections with a Chicago public relations firm, and he did so, Downey formed a fictitious partnership called Ames, Mahan, and Draw. Ames and Mahan were female business associates of his, and Draw his middle name spelled backward. Payments were made to the fictitious firm by entities

174

interested in public policy, such as the Master Plumbers Association, Chicago Downs Race Track, Maywood Park Trotting Association, and Mid-States Trailer Transport Association. It was blatant influence peddling, and Hayes Robertson had charged as much during the primary. It was income from that activity on which Downey had not paid sufficient taxes.[38]

The Downey case was once again in the news, and in the public consciousness, when Downey pleaded guilty on all four counts of the indictment on September 1. He was fined five thousand dollars and placed on three years' probation, during four concurrent suspended sentences of three years each. Three years later he still owed eighty-five thousand dollars in taxes and penalties and his probation was continued for two years.[39] Like the Hodge case, it was a ghost that simply would not go away. Ed Pree feels that the Downey conviction hurt Stratton in the 1960 election campaign, though not decisively.[40]

A happy event for the Strattons took place early in September, when Diana was married to Norman Weiskopf of Springfield. His father was one of the governors' close associates in politics. Diana was twenty-one and had attended DePauw University for three years. In a formal ceremony in St. John's Lutheran Church in Springfield the bride was radiant in the usual white wedding gown, and the crew-cut groom wore formal attire. Sandra was her sister's maid of honor. The ceremony was followed by a reception at the executive mansion.[41]

After the wedding, the Strattons plunged into campaigning, for it was clear that the fight for reelection would be a hard one.[42] The governor decided on a campaign style that was new for him and little practiced by others in Illinois. He and Shirley toured the state by helicopter. He recalls that experience with pride in its boldness. It allowed him as many as two dozen appearances a day, many more than travel by automobile would have permitted. By the end of the tour, Stratton had landed at 418 communities. Often the day would begin at factory gates at 6:00 A.M. before it was light enough to fly.[43] Stratton personally worked out the route and schedules for the helicopter, as penciled notes in his hand on a county outline map of Illinois attest.

The helicopter tour went on from September 13 to October 22, touching almost every county.[44] From time to time Stratton was able to join Sam Witwer, Charles Carpentier, and William Guild, the other Republican candidates on the statewide ticket as they campaigned by automobile.[45] With the end of the helicopter rounds, Shirley observed that she and the governor had been campaigning every day for six weeks, and during that time they had been at home in Springfield together only three times, once for only twenty minutes.

Shirley claimed to enjoy the campaign pace and the opportunity to see old friends. While she still did not make political speeches or answer questions about politics, she did talk about the executive mansion and her campaign experiences. She insisted that she did not grow tired of campaigning, even with 5:30 A.M. risings and much handshaking and smiling, but she had lost eight pounds.[46] As the campaign neared its end Shirley was busy at teas and coffees, Republican women's group meetings, luncheons, and rallies.[47] Many years later Stratton recalled that she had accompanied him on every campaign trip in 1952, 1956, and 1960.

At the same time the governor was plagued with state revenue shortfalls. An audit, which the Democratic candidate Otto Kerner commissioned, suggested a possible deficit of thirty-one million dollars by the end of the fiscal year. There was also a shortage of judges and a sizable backlog of cases awaiting trial. This hurt Stratton politically. If the judicial reform amendment had been approved in 1958, that problem might have been avoided.

Stratton still suffered from the aura of scandal, following the Hodge and Downey cases, and just a few days before the election there was a charge that state funds had been used to make a campaign film. It was denied, but it was still damaging. Kerner was challenging Stratton to a televised debate and bringing up the five-thousand-dollar boat that he said the governor had been given by Andy Fasseas, director of the Department of Revenue. Fasseas asserted that Stratton had in fact paid him forty-seven hundred dollars of the boat's cost, although earlier and later the boat was said to be a gift from a number of his friends.[48]

Charles Burgess, chairman of the Toll Highway Commission, wrote Stratton late in September to say "your helicopter campaigning is apparently paying off." He also said "I have talked to a good many people ... relative to your pitting downstate Illinois v. the City of Chicago. They think it is good psychology." Stratton followed Burgess' advice. In an October 28 news release he was quoted as saying: "It becomes more and more apparent ... that my opponent is the handpicked candidate of Daley.... Kerner ... is subservient to the Chicago Democratic machine and will continue to be so in the future." He had made the same charge against his opponent in 1956.

Three thousand party faithful cheered Stratton at a rally in Chicago's Hilton Hotel on November 2, and on the fourth John F. Kennedy, the Democratic candidate for president, came to Chicago to take part in a huge parade. Shirley greeted twelve hundred women at a rally in Park Ridge. Mayor Daley admitted on November 6 that Kennedy was running behind the ticket in Illinois. Both candidates for governor spoke from the steps of the Old Capitol in Springfield on the sixth. Richard Nixon appeared at a rally in Chicago on the seventh. A record turnout was expected in Illinois and the nation.

The Republican attorney general of the United States had taken steps to impound, if necessary, ballots and voting records in Democratic Chicago, to prevent fraud. And fraud was anticipated by some. E. L. Bost, of Harvard, Illinois, had sent a letter of warning to Stratton on October 31. "I presume all precautions have been provided for at Election Polls," he wrote. "The Democrats, I believe, would steal the vote or votes to steal the throne of God. . . . They are viciously determined to get possession of the government in every department, local, State and Nation. I hope you and the constituted authorities will spare nothing."[49]

The Strattons went to their house in Morris to vote on November 8 and wait out the results. It did not take long after the polls closed to determine the winner of the contest for governor. Otto Kerner beat Stratton by 524 thousand votes. Kerner won in thirty-nine counties, many of them the more populous ones, while Stratton carried the rest. Kennedy, who carried only nine counties, beat Nixon by 8,858 votes. Paul Douglas kept his Senate seat, winning over Sam Witwer by 437 thousand.

Up and down the ballot there was evidence of much ticket splitting. The Democratic candidate for lieutenant governor, Sam Shapiro, won by 236 thousand votes, beating the incumbent John W. Chapman. For secretary of state, the Republican incumbent Charles Carpentier won by 385 thousand. Democrat Mike Howlett beat the incumbent Auditor Elbert Smith by 49 thousand votes.

The two bond-issue referenda for permanent improvements, one for mental health and the other for higher education, both carried. This must have been gratifying to Stratton, since he had supported both propositions during the preceding four years.

Stratton was beaten in Cook County by almost the full margin of Kerner's victory. He lost in Peoria County and in its neighbor Tazewell County, in the populous Democratic strongholds Madison and St. Clair (Alton and East St. Louis) counties, and in urban Rock Island and Winnebago (Rockford) counties. Among the collar counties around Cook, he lost in Lake, his birthplace, and Will. He lost in Macon (Decatur) and Kankakee counties. Where labor was strong he did poorly, especially in centers of United Mine and United Auto Workers strength. Kerner did better than Kennedy in Chicago, and even more so in the Cook County suburbs and townships. Stratton won in the university counties, perhaps in part because of his support for the education bond issue, and in the collar counties of DuPage and Kane. Significantly, he lost by 814 votes in Sangamon County, where patronage might have been expected to make him strong.

Why did Stratton lose? The third-term issue and the convictions of Hodge and Downey provide some of the explanation. Changes in life-style, such as the annual ski trip to Idaho, the lodge, and the houseboat on the river, may also have damaged him politically during his second term. After Richard Ogilvie was beaten in 1972 his "attitude was you put a ship in the water, its clean, and the first day or two its got barnacles and it keeps picking them up until it won't perform as a ship anymore."[50] Stratton's political hull had accumulated a great many barnacles by 1960. He was a patronage governor, and as time goes on patronage is less and less able to sustain its political force.

Ed Pree believes that the Hodge scandal hurt Stratton during his second term. "It badly damaged Governor Stratton's political career and made it impossible for him to be elected" in 1960. Without that burden Stratton might have won a third term, but Pree doubts it. Instead, he is of the opinion that "the people who were responsible for inducing [Stratton] to run did a disservice . . . They concluded a career that should have had another decade or two." He "could never understand why Governor Stratton let them talk him into running for a third term." Stratton might have run for the Senate in 1960 or in 1966, when Charles Percy beat the incumbent Paul Douglas. But "when he ran for the third term and was beaten so decisively, it really finished his career. And it was a real tragedy because he had so much to contribute. . . . He would have made an outstanding senator."[51]

Of course, it was Stratton himself who made the decision to run for reelection in 1960, not his friends and advisers. Their opinions probably did not make much difference in the long run. He strongly wished to continue as governor and Shirley concurred. Her feeling, from several accounts, was stronger than his. He must have known, from going down with Green in 1948, how hard it was to gain a third term. Stratton had unfinished business as governor and once said that he believed that if he had won and Nixon had lost it might have been possible for him to "pick up the pieces" for the Republican party and take the nomination for president in 1964.[52] He has never indicated any regret about having run in 1960, nor has he had any second thoughts about the wisdom of running and its impact on Nixon's campaign in Illinois.

For, in a real sense, Richard Nixon was a victim of Stratton's insistence on running for governor in 1960. Considering the votes each man received, a more popular candidate for governor would probably have carried the state for Nixon over Kennedy, and in view of the closeness of the race for president across the nation, that difference might have been decisive and changed the course of history. Faced with a less urgent need to campaign in Illinois, Nixon might have effectively employed his resources in another state or states. Fred Selcke believes that "if [Charles] Carpentier had run for governor in 1960, he would have beaten Stratton in the primary and ... would have been elected."[53] In view of Carpentier's performance in the 1960 election—the only Republican winner and that by a wide margin—Selcke was probably right.

In the light of later events, was Stratton already in 1960 fearful of prosecution on an income tax charge, and if so, did he run with the thought that he would be safer as governor than not? If he and Nixon both had won, there would have been little danger of a federal prosecution. He might have chosen not to run and thrown his campaign weight behind Nixon, hoping to become a member of a Nixon cabinet or at least winning favor with a Republican president. If he had declined to run in 1960 and had announced permanent retirement from politics, he might have avoided later prosecution, but that would have been out of character.

Stratton returned to Springfield from Morris soon after the election without making any public comment on the result. From November 11 to 20 he and Shirley vacationed outside the state. As chairman ex officio of the State Electoral Board he held up certifying the result of the presidential election in Illinois for a brief period, until Nixon asked him to validate Kennedy's victory. The closeness of the result and the often-heard charges of vote fraud in Chicago in Kennedy's favor raised the possibility that his win in Illinois might be challenged. According to Stratton, Nixon did not want the nation to be kept in suspense during the lengthy period that a challenge in Illinois would have taken.[54] It is possible that even that brief delay in certification earned Stratton ill feeling on the part of the president-elect and his brother Robert, who was to become attorney general and the nation's chief prosecutor.

Illinois had changed a great deal during the time Stratton was governor. From 1950 to 1960 the population increased by 15.7 percent, to just above ten million persons, the next-to-last decade in which such great growth occured. The median family income almost doubled, from $3,667 to $6,566.[55] The toll highway system in the northeastern part of the state was substantially completed and the interstate highway network well under way. Suburbs were growing rapidly and there was much residential and commercial construction in progress. The decline of Illinois as a heavy-industry state had already begun, though this was little understood. The baby boomers were flooding into the schools throughout the decade in a series of waves that were to remake the system of public education. Although increases in the property and sales taxes had kept sufficient revenue coming into local and state coffers to maintain basic services, there was a revenue crisis looming ahead. But that was not Stratton's official concern, as early in January he left the office he had held for eight years.

13

Years of Trial

Although he had lost the election, in 1961 Stratton was pleased to have time he could call his own. He and Shirley took several trips during the first three-quarters of the year. They divided their time at home between the farm, which became their source of income, and their house in Morris. Skiing in Colorado and Michigan during the winter and several summer days boating on the Sangamon and Illinois rivers provided outdoor recreation. Stratton seems to have had no intention of finding nonfarm employment, and took part in activities that suggested he may have considered running again for public office.

In June the Strattons attended the "global strategy" discussions at the Naval War College at Newport, Rhode Island, at the invitation of the secretary of the Navy. Stratton's old service friend, Captain Don Christensen, who had remained in the Navy, was in attendance and entertained them there. Their trip included Norfolk, Virginia, where Stratton recalled his service days. While he told a reporter there that he had "no particular political plans," neither did he admit retirement from politics. In New York City they stayed at the Waldorf-Astoria and went from there to visit the submarine base at New London, Connecticut. Their last stop was at White Sulphur Springs, West Virginia.[1]

After Stratton returned to Illinois he wrote to thank Christensen and added, "In case you hadn't heard, we are expecting an addition to the family in February." He was then forty-seven, Shirley nine years younger. His two daughters were grown and both were married. It would be Shirley's first child. Late in July they went to San Francisco; it seemed they were trying to get in as much travel as possible before Shirley's pregnancy was well advanced.

The first few months of 1961 must have seemed like an extended vacation to the Strattons after eight years in the executive mansion. But on June 5 the good times were marred by a visit Stratton received at Morris from Agent Leo Dehen and Special Agent Charles Francisco of the Internal Revenue Service (IRS). They interviewed him at length, and Dehen spent five days working in his records. Stratton knew that an agent of Francisco's stature was never brought into a case until it was decided to seek criminal prosecution.[2] The episode must have been profoundly disturbing to him.

Smokey Downey, who had pleaded guilty to a tax evasion charge a year earlier, recalls that the IRS tried in 1961 to get information from him about political contributions to Stratton. The agents quit coming around, he remembers, when he told them that President Kennedy's father contributed in 1956. He was seeking utility rate changes that would provide cheaper electricity for his motion picture theaters in Illinois. Downey feels that his own indictment had occurred because the IRS was "after Stratton."[3]

The IRS agents made it clear to Stratton that they felt he had failed to report taxable income during his second term. The IRS view was that a portion of the money that had been contributed to Stratton was spent for personal purposes, and thus was taxable. Their intention was to show that his net worth had grown more rapidly than his reported income would allow. He denied any wrongdoing, telling Dehen and Francisco: "I did not solicit for campaign funds between campaigns. I did not have an office fund that people had to contribute to in order to work for me or to do business with the state.... I think we ran a pretty clean operation." He explained to the agents his multiple roles as governor, head of the Republican party in the state, and candidate for office. He had been too busy, he said, to keep detailed records of all political expenditures.

Stratton told his interrogators that in the past "he would raise as much as $500,000 in a campaign year, and when the bank account was closed out ... would transfer the remainder [presumably in cash] to a vault in the First National Bank in Springfield." That amount seldom exceeded five thousand dollars. He estimated at the time of the interview that there were between five and six thousand dollars in his campaign fund. This suggests that he considered himself to be a potential candidate in some future election.

Political campaigns in Illinois last one and one-half years, Stratton told his visitors, and they are costly. In Cook County, campaigns are funded by the candidate, with delivery of a certain amount of money to each precinct. "I don't have any personal automobiles," he told the agents, considering the Lincoln and the Chevrolet he was using to be "campaign cars," one purchased in 1956 and the other in 1960. It is true that if he again became a candidate they would undoubtedly be used in his campaign, and it is reasonable to argue that they would have political uses in preparing for a candidacy. By the same rationale, he felt that the lodge at his farm, the farm itself, and improvements in his house at Morris were political assets, as clearly they were.[4] The question remained, were they also personal assets, and in what proportion?

Stratton was sufficiently sophisticated in politics to realize the dilemma he faced. All of his actions indicate that he hoped again to be a candidate for public office. He was pure political animal, with a high level of competitiveness, and probably saw himself running for governor in 1964, defeating Otto Kerner and regaining the office he so deeply enjoyed. The Senate seat held by Paul Douglas would come up again in 1966, and after eighteen years in office, an aging Douglas might be vulnerable. It is conceivable that Stratton might have sought the office of secretary of state in 1964, whether or not the incumbent Charles Carpentier wished to succeed himself.

Stratton must have suspected that the investigation of his tax liabilities was motivated by a desire of the Democrats to neutralize him, to keep him from again being a candidate for any public office. If he announced a candidacy, he could expect the pace of the investigation of his finances to quicken. On the other hand, if he retired from politics, the investigation might in time be abandoned. It was a problem that he attempted to meet by halfway measures in the following years, neither eschewing politics nor throwing his hat in the ring.

He knew he had political enemies in Washington who were capable of employing an IRS investigation for political ends. President Kennedy and his brother Robert, now attorney general, perhaps remembered that as chairman of the State Electoral Board Stratton had for a time delayed certification of Kennedy's win in Illinois. Nor had Senator Douglas forgotten that Stratton had beaten his wife Emily in a hard-fought congressional race in 1946. Governor Kerner was closely allied with Mayor Daley, and the latter held political due bills from the Kennedys. Stratton must have suspected that any vigorous try for office on his part would bring about his indictment.

In 1961 Stratton often appeared to be a potential candidate. He publicly criticized the Kerner budget as "extravagant," feeling that Kerner could have gotten by with fewer tax increases if he had practiced economy, "assigned priorities," and "put his foot down" on departmental requests. It had been a "big revenue year," according to Willard Ice, "where they increased motor fuel taxes, and cigarette tax rates, and liquor tax rates, as well as the sales tax. 1961 was a crisis year ... the till was about at rock bottom and so they really had to go out and raise some revenue."[5]

Stratton had no definite answers to questions about his future plans.

They might involve politics, business, or continued farming. "I hope," he said, "to make up my mind by September."[6] During the summer friends urged Stratton to continue in politics, and it is probable that some made contributions to him for political purposes. Dr. Austin C. Kingsley of Jacksonville wrote a salty letter of political commentary and advice in August. He urged Stratton to run again for governor, saying: "Carpentier . . . *sold* his ticket down the river. . . . I never voted for that— G.D.S.O.B. in my life—wouldn't you feel good if you could say the same? R. Y. Rowe had no braine [*sic*] or he would not have taken in after Bill Erickson—hell—Bill's votes went to another Bill and that bill [*sic*] was elected Governor. LISTEN—to me Bill . . . you can win and tell Warren Wright to go to *HELL*."

The fall brought activities of the sort a potential candidate would favor. Early in November Stratton spoke to a luncheon of the League of Women Voters at the Sherman Hotel in Chicago on needed changes in the executive article of the Illinois constitution. He called for expansion of the governor's powers, reduction in the number of elected executive officers, and a realignment of their functions. He also recommended annual sessions of the General Assembly, annual budgets, and a modernized revenue article. The relationship of state executive authority to local government, as in law enforcement appointments and finance, should be redefined. The scholar W. Brooke Graves found it a "very interesting address" and asked Stratton for a copy.

Later in November, Stratton voted the proxy of James Kemper at a meeting of the Republican National Committee. On December 1, he spoke to the High Twelve Club of Oak Park; and went to a stag dinner held by the Indiana Society of Chicago on December 2 as a guest of Thomas J. Downs, whom he had once appointed public administrator of Cook County. On December 12, he spoke at lunch to the Phi Alpha Delta legal fraternity at Northwestern University, and later in the day at Downers Grove to a University of Illinois extension class on political parties.

As 1961 ended, Stratton had kept up his political contacts and made a number of public appearances, without declaring himself to be either in or out of politics. The IRS investigation still hung over his head; but with 1962 his concern was increasingly with his family.

The Strattons kept close to their farm home in January. For the first time in five years they did not go to the mountains for skiing. "We have had so much snow," Stratton wrote to a friend, "that we have had most of the Springfield skiers out at the farm. We have a wonderful spot on a north hill . . . about a one thousand foot run. We even put up a rope tow and it has been a good deal of fun." To another he wrote: "For the first time in twenty years I am neither a candidate nor burdened with the responsibilities of office.... Now that I am an elder(?) statesman, I can give a lot of free advice."

Both skiing and politics came to an end for a time, however, when on February 15 the Strattons welcomed a daughter, whom they named Nancy Helen. Four days later Shirley suffered a pulmonary occlusion and was obliged to remain in Springfield's Memorial Hospital for three and one-half months. Stratton moved into a room across the hall and spent most of his time in the hospital. Later he wrote to his friend Richard Amberg, publisher of the *St. Louis Globe-Democrat,* "I spent so much time in the maternity section that everyone began calling me 'Dr. Casey,'" (after the early 1960s television character).

When Shirley left the hospital, they went to the farm and remained there for most of the rest of the year. The lodge was on one floor, as their home in Morris was not, and better suited to Shirley's convalescence. With a great deal of time on his hands and travel not practicable, Stratton was much in correspondence with friends during mid-1962. Like most new fathers, he found his daughter to be a great source of pleasure. On July 24 he wrote proudly, "Nancy, now five months old, is trying to say something as she sits in her play pen right next to my desk." To Evan Howell he wrote in September, "Nancy is the best baby anybody could have—happy and healthy.... [She is] sleeping right on through until 8:00." Often Stratton urged friends to visit him at the farm, enclosing a map so they could find their way. Richard Nixon, out of office like Stratton, and running for governor in California, sent an autographed copy of his book *Six Crises.*

In a letter to Sam Witwer, who had been with him on the ticket in 1960, Stratton said, "There are so many things I would like to discuss with you." He was impatient for political action, and the peace and quiet of a Sangamon River farm seemed dull. Glen Palmer sent a cordial letter in July, saying "I have thought of you many, many times in the past year," and wrote again in August to say that a Springfield audience, which had come to hear Senator Dirksen, was "still *interested* in Bill Stratton," judging from their applause when his name was mentioned. Perhaps Palmer was interested in coming back as director of the Department of Conservation.

Richard Amberg wrote in August to suggest that Stratton become a candidate for governor in 1964 and promised his help. "Nothing would give me greater joy," he said. "I am confident that the voters appreciate you even more now." Of Governor Kerner he offered the opinion that "while he is a personable man, he is ... completely under the domination of Daley."[7]

Stratton was interviewed again in 1962 by the IRS agents. This time he was informed that a criminal prosecution was being prepared. He repeated to them his feeling that he "had no under-the-table business or dealings that were illegal, and was given no funds that weren't in the public interest or that were improper." He was "very proud of that record."[8]

A criminal prosecution seemed extreme because a civil suit could have settled the question and extracted any back taxes Stratton in fact owed. But at least he was kept aware of what was happening. He knew very well that a declaration of candidacy on his part would hasten the criminal investigation; and he hoped that his silence might delay it, perhaps indefinitely. It must have been a frustrating period for him.

The times were running on for Stratton. In September one of his oldest political friends, Jim Heidinger, of southern Illinois, died. Stratton wrote to Bob Miley that "Jim and his Dad [a former congressman] . . . were always our loyal friends." In October, Marion Keevers wrote from Washington asking for help. The Automotive Canteen Company of America, for which she had worked, had closed its Washington office and she had tried and failed to get a job with Congresswoman Reid. Nor had the University of Illinois offered a position, as she had hoped. She was turning for assistance to Stratton, and soon she went to work for the Senate Special Committee on the Aging.

The Strattons first venture from the farm of any distance, following Shirley's illness, was a trip to Chicago, which their friend James Kemper helped to arrange, in mid-October. There they enjoyed the opera. Not until mid-November were they able to attend a football game at Champaign, as they so often had in the past. A letter to Stratton from political science Professor John E. Jurgensmeyer a few days later mentioned "your next campaign."

Though he had announced no candidacy, Stratton kept in touch with political figures such as his friend Governor Nelson Rockefeller of New York. He attended a campaign dinner for Ray Page and commented upon it in a cordial letter to Secretary of State Charles Carpentier. He was corresponding with Charles Percy, who was to run for governor two years later and for the Senate in 1966. Tom Downs invited Stratton, on the eve of election day in November, to be his guest at the Indiana Society dinner. "I should like very much to have you as my guest again this year," Downs wrote. "It is one of the best ways I know, without making it too obvious, to keep you in the public eye." Stratton accepted.[9]

Election day in 1962 was a lonely one for the former governor. For the first time in many years he was not a candidate, nor was he in office with concern for the election of others who would be working with him. There was no election-night crowd at Morris this time, nor members of the news media with their microphones, cameras, and persistent questions. There was just Stratton and his little family to await the results at the farm.

His friend Everett Dirksen won a third term in the Senate, beating Congressman Sidney Yates by 213 thousand votes. Republicans Bill Scott and Ray Page beat Francis Lorenz and one-term incumbent George Wilkins for treasurer and superintendent of public instruction, respectively. If Stratton had wished to consider a candidacy in 1964, the political trend appeared to be in the right direction.

An amendment to the judicial article of the Illinois constitution was again on the ballot and was approved by the voters. While somewhat changed, it was similar in its essentials to the proposal that had so narrowly missed approval four years before. Stratton was gratified that judicial reform, which he had advocated since 1952, had at last been accomplished. It did much fully to professionalize the judiciary in Illinois and to integrate all of its courts into one system, with the state Supreme Court at its head.

Stratton continued to be in touch with the political world in 1963. Marion Keevers wrote to report on her new job, as well as to relay political gossip from Washington. She was interested in whom the Republican gubernatorial candidate in 1964 would be. Perhaps, like others, she hoped to return to her former position.[10] Stratton attended a dinner for politico Robert Canfield in Rockford in May. Ken Watson, columnist for the *Illinois State Journal,* wrote that Stratton was likely to be influential in selecting the Republican candidate for governor, but that few expected him to make a comeback try. "The governor," Watson reported, "after a two year hiatus from politics at his Sangamon River farm, is once again plunging full force into his favorite pastime." Party leaders and would-be candidates, including Charles Percy, were seeking him out.[11]

In August, Stratton sharply criticized Governor Kerner's veto of the legislative redistricting act, an action that eventually led to the at-large election of all members of the Illinois House in 1964—a bonanza for the Democrats, since it was a Democratic year. Stratton called Kerner's veto an "arbitrary and arrogant abuse of power." He contended that the veto power did not extend to redistricting,[12] a view that does not seem to be valid.

On October 10, the *New York Times* reported that a federal grand jury in Chicago was investigating campaign contributions made during Stratton's administration. When a *Times* reporter reached Stratton, he said "he knew nothing of the investigation." If so, he must have been one of the very few in Illinois politics who were not aware of it, for 125 witnesses appeared during the month-long session, including two former members of Stratton's cabinet, Andy Fasseas and Conrad Becker.[13]

Early in January 1964, Stratton wrote his friend publisher F. Ward Just, in Waukegan, that "this is ... a busy time of the year for a cattle farmer." Since the time for filing for candidacy in the primary was at hand with no decision on his part to run, perhaps he was reconciled to that role, at least for the present. James Kemper had given the Strattons a bull for Christmas, so he too evidently thought of the former governor as a cattle farmer. In mid-January, Stratton wrote to Kemper in Palm Springs, thanking him for the gift and reporting that "we had a wonderful Christmas just watching Nancy; every minute of the day is so exciting for her." John H. Altorfer of Peoria, who was seeking the Republican nomination for lieutenant governor, had given Nancy a pony, and Stratton wrote him to report that "she is a real pet and follows us around like a dog. I built a barn for her ... and each morning Nancy looks forward to taking her Pony her oats. She is so happy to have her."[14]

Stratton attended a dinner for Charles Percy in January and contributed to his successful campaign for the Republican nomination for governor. Percy decisively defeated State Treasurer Bill Scott, "in the most bitter governor primary in years."[15] There were no contests on the Democratic side. Otto Kerner for governor, Michael Howlett for auditor, and Paul Powell for secretary of state were all unopposed.

Stratton was indicted immediately after the April 14 primary election. Timing of the indictment could not have been better if one of its purposes was to keep him from being a candidate. Instead, his role was that of election night commentator on a television program. His indictment had been returned by the grand jury on April 9, but it had been ordered suppressed by the judge until after the primary, "to avoid the possibility of affecting an orderly election." For him to be indicted less than a week before the primary surely would have reflected badly upon Percy, whom he was supporting. If Stratton himself had been a candidate, the timing of the indictment would have been utterly ruinous.

The indictment charged that Stratton had evaded $46,676 in taxes upon $82,542 of unreported income during the years 1957 through 1960. "The case was built on the 'net worth theory'" that Stratton's holdings had increased more in value than his reported taxable income would allow. In income tax cases, "net worth" was an approach formerly used chiefly for underworld figures for whom reliable data on income were lacking. The governor's annual salary had been no more than thirty thousand dollars during the period in question, and was twenty-five thousand during most of that time. He had reported taxable income of $86,097 for the four years and had paid income taxes of $23,311.

Stratton denied any wrongdoing, and pointed out that he had given IRS investigators complete access to his records for the years since 1961. "Agents have come to see me many times," he said. "I have talked to them completely and fully. There may be some technical differences of opinion ... but with respect to the charge ... I do not believe I have done anything wrong whatsoever."[16]

The case was assigned to federal District Court Judge Hubert L. Will, who as a young Chicago lawyer had been an early backer of presidential candidate Adlai Stevenson in 1952.[17] In the face of speculation that the indictment and subsequent proceedings would damage the Republican ticket in November, Victor Smith of Robinson, who was chairman of the party's State Central Committee, said he doubted that there would be any effect. "It is a personal matter," Smith said. "Stratton has been away from the party for four years. When he was defeated for governor, he practically withdrew from the party." In view of Stratton's persistent political activity, that was clearly untrue, yet Smith was simply putting the best possible face upon a potentially damaging situation.

Stratton pleaded not guilty on April 24. His attorneys were George D. Crowley and William A. Barnett, both former IRS agents. Barnett was also a former assistant United States attorney. Leading the prosecution was United States Attorney Thomas Hanrahan, who expected the trial to last about a month, and masterminding it was Vincent P. Russo, "a tax expert with the Justice Department in Washington. He handled the grand jury investigation."[18] The Justice Department was firing one of its biggest guns at Stratton.

Letters and calls from friends began to come to the Strattons with comments upon the indictment. Attorney Charles E. Mason of Waukegan suggested that the action was a Democratic backfire to the Billy Sol Estes and Bobby Baker cases, then on the national scene. Both had been associated with President Lyndon Johnson. "All they got away with is millions," Mason wrote. He also thought that the whole proceeding against Stratton was an effort to "resurrect" the Orville Hodge case—an implication that the government would try to show that Stratton had shared Hodge's loot.

Another attorney, Walter E. Wiles of Chicago, wrote: "There are several features about the matter ... that firmly convince me [it] ... is solely motivated by political partisanship. If it were not for political motivation there would have been adjustment by negotiation, and if it did go to suit it would have been a civil suit." Former Governor Harold Handley of Indiana, a personal friend, wrote to Stratton on April 23 that he "was distressed to read about your hassle with the Internal Revenue Department [sic] because you told me some time ago that the pressure was on as a result of your actions during the '60 campaign relative to the state of the Illinois electors." Handley's reference was to Stratton's role, as chairman of the State Electoral Board, in certifying the Illinois winner.

Not all of Stratton's mail was positive, however. One man wrote on the day the indictment was announced: "Dear Sir. It give [*sic*] me great pleasure to learn of your difficulties with the Government Tax Law. Since your administration abolished my job as Chief Engineer at the Dwight Reformatory ... in 1953. Very Truly Yours."[19] He must be credited with a good memory. Apparently he felt that the political axiom "What goes around, comes around" had been proved true.

The pattern of life for the Strattons in mid-1964 was to alternate two-week periods at the farm and in Morris, as they had done during the previous year. In spite of the fact that the ex-governor was working during the summer with his attorneys on his defense, the Strattons made a trip to New York. Nor did he ignore political matters, and in October he attended a major event in Chicago hosted by his longtime associate Sinon Murray and sat at the head table.

When election day came in November, it was a smashing victory for the Democrats, up and down the Illinois ballot. President Johnson overwhelmed Senator Goldwater by 891 thousand votes—a greater margin than Eisenhower's in 1956. Governor Kerner beat Charles Percy by 179 thousand, and Sam Shapiro was reelected lieutenant governor by 380 thousand over John Henry Altorfer. Paul Powell moved from the House of Representatives, where he had been for thirty years, to the office of secretary of state, beating Elmer Hoffman by 489 thousand votes. Mike Howlett won the office of auditor and Willian Clark that of attorney general, each by about a half-million plurality.

No doubt it was the contest between Johnson and Goldwater that explains most of the Democratic sweep in Illinois in 1964. Also a factor, though probably a minor one, was that the Republicans' former governor was under indictment and awaiting trial. Even so, Kerner trailed his ticket badly and could have been vulnerable to a challenge from an unblemished Stratton. Instead of celebrating victory, however, Stratton went on trial on January 4, 1965, the day Gerald Ford was elected Republican floor leader of the United States House of Representatives, where both men had begun their political careers many years before. Both were now fifty-one. Ford's course was to take him to the presidency, while Stratton's political life was virtually ended.

Jurors for the Stratton trial came to the courtroom at Adams and Dearborn streets in Chicago from places as distant as Blue Island, Elgin, Deerfield, and Roselle. By occupation they seemed quite ordinary—a stock clerk, a secretary, a homemaker, and a bookkeeper, for example. For two and one-half months they were to assemble five days each week, coming through the snow and ice of a northern Illinois winter to hear the arguments and view the evidence in the case of the United States against Stratton.[20]

The teams of attorneys were complete—Chester A. Emanuelson had joined the defense; Stephen Kaplan and John P. Crowley (not related to the Crowley on the other side of the case) the prosecution. Emanuelson was a political figure who had once run for Congress against Sidney Yates. The trial began badly for Stratton. Early on, he was reprimanded by Judge Will for "grimacing and laughing" while he was conferring with his attorneys. The judge warned that he did not want anyone "playing Hamlet." The case was serious business, he said, and he would tolerate no levity. "I don't see what's so funny about this, governor," he told Stratton. "These are not frivolous points we are trying to decide." The defendant was obviously startled, and asked if he had the right to confer with counsel. Told that he did, he said to Judge Will: "I have every confidence in your honor's conduct of this case.... I have never been in a courtroom in these circumstances."

The defense offered a motion to dismiss the case, arguing that since Stratton had received many tax-free political contributions, the net worth theory, used here for the first time in the prosecution of a political figure, was too weak, and "didn't promise proof of the case." Judge Will denied the motion. "I'm prepared to be educated," he said, "but I can't believe they can be treated as non-taxable gifts. The minute I reach that conclusion, I will cause politics to become the greatest business in America."[21]

On January 7 the government opened its case against Stratton with the first of two hundred witnesses it expected to call and the first of ten thousand documents it planned to offer. The thrust of the prosecution was relatively simple—to show that the gain in Stratton's net worth could not have been accomplished by means of his reported income. Central to the issue was this question: Were elements of net worth such as the house in Morris and the lodge at the farm essentially personal or political possessions? If the former, then the income from which they were acquired and improved should have been reported and taxed. If the latter, then that income could be considered a political contribution and not subject to tax. They might have reasonably been viewed as personal in part and political in part. The government proposed to show that a "wilful attempt" to evade taxation had been made.

The government explained that Stratton deposited his salary and other reported income in a Springfield bank and wrote checks upon it for personal expenses. It proposed to show that other personal expenses were paid in cash, which had not been reported as income. Witnesses for the prosecution testified that cash was paid for furnishings for the lodge and for clothing for both the Strattons. The defense suggested that the clothing in question might have been worn at such events as the governor's inauguration, the inauguration of the president of the United States, and the Strattons' entertainment of Queen Elizabeth.

That was to be the main thrust of the defense—that Stratton's roles as candidate, party leader, and public official made political expenditures out of what would have been personal ones for a private citizen. Less easily defended were such expenditures as the shoeing of Stratton's horses at the farm, and purchases from Abercrombie and Fitch in Chicago of such items as air mattresses, a book on wildlife, and a wine rack. Simply to show that such purchases were made, however, and with cash in some cases, did not prove that they were funded with unreported, untaxed income.

Stratton's old friend and cabinet officer Andy Fasseas testified on January 11 that the boat, which the Strattons used on the rivers and that presumably formed a part of his net worth, "was the scene of many political conferences. Senators, representatives, and civic leaders would be there. . . . There were barbecues. The Supreme Court justices came one time, and unfortunately one of them fell into the river." The prosecution would have wished the boat to be viewed as purely a social and not a political asset. In any case it had been a gift and thus not taxable as income.

Remodeling and electrical work at the house in Morris were shown to have cost $9,900, paid in cash and other disbursements. The defense contended that the Morris house was a political base and that as many as fifteen hundred persons gathered there on occasions such as election nights, which made improvements necessary.[22]

On January 12, Shirley Stratton's inaugural gown—of red satin—was brought into the "somber walnut-paneled courtroom." It was defense "exhibit #2"—evidence that her clothing was often worn on official occasions. Testimony was heard that Shirley made 155 visits to Francine's House of Beauty during 1958, 1959, and 1960, at an average cost of three dollars a trip. The operator of the shop, Mrs. Francine Patton, testified that Shirley usually had "a wash and set." "I talked to her when she had time," Mrs. Patton said, "but usually she was working, opening mail and writing letters. She was always busy." It was also shown that the Strattons gave Senator Dirksen a subscription to *Réalités*, "a sophisticated Parisian magazine with left-bank flavor."[23] Apparently the government was trying to show that the Strattons had lived on a more lavish scale than their reported income would allow. That was hard to do with three-dollar "wash and sets" as evidence, especially in view of the defense's argument that well-dressed hair was essential to Shirley's official appearances.

On January 13, Stratton's first wife, now Marion Munyon of Lynn

Haven, Florida, was a reluctant witness for the prosecution. The government's purpose in subpoenaing her was to establish Stratton's net worth in 1949 when they were divorced. It was next to nothing. The prosecution also put a reluctant Kenneth B. Carroll, a Springfield photographer, on the stand, to give testimony about the number of times the Strattons had had portraits made. The weight of his testimony seemed to come down on Stratton's side, however, when defense counsel asked him, concerning a bill for four glossy photographs of Diana, what she was doing in them. "She was sitting on an elephant holding a sign saying 'Stratton for Governor,'" Carroll replied.[24] He was a photographer and eventually half-owner, for many years, in the Herb Georg Studio in Springfield, and made portraits of many of the state's politicos. He gained a deep and clear understanding of political practices in "Mr. Lincoln's Hometown." Carroll felt strongly that the Stratton trial was a political harassment, unjustified by the facts.

On January 14, after John Doctoroff, an artist from Chicago, testified that he had done portraits of the Strattons for thirty-five hundred dollars each, the jury got their "first loud laughs," as Clinton Craggs of Mason City appeared as a witness for the prosecution. An ironworker, he testified that he had installed a stairway in the lodge for $2,359. " 'That was in 1958, wasn't it?' said Craggs, looking directly at Judge Will. 'If you don't know, I certainly don't,' " the judge replied. After Craggs explained that the Strattons thought the cost of the stairway was too high and that it was several months before he was paid, Judge Will asked, " 'Was it black iron?' . . . 'No Ma'm,' Craggs answered, and when the judge looked slightly startled, he added, 'I ain't so good at this.' " With a smile the black-robed judge said, " 'I assume you were confused by the gown.' . . . 'I knew I'd make a fool of myself,' Craggs said, throwing up his hands." As he left the witness stand he said to the jury, "I'm old enough to know better. It's just my nature."[25]

Robert D. Patton, who had bought the farm with Stratton, went to the stand as a government witness on January 19. He had been the Strattons' landlord in 1951 and 1952 and testified that the rent was usually paid in cash. He and Stratton each purchased a one-half interest in the farm on the Sangamon River, where the former governor and his wife had been living since 1961. Eleven months after he became governor Stratton paid ten thousand dollars in cash for his share. Patton testified that thirty bred cows were purchased for the farm in 1954, for thirty-six hundred dollars, and the only animal acquired since was a heifer presented to Stratton. "Some time or other you must have acquired a bull," Judge Will commented.[26]

The government's argument regarding the farm was that, in expanding Stratton's net worth, it was evidence of unreported and untaxed income that should have been taxed, while the defense contended that since all political contributions were tax exempt by law, if no restrictions were placed on them by the giver, they could be used for personal benefit by the recipient. Both positions seem extreme, and justice probably lay somewhere between the two. It would not seem unreasonable for a political figure to acquire with tax-free contributions property or services that were principally for political purposes, without establishing tax liability because of an expanded net worth. When such property ceased to have political purposes, tax liability could be established by negotiation or by civil suit. The central question in the Stratton case seemed to be whether such property as the farm and house in Morris were essentially for political purposes during the relevant years, 1957 through 1960.

On January 21, the government brought Leo Dehen, the IRS agent who had first interviewed Stratton in 1961, to the stand as an expert witness. He was "ready to tell how Stratton, in the years in question, 'was spending terrific amounts of currency.'" Judge Will ruled that Dehen could not make conclusions about which of Stratton's expenditures were personal and which were political, that only the jury could do that.

On the following day the government introduced, for verbatim recital, the lengthy interviews the IRS agents had held with Stratton in 1961 and 1962. Stratton's lawyers offered to have him read his answers, but the prosecution apparently did not wish to have that much reality at work and preferred another arrangement. Chief prosecutor Russo read the questions and prosecutor Crowley the responses.[27]

Shirley Stratton made her first appearance at the trial on the day the lengthy interviews were read. "The governor proudly introduced her to the government's attorneys and the one or two newspaper reporters who did not already know her." On this day, and most of those of the trial that followed, she sat on a bench usually reserved for witnesses, little more than eight feet behind her husband.

During a recess Shirley talked to reporters at an informal press conference. "I have been told," she said, "that over a million dollars has been spent on this investigation," during three years, with "trips to Florida, New York, [and] Oklahoma and that unprecedented numbers of investigators have been used." She compared such prosecution resources to the limited private funds available for the defense. She was suggesting political persecution, and hardly would have done so if she and Stratton had not been in agreement on that score. "I am proud of my husband," she said, "and proud that he had the courage to fight back."[28]

The verbatim recital of earlier interviews with Stratton illuminated his manner of handling political contributions and his rationale about their use. Prior to 1952, he often had to fund his own campaigns in part, and to borrow from friends to do so, especially for the primary, when his eventual candidacy was uncertain. "Sometimes you can get that back and sometimes not," he said. After he won nomination for governor in 1952, money was easier to get. His practice was never to solicit contributions until he had announced his candidacy (typically he announced quite early), to distinguish carefully between contributions to the party and to himself personally, and to refrain from intermingling personal and campaign funds.

Stratton explained that at the end of each campaign for governor he had a cash reserve in the political fund. Late bills might come in. He did not invest those funds, and thus there was no income from them and no record was kept of them. "There is no particular reason to keep a record," Stratton said. "I know where it is, it is mine, and I can use it. I wouldn't say it would be mine in the sense I could use it for my personal benefit. I could use it . . . to enhance my political career." Earlier Stratton had explained, in speaking of his campaign fund, that "if I were actively engaged in campaigning, I would certainly pay the increased cost of my personal living with it."[29]

Even though Stratton did not solicit contributions before announcing candidacy, some did come in. He explained that, while he was governor, each year one to two thousand dollars would be found in Christmas and birthday cards, "some from people [we had] never even heard of." Such contributions were placed in a petty-cash fund and were useful, for simply to announce a statewide candidacy would cost up to ten thousand dollars or more.

The former governor agreed that the costs of official travel were reimbursed to him personally while he was governor, even though they might have been initially paid from campaign funds. The source of the initial expenditure seems not to be significant if he was entitled to reimbursement. At least a portion of the cost of building the lodge was funded by Stratton out of personal resources derived from previously taxed income. "I sold some stock," he said, and "drew out all my reserves."[30]

The government's last witness—of eighty-five, falling far short of the expected two hundred—was Robert Dyas. An employee of the IRS, his specialty was investigating the incomes of public officials. He had audited at least two governors, a state senator, a state party chairman, two former mayors, and a councilman. "Like 'The Twelve Days of Christmas,'" commented Judge Will.

During fourteen days of the trial Dyas presented dozens of summaries for the prosecution. One showed that Stratton's net worth had gone from $1,406 in 1949 to $209,116 in 1960. Dyas' final summary indicated that Stratton owed $40,945 in taxes, over four years. The defense attacked his ability to determine which expenditures were political and which were not. When Dyas was asked what trade or business Stratton had been in, he replied "public official." Then he was "asked . . . whether expenses incurred in a trade or business are deductible items, and [he] replied, 'Yes, Sir.'" Later Dyas agreed that political contributions could be used for campaign purposes without tax liability. He "testified that there was no direct evidence that Stratton diverted campaign funds for personal purposes." That he had done so was one of the government's chief contentions. When asked if a car purchased with contributed funds for use during a campaign would still be a legitimate political tool during following years before the next campaign, he replied, "I think possibly it could."[31]

On February 23, the thirty-fifth day of the trial, the government rested its case. Stratton's mother, now seventy-seven, was in the courtroom for the first time. The defense moved to strike all of Dyas' testimony on the ground that he was not qualified to distinguish between personal and political expenditures. Judge Will denied the motion, holding that the matter was one for the jury to decide.

Then the defense moved for a directed verdict of acquittal on the ground that the government's case had not been demonstrated, that no evidence of the improper use of money had been offered. Judge Will disagreed, "saying that many of the expenditures were for personal clothing, including women's apparel, both 'inner and outer.' 'Do you mean you don't know what a brassiere is for, Mr. Barnett?,' said the judge. 'I do.'" He denied the motion; and called the question of Stratton's intent the most sensitive one of the trial. He appeared to be leaning toward the defense's contention that there had been no wilful intent to defraud, but still considered the question to be one for the jury.[32]

Stratton kept himself fit during the trial by taking long walks through the Chicago Loop, usually in the company of defense attorney William Barnett. It was almost his only opportunity for exercise. He and his family were living in a hotel near the courtroom. Of their daughter Nancy, Shirley said, "She's a very happy child and I brought her up [from Morris] so Bill could have breakfast with her. That was a source of joy for him." Since her first appearance in the courtroom, Shirley had been there each day of the trial.

The defense counsel recognized Stratton as their chief strategist. He sat "at the right end of the defense table, about a yard from the press table, [and] frequently throughout the trial . . . summoned his lawyers to his side for strategy conferences. . . . [He] invariably accompanies counsel into Judge Will's chambers for conference on legal points."[33]

The defense brought a parade of witnesses to the courtroom in an effort to demonstrate conventional political practice. Judge William L.

Guild of Wheaton, who was the Republican candidate for attorney general in 1960, testified on February 24 about the persistence of campaigning. "I ran for political office" nine times, he said, "and you start campaigning the day you win or lose." He had visited the lodge twice in 1960 for political meetings. At one, others present included Stratton, Charles Carpentier, John Chapman, and Sam Witwer, all, like Guild, on the statewide ticket, and Shirley Stratton, "who cooked dinner."

On February 25 three expert witnesses—experts in politics— appeared. They were Republican state Senator George R. Drach of Springfield, Timothy P. Sheehan, chairman of the Cook County Republican Central Committee, and Francis X. Connell, a Chicago ward committeeman who had been county chairman from 1958 to 1962. All stated that political contributions were tax exempt, even when used for personal expenditures. Sheehan challenged the IRS rule, numbered 54–80, to the contrary. He asserted it had "never previously [been] tested in court," and called it a faulty interpretation of the law. Drach stated that "many candidates use campaign money for subsistence,"[34] as Stratton probably had in 1950 and at other times.

State Representative John W. Lewis of Marshall, who was Speaker of the House in 1963, testified for the defense on February 26. He told the jury that he had served under four governors, from Green to Kerner, and that Stratton had a better command of state government than had the others. "I hope he's a candidate for public office again," Lewis said. As he left the witness stand he offered Stratton fifty dollars, "to do with as he sees fit, to use ... in any way he wants." Taken by surprise (perhaps), Stratton asked, "Your honor, may I have your permission to accept this? ... It's my 51st birthday." Judge Will smiled and said, "I don't control contributions."[35] Lewis was seeking, of course, to make the point dramatically that money given to a political figure often had no strings attached.

Fred Selcke recalls that when he gave Stratton money he said: " 'You do what ever you want with this.... You buy Shirley a coat with it if you want to; they [the contributors] don't care what you do with it.' ... Back in those days when you gave money to a candidate, you didn't care what he did with it."[36] Former longtime state Representative Charles Clabaugh expresses himself somewhat more directly on the subject. "They accused Bill Stratton ... of using campaign money to buy his wife a coat. Well Bill Stratton didn't have a pot.... I think all that kind of stuff is ridiculous."[37]

Julius Klein, former major general in the Illinois National Guard, political publicist and consultant, and an old friend of Stratton's, testified for the defense on March 1. He seemed to be shocked by the nature of the proceedings. "Your honor," he protested, " 'the prosecutor referred to Governor Stratton as the defendant.' Black-robed Judge Will peered down from the bench and replied softly: 'Mr. Stratton happens to be the defendant in this case.'"[38]

Klein recovered sufficiently to tell the court that two or three days before the 1960 election he gave Stratton one thousand dollars, saying "Bill, you're not going to win. You'll need money after the election." (He did not say that he had been one of those who had urged Stratton to make the try for a third term.) That brought the total of his contributions to Stratton to approximately ten thousand dollars. "I never put any restrictions on any contribution," he said. "I am a great admirer of the Governor.... He was good to the poor people."

Other defense witnesses included state Senator Dwight Friedrich of Centralia, who recalled that he gave Stratton five thousand dollars in 1960 with no restrictions on its use. Frank A. Frisch of the Republic Printing Company—which never had any state business, he alleged— told the court that he gave a total of thirteen thousand dollars to Stratton, including five thousand in 1953. At that time he said: "Bill, I think you need some money. I can spare it and you can use it." At the time of another contribution he said, "Bill, this is gift from me and my wife to you and your wife."[39]

Another longtime Stratton friend and political associate, Andy Fasseas, testified on March 4. He gave Stratton five hundred dollars on Christmas day in 1950, when he "was about to marry Shirley Breckenridge." Every Christmas thereafter he gave Shirley five hundred dollars until 1960, when it was seven hundred. He set the total at fifty-two hundred dollars. When he made the contribution in 1960 he remarked to the Strattons, not completely logically, "We can thank God we live in a country where money doesn't control the election of officials." The defense was straining to make the point that many contributions had been unrestricted, leaving the Strattons free to use them as they saw fit.

Sergeant Leonard E. Wirtz of the Illinois State Police, who was Stratton's driver and one of his security detail for eight years, testified that as governor Stratton never spent a night at the lodge. That was in support of the defense's contention that it was not a personal home but a political facility. Wilma Schuey, Shirley's secretary, testified about the many political functions held at the lodge and houseboat, and to Stratton's writing checks out of his personal account for purposes that were clearly political. S. James Holderman of Morris, a lawyer and Stratton's friend who had been chairman of the Illinois Industrial Commission, testified about the use of the house at 437 Vine Street for political events such as announcements of candidacy. Those affairs in 1951, 1956, and 1960 had cost two thousand, thirty-five hundred, and forty-five hundred dollars, respectively, to stage, all paid in cash. Holderman's son James "told of driving Stratton's 1960 campaign station wagon and acting as paymaster on the campaign trail. He said he spent six hundred dollars a week, which Stratton gave him in cash."[40]

John Drieske, political editor of the *Chicago Sun-Times,* testified that he had visited Stratton at his Morris home and at the farm. He never gave the governor money; but Stratton gave him Christmas gifts—"a silver tray, a book, a small desk set, that type of thing." He denied that he wrote more favorably of Stratton as a result. Such generosity on Stratton's part, clearly for a political purpose, would explain some of his purchases from local department stores.

After Chief Justice Ray Klingbiel and Judge Byron House of the Illinois Supreme Court testified to their need for campaign contributions in running for the court—House said, "I fell far short of my needs and had to dip into my personal reserves"—the defense brought its star witness to the stand on March 5: the "silver-tongued" Senator Everett Dirksen, who made a dramatic appearance. While the government's attorneys challenged his standing as an expert on tax laws generally, he claimed that status so far as the taxing of political contributions was concerned. "Congress has passed no laws to tax political contributions as such," he said, and "nothing by law restricts" the use of such contributions.

Dirksen called himself "an old friend" of Stratton, saying he had known him "man and boy" since Stratton was twelve. Speaking "in a low, sonorous voice. . . . He expounded the philosophy that a politician must have wide latitude in deciding what is a personal and what is a political expenditure." In 1944, when Dirksen was seeking the Republican nomination for vice-president, he obtained a ruling from the IRS that unrestricted political contributions were not taxable, and could be spent in any way the recipient chose.[41]

The courtroom was crowded for Dirksen's testimony. Sipping water as he spoke, he declared that in politics "he has 'never yet found a substitute for money.' " The politician in office or seeking office must maintain an image, which often requires spending. A governor makes many ceremonial appearances and receives many requests for contributions of money and objects of value. From long-term records he estimated that such requests coming to him averaged one hundred dollars a day. "Fortunately, there are people [contributors] who recognize the difficulties public service imposes," Dirksen said. He felt that partial upkeep of an official's home was a legitimate use of contributions, since it was also a political center.[42]

Judge Will asked Senator Dirksen if he had ever spent contributions on clothing for himself. "I came very close on one occasion, your honor, and it might have been a sizable sum," Dirksen answered, "settling into his chair for a good anecdote. As a freshman congressman in 1933, he arrived in Washington for Roosevelt's inauguration without a dress suit and was described in the newspapers as 'the man who attended the inauguration in a rented suit.' 'It was a frightful embarrassment,' " Dirksen recalled, " 'and it resulted promptly in the raising of a fund of $2,700 to buy me a white tie and a long-tailed coat.' He said that he had not used the money for that purpose, finally giving it to charity, but added, 'I felt I might have been justified in doing so.' "[43]

The senator also felt it was important for an official's wife to be properly dressed. "I've said a thousand times that Mrs. Dirksen is the most valuable unsalaried member of my staff." His feeling was that such partners should be adequately clothed as a legitimate political expense: "If a wife attends two functions in the same dress, 'the next time around there ought to be a new gown.' " With that opinion the senator surely did himself no harm with the women's vote.

With the completion of Dirksen's testimony the defense unexpectedly rested its case. He was its twenty-seventh witness. "When the jury filed out at the noon recess, Dirksen stood in the witness box, bowing, smiling and saying hello as each one passed. Stratton and Dirksen made their way arm in arm through spectators outside the courtroom where television cameras faced them." An estimated two hundred spectators surrounded them there. The impact of Dirksen's testimony was great, due to his office, his prestige, his persuasive talents, and the examples he cited. The government's attorneys must have felt a sense of foreboding as he spoke.

With Dirksen the last witness for the defense, the trial went to summary statements from both sides, and for the prosecution, four rebuttal witnesses. In closing, the government made much of the lodge's existence as a personal rather than as a political asset. Again, on March 8, the defense moved for a directed verdict of acquittal, arguing that the government had not proven its case that Stratton had no known source of nontaxable income, nor had it proved "wilful and knowing" intent to evade taxes, as charged in the indictment. Again Judge Will denied the motion.

In his closing argument, George D. Crowley, for the defense, "declared that the trial was a 'political case', and that the indictment was voted before the primary election and the case scheduled before the general election."[44] He asserted that "the former Governor was the victim of an unprecedented, political line of argument based on 'guesswork' and derived from a method originally used to prosecute hoodlums and racketeers." In rebuttal, the prosecution charged that the defense had lied.[45]

During the trial the Strattons received a heavy volume of supportive correspondence—"thousands" of letters, they reported—often with contributions of money toward the cost of the defense. On March 1, Stratton's second cousin, Sister Mary Charlesita, B.V.M., a teacher in the Regina convent in Dubuque, Iowa, wrote that her prayers were with Stratton as the trial neared conclusion. She made a significant point as she wrote: "There are few whose lives could be scrutinized as was yours in this endless presentation of minutiae without revealing weakness or vice." Perhaps that was the most significant finding of the trial—that no incident of bribery or kickback, no ownership of racetrack stock or other suspect activity could be found—and it was a person with spiritual insight like Sister Mary who could observe it. She closed her letter with "God be with you, and I certainly will continue to speak to Him about you."[46]

The case went to the jury for deliberation late in the day on March 10. As the hours went on, Stratton's mother, who had been in the courtroom every day since the defense began its testimony, observed that "this is worse than a pregnancy. You can't do anything to be comfortable." By one account "the most relaxed man in the walnut-paneled courtroom was Stratton. Jokingly he asked newsmen if they had 'heard from the first precinct yet.'" Apparently his election-night instincts were at work, but the impending verdict was more critical to him than any election result had ever been.

The jury took an hour for dinner, then continued its discussion. The evening wore on. Ten o'clock came, and Judge Will sent the jurors home for the night. There was to be no relief from the tension until the next day. The jury resumed its work at 9:30 A.M. on March 11, and by 11:40 it had reached a decision. The court came back into session. As the Strattons entered the courtroom, Shirley "squeezed her husband's hand tight, leaned close, and whispered to him."

Shortly after twelve o'clock the decision of the jury was read. It found Stratton not guilty. As the verdict was announced, there were shouts of joy among the spectators. The Strattons were silent with no signs of emotion, as Judge Will examined and read the verdict. Without comment upon their decision, he thanked and complimented the jury, saying, "You have earned the right to freedom in our free society. You are entitled to walk a little taller from now on." He discharged the jury and then the defendant. Journalists crowded around the Strattons, and at last he showed emotion, his voice breaking as he said: "I felt we were right all along. . . . It was worth fighting for." One competent observer reported that Stratton "has been probably the most confident defendant ever to face a federal court jury on a criminal indictment."

Shirley Stratton said: "I never lost faith in my husband. I am proud of my husband's profession. There is no more honorable profession."

The governor's mother said she "never doubted that he was right. Will we celebrate? Yes, I guess we will celebrate this for a long time." When asked if the trial was "one of the roughest times" she'd been through, she replied, " 'In politics and life, there are lots of ups and downs,' with a smile."[47] Perhaps she was remembering the hard times of the 1930s, her husband's death, and her struggle for the bare necessities of life in the years that followed.

After their first round of statements to the media, the Strattons and Judge Will spent twenty-five minutes chatting with the jurors in the judge's chambers. It had been quite a different sort of gathering when the government's counsel met, minutes after the verdict was announced, in the fifteenth-floor offices of United States Attorney Hanrahan, who "appeared chagrined." Prosecutor Crowley was their spokesmen. He said that the evidence presented by the government "was irrefutable." He felt that the verdict was based, not on the evidence, but "on other considerations," that the defense had created an "atmosphere of politics." Hanrahan said that "the evidence was just disregarded."[48]

One of the jurors revealed that eight ballots were taken before unanimity for acquittal was found. The decisive elements of the trial, he felt, were Dirksen's testimony (Stratton agreed), the failure of the government to credit Stratton with cash reserves that he might have had, and its failure to reveal any unreported, taxable sources of income.

The Strattons spent that night in Chicago, then went to Morris the next day. An informal reception took place, arranged by the governor's mother, with friends and neighbors coming to the Strattons' home to offer their best wishes. Much of the talk was of the nature of the trial that Stratton had endured. Magistrate Chester P. Winsor recalled: "There were agents all over the town [before and during the trial]. One . . . even wanted to look at the books of Bill's church to see if he gave any money. The minister told him he'd have to get a subpena [sic]." Circuit Judge Leonard Hoffman remarked that "this thing had to be political."[49]

Others long experienced in politics shared the judge's opinion. Fred Selcke recalls: "I think it was . . . a political harassment deal. . . . They [the Democrats] stole the election [in 1960]. They thought, 'we'll shut them [the Republicans] up, we'll indict the . . . ex-governor.' " When asked if there was a "defense fund" for Stratton, Selcke said that there was no organized effort. "I sent him a check," he remembers. "Not that I was solicited, but I think I sent him a hundred dollar check."[50]

The expenses of the defense amounted to over one hundred thousand dollars. The team of attorneys had worked together beginning in June 1964. Crowley said: "We worked every night, often well beyond midnight, and every weekend and even New Year's Day. Often, it was brutal, hard work." Time spent in preparation had to be compensated.

Each day of the trial meant more than fifteen hundred dollars in legal fees, plus nine hundred a week for transcripts. Weeks of living in a Chicago hotel were costly for the Strattons. Loss of potential earned income probably amounted to as much as legal expenses. Stratton reported that much of the cost of the trial was "borrowed from friends."[51] To one contributor he wrote, "The ordeal at Chicago placed a heavy financial burden on me and I certainly welcome the kind interest of such friends as yourself."[52] Twenty years later he recalled that the cost of the defense reduced him to near-bankruptcy.[53]

Many friends, like Selcke, made voluntary contributions. Democratic Secretary of State Paul Powell had sent money, saying, when asked why he was aiding a Republican, "If they get Bill Stratton on this charge, they'll get us all." After the trial Powell wrote again to Stratton, "I am herewith enclosing my personal check in the amount of $500 to assist you in a small way in paying part of your legal expenses incurrred in what I consider a 'great victory,' not only for yourself but every other person who is in political life."

Republican state Senator Everett R. Peters, chairman of the Senate Appropriations Committee, sent twenty dollars, writing, "You fought the battle for everybody in politics ... and you should be lauded by all politicians." A "Springfield Republican" sent four dollars, saying "the Government should be made to pay for trying to defame your character." All this raises the interesting question, was money so contributed subject to taxation? If the trial was regarded as a political proceeding, probably not. If instead the costs of the defense were personal expenditures, in the eyes of the IRS, probably so.

Others shared in the opinion that the trial was "political harassment." Paul Prehn, veteran Urbana politician who had himself endured indictment and prosecution, wrote: "I am sure this is correct—Bob Kennedy and his associates decided four years ago that if his brother was going to be reelected they had better smear the Republican party in this state—and you were the victim." Former Indiana Governor Harold Handley wrote to Stratton on March 12, saying "you and Shirley had to go through the kind of persecution that seems to be the order of the day for public officials other than those aligned with the administration in Washington."[54]

The *Tribune* editorialized on March 12, "If there ever was a case of prosecution for political purposes, this was it." The jury was congratulated. The editorial alleged that Democratic politicians had often been spared such problems, recalling that former Chicago Mayor Ed Kelly, after he "acquired a fortune" while Park Board president, was allowed to negotiate a tax settlement of $105,000 after he became mayor in 1933.

A few days later in another editorial the *Tribune* quoted Timothy P. Sheehan, chairman of the Cook County Republican Central Committee, as saying, "After I left the witness stand in the Stratton case, I wished I had said what I believed—that, if he was stuck on this charge, anyone who ran for office would need Joe Kennedy for a father." There were three ways to run for high office, in the *Tribune*'s editorial opinion: be wealthy, be a complete demagogue, or rely on contributions. "The last is the cleanest of all, and the government case, in effect, was that Stratton had been successful using this approach." In a *Chicago Sun-Times* editorial Milburn Akers expressed the opinion that Stratton was not guilty, and called for a better accounting of campaign contributions in Illinois.[55]

Ed Pree feels that the trial "was a political prosecution." He suggests that it took place because Stratton defeated Emily Taft Douglas for Congress in 1946. In 1965 her husband Paul was still a United States senator and his former Senate colleague Lyndon Johnson was president. In Pree's opinion, "Governor Stratton felt it was largely a politically-inspired prosecution and that he was the victim of it all." Pree also recalls that Stratton "demonstrated remarkable personal courage before and during the trial, and his usual optimism." He suggests that the Stratton trial was the beginning of a series of such political harassments, with the Kerner prosecution "retribution" for Stratton's ordeal, and that of Attorney General Bill Scott a response to Kerner's.[56] (If one subscribes to that line of reasoning, it would be logical to conclude that Governor Walker went to prison because Scott did, which leaves the interesting question, who's next?) In lengthy interviews, Stratton has consistently made it a point, when the subject came up, *not* to say that he believes his trial was a political one. That is not the same, however, as saying it was not.

The themes that ran through the many letters Stratton received during the spring and summer were recognition of his courage and persistence, his return to party leadership, and the opportunity for him to run for the Senate in 1966.[57] Such appeals were not sufficient, however, to cause him to seek a return to political life. He had been noncommittal on that score when the trial ended. As 1965 went on, he made the decision to take a position in the business world. Many letters of the sort he ordinarily would have responded to lay unanswered in his file, in the latter part of 1965. The curtain was coming down on his political career.

14

After Politics

When his trial ended Stratton faced another of the critical decision points of his career. For a time during 1965 he considered running against the aging incumbent Senator Paul Douglas, whose third term would end early in 1967. In replying to a congratulatory letter from his friend Harold Handley, Stratton wrote in June: "Now that the long ordeal is behind us, many people have been in contact with me about the race in '66 for the U.S. Senate seat. Although, it is too early to make any decision, I am giving it considerable thought."[1]

He attended such obviously political events as the Sangamon County Young Republican picnic on July 4, a meeting of the Antioch Township Republican Club in September, and other party functions. Pictures taken during a political swing through northeastern Illinois in August show the extent to which the events of the 1960s had aged him. He told a reporter in DuPage County, without committing himself to the race, that he thought he could defeat Douglas, but he recognized that he might have a primary fight if he chose to run.[2]

The Strattons were vacationing in Boulder, Colorado, when he received a telegram from Governor Kerner inviting him to a memorial service in the capitol rotunda for Adlai Stevenson, who had died in London on July 14 at the age of sixty-five. Stratton was fourteen years younger. Stevenson, one of the few political opponents toward whom he felt real antagonism, was dead, while Stratton was perhaps near the point of resuming his political career. He sent his regrets to Kerner.[3]

Stratton and Stevenson were much alike and yet much different: each grew up in Illinois in a political family; each served his state as governor; each suffered a failed marriage. There the similarities end. Stevenson was educated in the east at one of the nation's oldest universities, Stratton in the west at one of its newest. The older man was primarily interested in foreign relations, yearned to be in the Senate or to be president. He knew little at first about the detail of being governor. Twice the candidate of his party for president, a role he enjoyed even while he appeared to reject it, he would have relished a third nomination, but characteristically refused to seek it and watched it go to another, who gained the office as Stevenson could not. Stratton, in contrast, was vastly absorbed in the detail of being governor, enjoyed the role, and in it was almost everything that Stevenson was not. Stratton deeply wished to be on his party's national ticket, as Stevenson had been on his, but that experience was denied him even though he pursued it actively.

The primary election in 1966 was scheduled for June, the later date that Stratton had advocated when governor, with final filing not until late March, so that he had adequate time to review his chances of winning a Senate nomination and election. Apparently he had decided by late 1965 that the business world was more attractive than politics, for early in November his longtime friend James Kemper announced that Stratton was joining the Kemper Insurance Company in Chicago as "a general agent and marketing and business consultant."

Early in 1966 the demands of Stratton's work in Chicago made continued ownership of the house at 437 Vine Street in Morris impracticable, and it was sold.[4] After twenty-five years in which it served as his political headquarters—though hardly as a home for he was seldom there—giving it up was a symbol of his decision to abandon politics and government for business.

Even though Stratton made known his intention to devote the rest of his career to the insurance business, he could not escape one "last hurrah" in the world of politics. Few remember today that he ran in the Republican primary for governor in 1968. The principal contenders for the nomination were his friend John Henry Altorfer of Peoria and Richard B. Ogilvie of Cook County, president of the County Board and former sheriff. Against those political heavyweights Stratton's candidacy went nowhere because he lacked the essentials that a campaign must have to be successful—money and organization. The baggage he carried—still burdened by the Hodge scandal, loser by half a million votes in 1960, the indictment and trial—all weighed heavily against him. Ed Pree recalls that "his old appeal, the Stratton name, the vote-getting power of the name was virtually gone." Pree thinks that perhaps Stratton felt he could win in a three-way race.[5] Fred Selcke suggests that Stratton might have been trying to tilt the balance one way or the other between the other two, but says, about why he ran, "I don't know . . . there was not much enthusiasm for Stratton . . . he wasn't real aggressive."[6]

Stratton says that he thought he could win in 1968, that either

Altorfer or Ogilvie would drop out of the race and he would be the beneficiary.[7] That expectation hardly seems to have been realistic. Both of his opponents were committed, experienced political figures with powerful backing and extensive resources. The contest between them was a close one—Ogilvie won with 336 thousand votes to Altorfer's 289 thousand. Stratton received only 50 thousand. He had no strength in Cook County, where he lived, and none in the suburban collar counties, so vital to success in the Republican primary. In only a few rural counties where remnants of his former glory still lingered did he have any following comparable to that of his opponents.

It is possible that Stratton had not found satisfaction in the insurance business, and that he was making one last, ill-prepared grasp at the brass ring as it went by. That he left Kemper and accepted employment with Canteen Corporation in the fall of 1968 suggests that he was ready for a career change. Still it does not seem that one so experienced in politics would make so feeble an effort if winning the nomination were his true goal. I believe that the real reason for his unprofessional, uncharacteristic, and completely unsuccessful candidacy in 1968 (it hardly can be called a campaign) was simply to establish that he was still a politician, still a seeker of public office.

During his trial in 1965 his defense had contended that the farm and lodge in Sangamon County and the house in Morris were political, not personal, properties and thus not evidence of net worth built on taxable income. The house had been sold in 1966, and the farm was soon to be sold. The tax liability upon the proceeds was to be settled by negotiation. Perhaps Stratton wanted still one more bit of evidence that he continued to be a political figure in 1968, even though unsuccessful, for use in his dealings with the Internal Revenue Service. In any case, the 1968 primary revealed that as a candidate he was completely lacking in viability, and the curtain finally came down on a political career begun more than thirty years before when "young Bill Stratton" joined the Young Republicans and started working his precinct in Morris.

Since Stratton went on to a career in business and civic affairs, it is appropriate here to sum up and evaluate his life in politics. Governors of Illinois fade quickly from public view and are little remembered or remembered wrongly, or both. Much of what a politician becomes is shaped by personal experiences long before he or she first seeks office or casts his or her first vote. Stratton's parents were powerful influences upon him. The strong character and intellect of his mother were especially telling because of the unusual amount of time they spent together. He watched his father win and lose high office and then endure a wilderness period in which his health and fortune were shattered and during which he died.

Stratton's positions as a young congressman—isolationism, fiscal conservatism, and near-hatred of Roosevelt and the New Deal—can be understood from his background and early life experiences. The younger man was at first under a strong compulsion to achieve the highest office his father had held, and from the start he was very much a patronage politician, as his father had been. It was the system he knew and took for granted. When he found himself out of office in 1945 he sought and gained a commission in the Navy—a way of filling time by serving his country until the next election and of gaining a service record, almost always a political plus. Service overseas broadened his intellectual and political horizons. His second term in Congress showed him to be less an isolationist—and in fact a mild internationalist—even though he was still a fiscal conservative. After his political defeat in 1948, the ensuing dissolution of his first marriage, his own wilderness time, and his entry into another marriage seemed to bring him the maturity to end his bondage to his father's record and to expand his political ambitions. The defeat of both Governor Green and Senator Brooks in 1948 paved the way for Stratton to contend for leadership of the Republican party in Illinois and within four years to run successfully for governor. His second marriage supplied him with a working partner in the enterprise of governing the state. To an extent seldom equaled, he had the assistance of his wife, a much younger and more energetic woman than governors' wives usually are, in the role of official hostess and in countless other ways.

As is often the case with accomplished and durable officeholders, good luck in electoral matters seemed to follow Stratton about. In 1952 his strongest primary rival had to abandon the race; and in 1952 and 1956 his Democratic opponents were replaced during the summer with weaker candidates. In spite of the myth of the great power of the Stratton name in attracting votes, he trailed his party's ticket in 1946 and in 1952, and did so by great margins in 1956 and 1960. At no time in his several campaigns for governor was he a strong vote-getter.

Stratton's performance as governor, however, must be rated as one of the best that Illinois has known. Reared in a political household, educated as a political scientist, experienced as a legislator during two terms in Congress, and trained as an executive and in public finance as state treasurer, he was ready for action when he was inaugurated as governor in 1953. Study of his inaugural addresses and state of the state and budget messages indicates that he was remarkably consistent in his goals. They can be summed up as greater aid to education, highway

enhancement, including the building of toll roads and interstate expressways, better mine and traffic safety, and improved mental health services.
He also sought the constitutional changes of reapportionment and judicial reform.

Conspicuously to Stratton's credit during his first term are reapportionment, the first since 1901, formation of the Toll Highway Commission and authorization of its program, enactment of a Personnel Code,
and an imaginative and politically adroit sales tax increase shared equally
by the state and municipalities that choose to participate. During the
second term his main accomplishments were implementation of the
Personnel Code, better funding of education, completion of the toll
highway system, another half-cent increase in the state sales tax, and a
successful bond-issue referendum for the benefit of higher education
and mental health facilities. The judicial reform amendment, approved
in referendum in 1962, had come very near approval four years earlier.
Its implementation in the years that followed placed Illinois among the
leaders of the states with the most modern judicial systems.

The lasting and most significant monument to Stratton's tenure as
governor is not the massive building in Springfield that bears his name
but the toll roads and expressways of the northeastern corner of the
state and the dozens of university buildings on campuses from De Kalb
and Chicago to Carbondale, from Macomb and Edwardsville to Charles-
ton. In a time of declining railroad traffic the toll road system and the
interstate network, which it facilitated and joined, have been vital to the
economic development of Cook and the collar counties and of the whole
state. This continues to be so during the decades of the 1980s and
beyond. The expansion of university campuses that took place while
Stratton was governor, and later with funds supplied by the bond issue
approved in 1960, continues to house much of the state's enterprise of
higher education.

Stratton was motivated to do good things by his early life experiences, and he was able to get good things done because he was an
experienced, pragmatic politician when he became governor. He did
not avoid using the standard political tools of the time in gaining his
ends. Ironically, though, it was use of those same tools, such as patronage
and vote trading with leaders of the Democratic party, that contributed
to his defeat in 1960.

It is not surprising to find that Republican legislators approved of
Stratton's programs; however, members of the other party in the General
Assembly generally got on well with him too. Such Democratic leaders
as Cecil Partee, who became president of the Senate, William Redmond,
Speaker of the House for three terms, and George W. Dunne, who was
majority leader in the House, all served in the General Assembly during

the time Stratton was governor. In their later memoirs they had nothing critical to say of him.[8] Democrat Esther Saperstein, who had a special interest in mental health programs, feels that Stratton's record of improvements in the mental hospitals was good. By the time he left the governor's chair there was at least one bed for every patient, which had not been the case previously. Democrat Robert W. McCarthy, who was in the General Assembly from 1955 to 1977, viewed Stratton less positively, feeling that he was "unpopular" in 1956 and later, and especially so because of the patronage of the toll road program.[9]

Stratton accomplished a great deal as governor because he saw clearly what it was he wished to do, pursued his goals steadily, and had the necessary skills of management and of dealing with the legislature. He was consistently conservative in taxation and conservative in appropriations as a control on spending. An adroit administrator, he chose cabinet officers carefully and they served durably, with little turnover, and appointment of the first black and first woman to cabinet status was much to his credit. He was a hands-on manager, actively and continuously engaged in overseeing the working of state government. Former legislator John Parkhurst, a Republican, states that his

> assessment of Bill Stratton as a governor is that he was probably the most active and informed chief executive that we have had.... He was on top of everything, he ran the show. There was no question about his authority. He was the boss. He was very effective. He dealt with problems very practically. He understood patronage. He understood how to twist arms.... He was a ... *consummate* politician.... He was a tough able executive. He *ran* the state.[10]

Former Republican legislator Charles Clabaugh believes that Ogilvie "and Bill Stratton—they were the two best governors I've ever served under. Stratton knew an awful lot more about the state of Illinois than any governor since Len Small.... They had a good deal of the same background.... They traveled the state and they knew the state." Both Small and Stratton had legislative experience—a qualification no other person elected governor since Small's time can claim. The veteran observer of political affairs Republican Joseph Immel feels that Stratton is "probably as knowledgeable about state government as any man that I've talked to in all the years that I've known state government." And not only Republicans felt that way; Clyde Lee, who was a Democratic member of the House from 1947 to 1967, feels that "Stratton was ... an outstanding governor" and that his knowledge of state government exceeded that of the other governors Lee had known.[11]

Donald O'Brien, a Democrat from Chicago who was in the state Senate all of the time Stratton was governor, and who became minority leader in 1958, also thought well of the governor—"He was ... very able ... and he did a good job." O'Brien recalls that Stratton, "If he needed some help ... would talk to some of us Democrats." O'Brien had easy access to the governor. He remembers that "Smokey Downey ... would come over to see me and he'd say, 'Can you stop in to see the governor?'"

"You know it gets hot and muggy down in Springfield in June," O'Brien remembers. "And the governor used to sit out on the back porch. And ... he knew I liked Wurtsberger beer so he'd always open up a couple of bottles.... He and I got to be good friends."[12] O'Brien's experience, as a Democratic leader in the General Assembly, helps to explain the governor's success in gaining legislation.

There is much evidence that Stratton has few peers among Illinois governors in terms of his grasp of the detail of state government and finance. Maurice Scott recalls that "one time he asked me to meet with him on the budget at the Leland Hotel. He was in his shirt sleeves with papers everywhere, and it just astounded me what he knew about each department, where he could cut and where he needed a little money.... What he carried in his head on state government was amazing."[13]

Not everyone looked on Stratton's budget-making practices with such favor, however. Democrat Anthony Scariano, who served in the House of Representatives from 1957 to 1973, believes that Stratton "preferred that kind of a budget system that we had because he wanted to be able to hide things.... You'd get big contingencies for instance.... They would lump everything and Stratton preferred it that way." Scariano "didn't like the way [Stratton] operated," but he also did not favor the way Speaker of the House Paul Powell and Governor Otto Kerner of his own party performed.[14]

There is no doubt that Stratton benefited greatly from having as mayor of Chicago a Democrat who was as fully in control of his party as Daley was. The two could bargain and trade General Assembly votes on behalf of programs that were in the public interest. Given the Democratic dominance in Cook County since the 1920s, over and over in Illinois politics it has been demonstrated that the state is best managed when the governor is a Republican, since the mayor is consistently a Democrat. When the governor is a Democrat, there is often rivalry between the two, or subordination of the governor to the mayor, and there is no central Republican figure capable of entering into binding and fruitful agreements.

Perhaps the greatest single political misfortune that has befallen longtime Governor James Thompson is the death of Mayor Daley just a few days before Thompson took office. Chicago and the office of its mayor were plunged into disorder and controversy that were still prevalent twelve years later. At no time, at least until 1989, has Thompson had the opportunity to bargain productively with the mayor, as Stratton had. Richard M. Daley, elected mayor of Chicago in 1989, could do much worse than to seek earnestly to consolidate his position as leader of Cook County's Democrats and then to bargain effectively in the public interest, as did his late father, with the Republican governor until 1991 and thereafter, if electoral fortune so permits.

The Hodge case was the greatest burden Stratton had to bear during the last half-year of his first term, throughout the second, and thereafter. It simply would not go away. In the public mind the governor was responsible, a judgment that was understandable. Stratton had no part in Hodge's embezzlement, and he acted quickly and decisively to repair its damage. However, he had the authority and the tools to have prevented it or to have limited its scope, even though that would have been politically very difficult, and he failed to do so. The public judgment against him for that failure haunted him for the rest of his political life.

As is the case with each of us, Stratton was the prisoner of his limitations. He would have been a better governor with a somewhat larger staff. He wished not to spend what it would have cost and not to relinquish the control that personal management allowed him. A child of the Great Depression, he was never able to escape conservatism in taxing and spending, which was deeply ingrained in him. He became the captive of his own patronage system, and when it could no longer satisfy the insatiable demands of his party, he paid the price in reduced popularity and at the polls.

Regarding the office of governor generally in the United States, while Stratton held the office, there were significant developments in planning, budgeting, personnel, and central administration. In only one of those areas—personnel—could he be considered to be near the forefront of change.[15] In the staffing of the new Department of Personnel during his second term he took care that it offered minimal interference with his patronage system.

Stratton's programs in education and highway improvement affected every community in the state positively. His other accomplishments were generally favored by the public. Why, then, did he fail so badly when he sought reelection in 1960? As suggested, the Hodge case was damaging. The toll highway system, his proudest accomplishment, had aroused criticism over patronage, routing, and the taking of property by eminent domain. Stratton also defied tradition by seeking a third term. His party could not be satisfied with the patronage remaining to him during his later years as governor. He had hung on too long, and might better have voluntarily left office after 1960, or he might have tried that year for the Senate. He was kept from seeking office and suffered a great deal of harassment in the investigation, indictment, and trial from 1961 to 1965.

During the first few months he was with Canteen Corporation in 1968 Stratton was an assistant to its president. He then became a vice-president and continued in that capacity until he was seventy, in February 1984. At that time he retired from Canteen Corporation and went to work for the Chicago Bank of Commerce. He was active in a number of trade associations during the Canteen Corporation years, including the Illinois Restaurant Association, which he headed for a time. He was actively involved in many civic positions and boards, such as in the Rotary Club and the United Fund, the governance of Mundelein College, and mental health concerns. At seventy-two, in 1986, with the assistance and encouragement of his wife Shirley, he still pursued a heavy schedule of civic activities during the evening hours. During those years in Chicago they had watched their daughter Nancy grow up, graduate from the University of Missouri, and return to Chicago to begin a career in governmental relations. In 1987 Stratton was co-chairman with Robert Gibson of the AFL-CIO of a "Committee of 800" formed by Governor Thompson to help seek a tax increase. More and more often in his later years he was called upon to serve in such an elder statesman's role.

Eventually, in his honor, on May 14, 1987, a plaque was placed in the Stratton Office Building in Springfield, which had been named after him only in 1977, more than twenty years after it was completed and more than fifteen after he had left the governor's office. Its inscription was simple:

William Grant Stratton

Governor of Illinois

January 12, 1953–January 9, 1961

This state office building is named in honor of William G. Stratton, who served the people of Illinois with energy and dedication for sixteen years. Born February 26, 1914, he was elected to Congress in 1940 as its youngest member. Adopting the slogan "Good government is good politics," he twice served as State Treasurer and brought to that office many needed economies. Elected Governor in 1952 and again in 1956, he strove to open the doors of government to all citizens of Illinois. His belief that public officials should not be isolated from the people they served was reflected in his actions. Governor Stratton regularly invited the public to visit with him personally in the State House to discuss how government was affecting them. He worked to strengthen Civil Service programs and also appointed the first woman and first black in Illinois history to cabinet-level positions.

Governor Stratton's legislative success reflected his high degree of personal political ability. He was able to obtain the first reapportionment of legislative districts in more than 50 years and did much to improve mine safety and enhance the growth of Illinois' universities. Perhaps his most lasting accomplishment during his tenure was the massive road-building program that linked Illinois with the nation's new interstate system.

In recognition of his many years of outstanding loyalty and service to the citizens and institutions of Illinois, and of his ability skillfully to administer the affairs of state government, we here today affix this plaque in the building which was named in his honor in 1977 by the General Assembly of the State of Illinois.

NOTES
BIBLIOGRAPHY
INDEX

Notes

Chapter 1. Father and Son

1. WGS:ISHL. Box 9, "WGS Personal"; Box 134, "File [1964]." The Stratton collection in the Illinois State Historical Library was a major research source for this work. It will be cited as WGS:ISHL. The collection is kept in numbered boxes, with the papers in each box for the most part in file folders, which are labeled. For each citation of the collection, the box number and file folder label will be given.

2. Interview, William G. Stratton, 12/20/85. Hereafter, interviews with Stratton will be cited as WGS:Interview, followed by the date.

3. WGS:ISHL. Box 4, "Congress 41–42."

4. Interview with Charles Mansfield, 2/77. The veteran newsman and historian Robert Howard also told me this story.

5. WGS:ISHL. Box 4, "Congress 41–42."

6. WGS:ISHL. Box 14, "Personal—Letters from Mother 1945–46." WGS:Interview, 12/20/85.

7. William J. Stratton, Secretary of State, ed., *Illinois Blue Book, 1929–30* (Springfield: The Secretary, 1930), p. 92.

8. *Chicago Tribune,* May 9, 1938, p. 22.

9. Edward Pree, *Memoir* (Springfield, IL: Sangamon State Univ., Oral History Office, 1984), p. 27.

10. WGS;ISHL. Box 12, "County Campaign Chairmen, etc." Meeting of William G. Stratton with the Executive Committee of the Republican County Chairmen's Association, 12/6/43, verbatim account, p. 15.

11. William "Smokey" Downey, *Memoir* (Springfield, IL: Sangamon State Univ., Oral History Office, 1984), p. 10. WGS:ISHL. Box 142, "Downey Personal File." Speech to the Izaak Walton League.

12. WGS:ISHL. Box 23, "1950 Campaign General Correspondence," letter, 11/3.

13. WGS:ISHL. "1950 Campaign Volunteers," letter to WGS, 8/3.

14. Louis L. Emmerson, Secretary of State, ed., *Official Vote of the State of Illinois, 1928* (Springfield: The Secretary, 1929), p. 5. All election data in this and later chapters are from this series. It will not be cited subsequently.

15. WGS:ISHL. Box 127, "Kemper Insurance," 12/18.

16. WGS:Interview, 12/20/85.

17. WGS:ISHL. Box 147, "Speeches, Dec. 17, 1959–Apr. 23, 1960." WGS:Interview, 12/20/85.

18. *Chicago Tribune,* May 9, 1938, p. 22.

19. WGS:ISHL. Box 147, "Speeches, Dec. 17, 1959–Apr. 23, 1960." McKendree College Distinguished Leaders Series, 2/8/60.

20. WGS:Interview, 12/20/85.

21. *Chicago Tribune,* Feb. 21, 1960, p. 6.

22. WGS:ISHL. Box 147, "Speeches, Dec. 17, 1959–Apr. 23, 1960."

23. WGS:Interview, 12/20/85.

24. WGS:ISHL. Box 119, "M–1959," letter from Mason, 11/30/59; Box 23, "1950 Campaign Correspondence."

25. WGS:Interview, 12/20/85.

26. Illinois State Historical Library Photograph Collection. This source will be cited hereafter as ISHL Collection.

27. WGS:ISHL. Box 134, "File [1964]."

28. WGS:ISHL. Box 14, "Personal—Letters from Mother 1945–46," 2/23/45.

29. WGS:Interview, 12/20/85. WGS:ISHL. Box 4, "Congress 41–42," letter to *The American Magazine,* 1/21/41.

30. WGS:ISHL. Box 4, "Congress 41–42," letter to *Guide,* 1/9/41.

31. WGS:Interview, 12/20/85.

32. Joseph Immel, *Memoir* (Springfield, IL: Sangamon State Univ., Oral History Office, 1984), p. 9.

33. WGS:ISHL. Box 5, "Congress '41–'42," 2/3; "Personal—Miscellaneous."

34. WGS:ISHL. Box 4, "Congress 41–42," letter to *Guide,* 1/9/41.

35. *Chicago Tribune,* Feb. 21, 1960, p. 6.

36. Jack Star, "'Billy the Kid' Makes Good," *Look,* Dec. 15, 1953, p. 77.

37. WGS:Interview, 5/9/86.

38. Star, "Billy the Kid Makes Good," p. 77.

39. WGS:ISHL. Box 12, "County Campaign Chairmen, etc."

40. WGS:Interview, 12/20/85.

41. "First Attempt at Politics Lands Him in Congress," *Future,* Dec. 1940.

42. WGS:Interview, 5/9/86.

43. WGS:Interviews, 5/9/86, 12/20/85.

44. *Chicago Sun-Times,* Aug. 20, 1957, p. 5.

45. *Chicago Daily News,* Mar. 5, 1960, p. 16.

46. Willard Ice, *Memoir* (Springfield, IL: Sangamon State Univ., Oral History Office, 1977), p. 80.

47. Edward J. Barrett, Secretary of State, ed., *Illinois Blue Book, 1943–44* (Springfield: The Secretary, 1945), pp. 46, 50.

Chapter 2. Young Congressman

1. *New York Times,* Apr. 25, 1941, p. 21.
2. ISHL Collection.
3. WGS:ISHL. Box 8, "Official Personnel."
4. WGS:ISHL. Box 2, "Congress '41–'42."
5. Ibid.
6. "Billy the Kid," *Time,* July 13, 1953, p. 24.
7. WGS:ISHL. Boxes 1–5, "Congress '41–'42."
8. WGS:ISHL. Box 5, "Congress '41–'42."
9. WGS:Interview, 5/9/86.
10. WGS:ISHL. Box 4, "Congress '41–'42."
11. Downey, *Memoir.*
12. WGS:ISHL. Box 11, "Wm. W. Downey," 10/15/41.
13. WGS:ISHL. Box 11, "Glen D. Palmer-General," 1/15/42.
14. WGS:ISHL. Box 4, "Congress '41–'42," 5/14/41.
15. WGS:ISHL. Box 2, "Congress '41–'42," 12/18/41.
16. WGS:ISHL. Box 10, "Job File."
17. WGS:Interview, 12/20/85.

Chapter 3. State Treasurer

1. WGS:ISHL. Box 5, "Congress '41–'42."
2. Pree, *Memoir,* p. 46.
3. WGS:ISHL. Box 14, "Campaign—Finances."
4. WGS:ISHL. Box 7, "R. Bippus Corr"; Box 9, "Publicity—State"; Box 11, "R. Bippus"; Box 14, "Misc. Information"; Box 23, "Report of Survey . . ."
5. WGS:ISHL. Box 9, "WGS—Official."
6. WGS:ISHL. Box 9, "War Bonds—4th Drive"; "WGS—Official."
7. WGS:ISHL. Box 9, "WGS—Personal Finances"; Box 11, "WGS Expense Accounts"; Box 135, "Check Stubs."
8. Pree, *Memoir,* p. 50.
9. *Verbatim Record,* meeting of the Executive Committee of the Republican County Chairmen's Association with State Treasurer William G. Stratton, Dec. 16, 1943, pp. 10, 26. In WGS:ISHL. Box 12, "County Campaign Chairmen."
10. WGS:ISHL. Box 6, "Unfiled Correspondence."
11. Ibid.
12. *Verbatim Record,* pp. 1–4, 9, 14–16, 27, 36–37.
13. WGS:ISHL. Box 124, "Advertising"; Box 14, "Sec'y of State Misc."
14. WGS:ISHL. Box 9, "De Kalb County."
15. WGS:ISHL. Box 14, "Secretary of State—Misc."
16. WGS:ISHL. Box 7, "Rupert Bippus Correspondence."
17. WGS:ISHL. Box 14, "Schedules, etc."
18. *The Fox Valley Mirror,* Mar. 1944, p. 154.
19. WGS:ISHL. Box 9, "Request File # 2."
20. WGS:Interview, 5/9/86.

21. Pree, *Memoir,* pp. 50, 51.
22. WGS:ISHL. Box 10, "Pay Rolls."
23. WGS:ISHL. Box 8, "Misc. 2."
24. WGS:ISHL. Box 9, "WGS—Personal"; Box 11, "Unfiled Correspondence."

Chapter 4. Anchors Aweigh

1. WGS:ISHL. Box 14, "Personal—Letters from Mother 1945–46"; "Personal Letters from Wife and Children '45–'46."
2. WGS:ISHL. Box 14, "Naval Service—'45–'46."
3. WGS:ISHL. Box 15, "46 Campaign Corr."
4. WGS:ISHL. Box 14, "Personal Letters from Mother—'45–'46"; "Personal Letters from Wife and Children—'45–'46."
5. WGS:ISHL. Box 15, "46 Campaign Corr."
6. WGS:ISHL. Box 20, "WGS Personal."
7. ISHL Collection.
8. WGS:ISHL. Box 18, "Boys Congressman Served With."
9. WGS:ISHL. Box 133, "1962 Pers. Corr."
10. WGS:ISHL. Box 15, "46 Campaign Corr."
11. Pree, *Memoir,* p. 89.
12. WGS:ISHL. Box 15, "Letters—Telegrams"; Box 135, "Check Stubs."
13. Downey, *Memoir,* p. 10.
14. WGS:ISHL. Box 18, "1946 Campaign."
15. WGS:ISHL. Box 15, "46 Campaign Corr."; "News Releases"; "Speeches—Statement"; Box 20, "Thank You Letters—1946."
16. Paul H. Douglas, *In the Fullness of Time* (New York: Harcourt Brace Jovanovich, 1971), p. 126.
17. WGS:ISHL. Box 18, "Burgess, Charles"; "Congratulations (1946)."

Chapter 5. Back to Congress

1. "Origins and Inclinations of the New Men in the House and Senate," *U.S. News & World Report,* Nov. 15, 1946, p. 21.
2. WGS:ISHL. Box 20, "WGS Personal."
3. WGS:ISHL. Box 17, "Logan."
4. WGS:ISHL. Box 19, "Glen Palmer."
5. WGS:ISHL. Box 19, "Perrine"; Box 18, "Burgess, Charles."
6. WGS:ISHL. Box 23, "Earl Madigan."
7. WGS:ISHL. Box 18, "Centralia Mine Disaster"; Box 23, "Earl Madigan."
8. WGS:ISHL. Box 19, "Glen D. Palmer."
9. WGS:ISHL. Box 15, "C"; Box 16.
10. "Pass the Stratton Bill," *Nation,* June 17, 1947, p. 164.
11. "Stratton Bill," *Commonweal,* July 4, 1947, p. 46.
12. WGS:ISHL. Box 15, "Letters Telegrams"; Box 18, "Rupert

Bippus"; Box 19, "Nickell, Vernon L."; "Perrine, George R."; Box 20, "WGS Personal"; Box 21, "Immigration Notes and Pamphlets."

13. WGS:ISHL. Box 18, "Campaign (1946)"; Box 19, "Panama"; "Office Correspondence"; Box 23, "1948 Secretary of State Campaign—Misc. Material"; "EM."

14. WGS:Interview, 5/9/86. WGS:ISHL. Box 22, "1948 Camp. Corr."; Box 20, "Unfiled Corr."

15. WGS:ISHL. Box 18, "Alphabetical."

16. WGS:ISHL. Box 18, "Burgess . . ."; Box 21, "D.P. Bill."

17. WGS:ISHL. Box 21, "Disp. Persons II"; and Box 22, "Displaced Persons Misc. Material."

18. WGS:ISHL. Box 18, "Burgess . . . "

19. WGS:ISHL. Box 18, "Rupert Bippus"; Box 21, "Displaced Persons II."

20. U.S. Congress, 80th Cong., 2nd Sess., Doc. No. 198, *Summary of Legislation Enacted by the Eightieth Congress* (Washington, D.C.: GPO, 1948), pp. 7, 28.

21. Downey, *Memoir,* p. 9.

22. WGS:ISHL. Box 22, "1948 Campaign Correspondence."

23. Charles W. Clabaugh, *Memoir* (Springfield, IL: Sangamon State Univ., Oral History Office, 1982), p. 79.

24. WGS:ISHL. Box 20, "Stratton—Private Desk."

25. WGS:ISHL. Box 19, "Office Correspondence"; "Burgess, Charles"; "1948 Sec'y of State Campaign"; "1948 Campaign Corr."

26. WGS:ISHL. Box 19, "1948 Campaign Corr."

27. Pree, *Memoir,* p. 50.

28. WGS:ISHL. Box 20, "Stratton Personal."

29. Pree, *Memoir,* p. 50.

Chapter 6. Wilderness Years

1. WGS:ISHL. Box 23, "EM."

2. Immel, *Memoir,* pp. 9, 12.

3. WGS:ISHL. Box 20, "WGS Personal"; "Stratton—Personal."

4. WGS:ISHL. Box 20, "Stratton—Private Desk."

5. WGS:ISHL. Box 20, "Unfiled Corr."; "Stratton—Private Desk"; "Stratton—Personal"; Box 23, "Misc. Notes, etc."

6. WGS:ISHL. Box 20, "Unfiled Corr."; Box 23, "Letters Handled."

7. Pree, *Memoir,* pp. 50, 51.

8. U.S. Senate, Committee on Banking and Currency, *Hearing,* Sept. 6, 1956, Chicago, Ill., p. 96.

9. WGS:Interview, 5/9/86.

10. Pree, *Memoir,* p. 51.

11. Downey, *Memoir,* p. 9.

12. Pree, *Memoir,* p. 51.

13. WGS:ISHL. Box 23, "Personal."

14. WGS:ISHL. Box 23, "1950 Camp. Gen'l Corres."; "Invitations"; "1950 Camp. Volunteers"; "Letters"; "Downstate Itenary [*sic*]"; "Letters Handled."

15. WGS:ISHL. Box 23, "Radio Talk—News Releases."

16. WGS:ISHL. Box 23, "Misc. Notes, etc."; "Invitations."

Chapter 7. State Treasurer Again

1. Pree, *Memoir,* p. 49.

2. Downey, *Memoir,* pp. 11–12.

3. Immel, *Memoir,* pp. 1, 3–5, 9.

4. U.S. Senate, Committee on Banking and Currency, *Hearing,* Sept. 6, 1956, Chicago, IL, pp. 4, 15, 19, 53, 55, 91.

5. Immel, *Memoir,* p. 12.

6. Ice, *Memoir,* p. 80.

7. Immel, *Memoir,* p. 13.

8. *Morris Daily Herald,* Sept. 24, 1951, p. 1. Also WGS:ISHL. Box 124, "Advertising," for the full text of the speech.

9. Edward P. Saltiel, *Memoir* (Springfield, IL: Sangamon State Univ., Oral History Office, 1985), p. 114.

10. WGS:Interview, 5/9/86.

11. Walter J. Reum, *Memoir* (Springfield, IL: Sangamon State Univ., Oral History Office, 1980), p. 75.

12. Immel, *Memoir,* p. 5.

13. Pree, *Memoir,* pp. 55, 103.

14. *Chicago Sun-Times,* Apr. 11, 1952, p. 12.

15. Immel, *Memoir,* p. 10.

16. G. A. Robichaux, "Springfield: Big Shoes, Middle-Sized Man," *New Republic,* Aug. 31, 1953, pp. 11, 13.

17. Harris Rowe, *Memoir* (Springfield, IL: Sangamon State Univ., Oral History Office, 1988), pp. 34–35.

18. Downey, *Memoir,* pp. 13, 15.

19. Johnson Kanady, *Memoir* (Springfield, IL: Sangamon State Univ., Oral History Office, 1984), pp. 3–4.

20. John Bartlow Martin, *Adlai Stevenson of Illinois* (New York: Doubleday, 1976), pp. 271–81.

21. Immel, *Memoir,* pp. 7, 11; Downey, *Memoir,* p. 9; Elbert Smith, *Memoir* (Springfield, IL: Sangamon State Univ., Oral History Office, 1982), pp. 73–75, 139.

22. Richard J. Jensen, *Illinois: A Bicentennial History* (New York: Norton, 1978), pp. 159–60.

23. John Fribley, *Memoir* (Springfield, IL: Sangamon State Univ., Oral History Office, 1981).

24. Leland J. Kennedy, *Memoir* (Springfield, IL: Sangamon State Univ., Oral History Office, 1988).

25. Martin B. Lohman, *Memoir* (Springfield, IL: Sangamon State Univ., Oral History Office, 1980), p. 63.

26. Donald J. O'Brien, *Memoir* (Springfield, IL: Sangamon State Univ., Oral History Office, 1988), p. 87.

27. Clyde Lee, *Memoir* (Springfield, IL: Sangamon State Univ., Oral History Office, 1988), p. 217.

28. Leland Rayson, *Memoir* (Springfield, IL: Sangamon State Univ., Oral History Office, 1987), p. 42.

29. Maurice Scott, *Memoir* (Springfield, IL: Sangamon State Univ., Oral History Office, 1984), p. 84.

30. Ice, *Memoir*, p. 79.

31. Bernice T. Van Der Vries, *Memoir* (Springfield, IL: Sangamon State Univ., Oral History Office, 1980), p. 243.

32. Immel, *Memoir*, p. 12.

33. Kanady, *Memoir*, pp. 3–4.

34. Pree, *Memoir*, p. 91.

35. Immel, *Memoir*, p. 10.

36. "Billy the Kid," *Time*, July 13, 1953, p. 24.

37. Downey, *Memoir*, p. 15.

38. Immel, *Memoir*, p. 7.

39. Illinois State Archives. Drawer 17, "Dixon Campaign." At the time of my research for this book in the Illinois State Archives, the Stratton papers were kept in twenty-two metal file drawers, contained in five, six-drawer file cabinets. The drawers were not numbered nor otherwise differentiated, so for the purpose of citing material from them I asssigned them numbers ranging from one to twenty-two, in a progression determined by their position in the collection. Some of the material was found loose in the file drawers, not contained in a file folder, but most of it was in such folders. In citing the Archives I ordinarily give the file-drawer number (of my assignment) and the file-folder label, as in this note. Hereafter the general source will be identified simply as Archives.

40. *New York Times*, Nov. 15, 1952, p. 9.

41. Martin, *Adlai Stevenson*, pp. 5, 21, 179.

42. Pree, *Memoir*, p. 44.

Chapter 8. First-Term Governor: First Biennium

1. Pree, *Memoir*, pp. 36–38, 56.

2. ISHL Collection. Box 2, "Misc. Groups."

3. Ronald D. Michaelson, *Gubernatorial Staffing* (De Kalb: Northern Illinois Univ. Center for Governmental Studies, 1974), pp. 8–9, 14, 53.

4. John C. Parkhurst, *Memoir* (Springfield, IL: Sangamon State Univ., Oral History Office, 1984), p. 71.

5. Pree, *Memoir*, p. 53.

6. "Billy the Kid," *Time*, July 13, 1953, p. 24.

7. Frederic B. Selcke, *Memoir* (Springfield, IL: Sangamon State Univ., Oral History Office, 1984), p. 6.

8. Corneal Davis, *Memoir* (Springfield, IL: Sangamon State Univ., Oral History Office, 1984), p. 140.

9. Immel, *Memoir*, p. 57.

10. WGS: Interview, 12/20/85.

11. Pree, *Memoir*, pp. 49, 74–75.

12. Downey, *Memoir,* p. 17.

13. *Chicago Sun-Times,* Jan. 12, 1953, p. 1.

14. WGS:ISHL. Box 140, "Notes—Gov's Address"; and Box 124, "Advertising."

15. *Chicago Daily News,* Jan. 14, 21, 1953, p. 8.

16. Immel, *Memoir,* p. 12.

17. WGS:ISHL. Box 107 to Box 122.

18. WGS:ISHL. Box 145, "CS. Survey Recommendations."

19. Downey, *Memoir,* p. 24.

20. Pree, *Memoir,* pp. 44, 46–47, 54, 71–73.

21. WGS:ISHL. Box 145. Archives. Drawers 9, 19–21.

22. WGS:ISHL. Box 101, "Public Health"; Box 30.

23. Pree, *Memoir,* p. 71.

24. Selcke, *Memoir,* p. 5.

25. Pree, *Memoir,* p. 47.

26. WGS:Interview, 12/6/85.

27. "*Life* Goes to a Governor's Open House," *Life,* March 30, 1953, pp. 146–47.

28. Ice, *Memoir,* p. 88.

29. Robichaux, "Springfield: Big Shoes, Middle-Sized Man," p. 13.

30. Selcke, *Memoir,* p. 6.

31. Pree, *Memoir,* pp. 48, 49, 71.

32. Michaelson, *Gubernatorial Staffing,* pp. 8, 9, 11, 13.

33. WGS:ISHL. Box 145, "Discuss with Governor."

34. Archives. Drawer 14, "4—Notices to Departs."

35. "Billy the Kid," *Time,* July 13, 1953, p. 24.

36. Pree, *Memoir,* pp. 109–111.

37. Selcke, *Memoir,* pp. 19–20.

38. Downey, *Memoir,* p. 38.

39. Paul J. Randolph, *Memoir* (Springfield, IL: Sangamon State Univ., Oral History Office, 1988), pp. 36, 94.

40. Downey, *Memoir,* p. 47.

41. William G. Stratton, "An Administration in Review," *Illinois History,* Oct. 1961, p. 5.

42. WGS:ISHL. Box 147, "Speeches, Aug. 31, 1960–Jan. 4, 1961."

43. William G. Stratton, "The Business of Being Governor," *State Government,* Summer 1958, pp. 146–47.

44. Russell Olson, "Illinois Faces Redistricting," *National Municipal Review,* July 1954, pp. 343–46.

45. Pree, *Memoir,* p. 104.

46. WGS:ISHL. Box 107 to Box 122, "Mansion File."

47. Downey, *Memoir,* p. 29.

48. WGS:Interview, 5/6/86.

49. WGS:ISHL. Box 140, "News Releases of Speeches."

50. Downey, *Memoir,* pp. 17, 28.

51. State of Illinois, *Financial Program for Illinois* (Springfield: The State, 1953), pp. 4, 5, 8.

52. Downey, *Memoir,* pp. 50, 59.

53. *Chicago American,* May 27, 1953, p. 10; Oct. 11, 1953, p. 8.

54. "Billy the Kid," *Time,* July 13, 1953, p. 24.

55. Archives. William Stratton, 1953–60, "Veto Message."

56. Robichaux, "Springfield: Big Shoes, Middle-Sized Man," p. 11.

57. Albert N. Votaw, "Chicago—The Machine Has Run Down," *New Republic,* Aug. 31, 1953, p. 10.

58. *Chicago American,* Oct. 11, 1953, p. 8.

59. Archives. Drawer 15, "3-Boys State."

60. Pree, *Memoir,* p. 99.

61. Ice, *Memoir,* p. 81.

62. WGS:ISHL. Box 131, "Pol. Corr. '54–'60."

63. Archives. Drawer 22, "Higher Ed. Comm."

64. Reum, *Memoir,* p. 129.

65. Saltiel, *Memoir,* p. 158.

66. WGS:ISHL. Box 116, "Reapportionment."

67. *Chicago Sun-Times,* Oct. 19, 1954, p. 4.

68. *Chicago Daily News,* Oct. 23, 1954, p. 2.

69. *Chicago Sun-Times,* Oct. 24, 1954, p. 4.

70. *Newsweek,* Jan. 3, 1955, p. 15.

Chapter 9. First-Term Governor: Second Biennium

1. WGS:ISHL. Box 137, "Message of Gov. Wm. G. Stratton to 69th General Assembly, Jan. 5, 1955"; Box 140, "Notes—Governors Address."

2. *Chicago Tribune,* Jan. 30, 1955, p. 5.

3. WGS:ISHL. Box 114, "Stratton 1955."

4. U.S. Senate, Committee on Banking and Currency, *Hearing,* Sept. 6, 1956, Chicago, IL, pp. 13–14.

5. WGS:ISHL. Box 142, "Matters to Discuss with Governor."

6. Ice, *Memoir,* p. 52.

7. Kanady, *Memoir,* p. 9.

8. Downey, *Memoir,* p. 84.

9. Ibid., pp. 31, 38.

10. Clabaugh, *Memoir,* p. 275.

11. *Chicago Tribune,* May 19, 20, 1955, pp. 1, 3.

12. WGS:ISHL. Box 147, "Stratton Speeches [#20], June–Nov. 1958."

13. *Chicago Tribune,* Apr. 29, 1955, p. 1; May 25, 1955, p. 1; June 1, 1955, p. 1; June 2, 1955, p. 14; June 3, 1955, p. 6; June 14, 1955, p. 1; June 15, 1955, p. 6.

14. *Chicago Sun-Times,* Aug. 26, 1963, p. 18.

15. Scott, *Memoir,* pp. 47–50.

16. Smith, *Memoir,* p. 162.

17. WGS:ISHL. Box 146, "Personnel Code."

18. WGS:ISHL. Box 106, "Racing Bd."; Box 146, "Pree's Political File, 1953–57." Pree, *Memoir,* p. 47.

19. *Chicago Tribune,* Aug. 20, 1955, p. 7.

20. *Christian Science Monitor,* July 20, 1955, Sec. 4C, pp. 1–2.

21. WGS:ISHL. Box 111, "Governor's Conf."

22. WGS:ISHL. Box 114, "Stratton—1955."

23. *Illinois Blue Book, 1959–1960,* p. 3.

24. WGS:ISHL. Box 112, "Campaign—1956."

25. Pree, *Memoir,* pp. 67, 103.

26. Archives. Drawer 20, "Minutes of Organizational Meeting." WGS:ISHL. Box 114, "Stratton—1956."

27. WGS:ISHL. Box 131, "Personal 1956."

28. WGS:ISHL. Box 146, "Public Safety." Rep. Simon's news release "Sidelights from Springfield."

29. *Bloomington Pantagraph,* Mar. 29, 1956, p. 2.

30. WGS:ISHL. Box 146, "Pree's Political File, 1953–57."

31. "Dark Horses for '56," *Newsweek,* Oct. 17, 1955, p. 34.

32. WGS:Interview, 5/9/86.

33. WGS:ISHL. Box 140, "Speech"; Box 147, "1956 Speech by Gov. S."

34. *Illinois State Journal,* Mar. 21, 1956, p. 7.

Chapter 10. The Case of the Errant Auditor

1. *Chicago Daily News,* June 6, 1956, p. 4. *Chicago American,* June 11, 1956, p. 11.

2. Davis, *Memoir,* pp. 157–58.

3. Scott, *Memoir,* p. 90.

4. *Chicago American,* June 12, 1956, p. 1.

5. Pree, *Memoir,* p. 59.

6. *Chicago Tribune,* July 5, 1956, p. 3. *Chicago Daily News,* Oct. 19, 1956, p. 1.

7. WGS:ISHL. Box 131, "3—Keevers 1957–60." Archives. Drawer 11, "1—Auditor—Orville Hodge."

8. *Chicago Daily News,* July 7, 1956, p. 1. *Chicago Tribune,* July 6, 1956, p. 6; July 10, 11, 1956, p. 1.

9. Downey, *Memoir,* p. 21.

10. Archives. Drawer 12.

11. *Chicago Tribune,* July 13, 1956, p. 2.

12. Archives. Drawer 11, "1—Auditor—Orville Hodge."

13. *Chicago Tribune,* July 12, 1956, pp. 1, 2; Oct. 19, 1956, p. 1.

14. Archives. Drawer 11, "1—Auditor—Orville Hodge."

15. Pree, *Memoir,* p. 61.

16. *New York Times,* July 17, 1956, p. 18.

17. *Chicago Tribune,* July 18, 1956, p. 1; Aug. 2, 1956, p. 1.

18. Downey, *Memoir,* p. 21.

19. *Chicago Tribune,* July 18, 1956, pp. 1, 4; July 19, 1956, p. 5.

20. Smith, *Memoir,* p. 147.

21. *New York Times,* July 22, 1956, p. 23.

22. *Chicago Tribune,* July 15, 1956, p. 1; July 16, 1956, pp. 1, 2.

23. Archives. Drawer 14, "Ill. Budg'y Comm. 1957."

24. *New York Times,* July 25, 1956, p. 10.

25. WGS:ISHL. Box 114, "Stratton—1956."

26. Pree, *Memoir,* p. 62. Selcke, *Memoir,* p. 10.

27. *Chicago Tribune,* Aug. 14, 1956, p. 1; Aug. 21, 1956, p. 1. *New York Times,* Aug. 16, 1956, p. 53.

28. Pree, *Memoir,* p. 61.

29. Clabaugh, *Memoir,* p. 214.

30. Selcke, *Memoir,* p. 10.

31. *Chicago Tribune,* Aug. 3, 1956, p. 1; Aug. 4, 1956, p. 1; Aug. 7, 1956, p. 3; Aug. 14, 1956, p. 15; Aug. 17, 1956, p. 14; Aug. 18, 1956, p. 1.

32. Helen Fuller, "Report to Stevenson," *New Republic,* Aug. 31, 1953, pp. 8–9.

33. *Chicago Tribune,* Aug. 27, 1956, p. 1; Aug. 30, 1956, p. 1; Sept. 1, 1956, p. 2; Sept. 4, 1956, p. 1.

34. WGS:ISHL. Box 20, "Unfiled Corr."

35. *Chicago Tribune,* Sept. 5, 1956, p. 1.

36. *Chicago Sun-Times,* Nov. 21, 1956, p. 3.

37. *Chicago Tribune,* July 20, 1956. p. 4; Oct. 9, 1956, p. 1; Oct. 17, 1956, p. 7; Oct. 19, 1956, p. 1.

38. Downey, *Memoir,* p. 15.

39. ISHL Collection. Box 1, "'56 State Fair."

40. WGS:ISHL. Box 125, "Political 55–56."

41. *The Clearwater* [Florida] *Sun,* May 15, 1956, p. 1.

42. WGS:ISHL. Box 112.

43. Pree, *Memoir,* p. 68.

44. *Chicago Tribune,* Oct. 30, 1956, p. 19; Nov. 1, 1956, p. III-2.

45. Len O'Connor, *Clout* (Chicago; Regnery, 1975), pp. 146–47.

46. Smith *Memoir,* pp. 149–50.

47. WGS:ISHL. Box 113, "H 1956."

Chapter 11. Second-Term Governor: Third Biennium

1. WGS:ISHL. Box 140, "Notes—Governor's Address."

2. WGS:ISHL. Box 137, "Budget Notes 1953–1959"; Box 147, "Feb–July '57 #9."

3. Ice, *Memoir,* p. 85.

4. Selcke, *Memoir,* p. 7.

5. WGS:Interview, 12/20/85.

6. Kanady, *Memoir,* pp. 1–2, 4.

7. Selcke, *Memoir,* p. 16.

8. Scott, *Memoir,* p. 88.

9. WGS:Interview, 5/9/86.

10. Downey, *Memoir,* p. 25.

11. WGS:ISHL. Box 147.

12. Pree, *Memoir,* p. 9.

13. Kanady, *Memoir,* p. 6.

14. Lloyd Morey, Albert E. Jenner, Jr., and John S. Rendleman, *Reports*

and Recommendations to Illinois Budgetary Commission, (Springfield: The Commission, 1956).

15. WGS:ISHL. Box 147, "Speeches, June–Nov. 1958, #13."

16. Archives. Drawer 19, "1—App't—Adv. B'd to the Dept. of Personnel."

17. WGS:ISHL. Box 102, "Dept. of Pers."

18. WGS:ISHL. Box 87.

19. Pree, *Memoir,* pp. 73–74.

20. WGS:ISHL. Box 85, "Personnel Corr. and Regulations—1958–59."

21. WGS:ISHL. Box 131, "Governor—Personal," letters of Oct. 30, 1957, and Jan. 26, 1958.

22. WGS:ISHL. Box 106.

23. WGS:ISHL. Boxes 85, 87.

24. August 14, 1958, p. 3.

25. Kenney, *Basic Illinois Government,* pp. 272–75.

26. WGS:ISHL. Box 147, "Speeches, Feb–July 1957"; Box 131, "Pol. Corr. '54–'60."

27. Clabaugh, *Memoir,* p. 189.

28. WGS:ISHL. Box 147, "Speeches, Feb–July 1957," Speech at Southern Illinois University, June 16, 1957; #23, Radio Address, WIND, Chicago, July 28, 1957.

29. Clabaugh, *Memoir,* pp. 177, 192, 204.

30. Downey, *Memoir,* p. 55.

31. WGS:ISHL. Box 147, "Speeches Feb–July 1957," #23, Radio Address, WIND, Chicago, July 28, 1957.

32. *Chicago Tribune,* Dec. 1, 1957, p. 5.

33. Pree, *Memoir,* p. 78.

34. WGS:ISHL. Boxes 144, 145.

35. Selcke, *Memoir,* p. 17.

36. Pree, *Memoir,* pp. 38, 66, 77.

37. WGS:ISHL. Box 145, "Governors Conf. 1954 NY."

38. WGS:Interview, 12/20/85.

39. WGS:ISHL. Box 117, "S 1958." Letter to Billy Magnuson, January 28, 1958.

40. WGS:ISHL. Box 109, "P—1954."

41. *State Journal-Register,* Oct. 7, 1962, p. 47.

42. *Chicago Daily News,* Dec. 6, 1958, p. 36.

43. *Chicago Sun-Times,* Aug. 20, 1957, p. 5.

44. Kanady, *Memoir,* p. 8.

45. WGS:ISHL. Box 121, "Biography of Mrs. Stratton."

46. WGS:ISHL. Box 141, loose.

47. Archives. Drawer 14.

48. *Chicago American,* Feb. 27, 1957, p. 4.

49. WGS:ISHL. Box 131, "3—Keevers 1957–60," Letter from Attorney General Castle to Stratton, Mar. 5, 1958.

50. *St. Louis Post-Dispatch,* Nov. 11, 1961, Sec. 3A, p. 2.

51. WGS:ISHL. Box 138, "Unemployment Comp. [1958]."

52. WGS:ISHL. Box 147, "Speeches, June–Nov. 1958," #9, Northwest Tollway Dedication Dinner, Aug. 20, 1958.

53. WGS:ISHL. Box 133, "1961 Pers. Corr."

54. WGS:Interview, 12/20/85.

55. Archives. Drawers 9; 11, "1—Att'y Gen'l."

56. WGS:ISHL. Box 132, "Pers. Corr. 58–59."

57. WGS:ISHL. Box 147, "Speeches, July 30–Dec 1957," Statement *re* clemency, July 30, 1957.

58. WGS:ISHL. Box 147, "Stratton Speeches, June–Nov. 1958."

Chapter 12. Second-Term Governor: Fourth Biennium

1. WGS:ISHL. Box 147, "Stratton Speeches, Nov. 25, 1958–May 1959," #6, State of the State Address.

2. Jan. 24, 1959, p. 1.

3. Kanady, *Memoir,* p. 8.

4. Davis, *Memoir,* p. 149.

5. *Chicago Sun-Times,* Jan. 9, 1959, p. 24.

6. WGS:ISHL. Box 117, "Governors Speeches."

7. WGS:ISHL. Box 137, "Budget Notes '53–'59."

8. WGS:ISHL. Box 147, "Stratton Speeches, Nov. 25, 1958–May 1959," #14, Budget Message, Apr. 22, 1959.

9. WGS:ISHL. Box 118, "Queen of England 7/6/59."

10. Archives. Drawer 11, "Atomic Energy Commission."

11. WGS:ISHL. Boxes 118, 119, 120, 131, 132.

12. WGS:ISHL. Box 119, "P–1959."

13. WGS:ISHL. Box 120, "S–1959."

14. Downey, *Memoir,* p. 56.

15. *Chicago Tribune,* Feb. 21, 1960, p. 6.

16. *Chicago Sun-Times,* Oct. 16, 1959, p. 38; Nov. 21, 1959, p. 3; Dec. 19, 1959, p. 19.

17. *New York Times,* Jan. 24, 1960, p. 1. *Chicago Sun-Times,* Jan. 24, 1960, p. 1.

18. WGS:ISHL. Box 131, "3—Keevers 1957–60."

19. *Chicago Sun-Times,* Jan. 24, 1960, p. 1.

20. WGS:ISHL. Box 131, "3—Keevers 1957–60."

21. *Chicago American,* Feb. 25, 1960, p. 1.

22. Smith, *Memoir,* pp. 158–59.

23. *Chicago Sun-Times,* Dec. 22, 1959, p. 20.

24. Pree, *Memoir,* p. 103.

25. *Chicago Daily News,* Mar. 5, 1960, p. 16.

26. WGS:ISHL. Box 131, "3—Keevers 1957–60."

27. WGS:ISHL. Box 122, "Campaign—1960."

28. *Chicago Tribune,* Mar. 5, 1960, p. 3; Mar. 12, 1960, p. 1; Mar. 13, 1960, p. 3; Mar. 15, 1960, pp. 3–4; Mar. 18, 1960, p. 7; Mar. 24, 1960, pp. 3, 8.

29. WGS:Interview, 12/21/85.

30. WGS:ISHL. Box 147, "Speeches Apr. 24–Aug. 23, 1960."

31. Scott, *Memoir,* p. 87.

32. Archives. Drawer 13, "1—Resignation—1960."

33. WGS:ISHL. Box 132, "Corr. re Nat'l Conv. 1960."

34. WGS:Interview, 5/9/86.

35. Pree, *Memoir,* p. 88.

36. WGS:Interview, 7/25/88.

37. WGS:ISHL. Box 132, "Personal 1960."

38. *Chicago Sun-Times,* July 30, 1960, p. 3.

39. *Chicago Tribune,* Apr. 16, 1964, p. 2.

40. Pree, *Memoir,* p. 78.

41. WGS:ISHL. Box 122, "Diana's Wedding."

42. WGS:ISHL. Boxes 131, 132, 133.

43. WGS:Interview, 5/9/86.

44. WGS:ISHL. Box 122, "Campaign—1960"; Box 127, "Campaign Chairmen..."

45. WGS:ISHL. Box 127, "1960 Misc. Political Material."

46. *Chicago American,* Oct. 25, 1960, p. 6.

47. WGS:ISHL. Box 122, "Campaign—1960."

48. *Chicago Tribune,* Nov. 1, 1960, p. 3.

49. WGS:ISHL. Box 127, "1960 Campaign File"; Box 133, "3—Political—1960." *Chicago Tribune,* Nov. 2, 1960, p. 7; Nov. 5, 1960, p. 11; Nov. 6, 1960, p. 9.

50. Fred Bird, *Memoir* (Springfield, IL: Sangamon State Univ., Oral History Office, 1984), p. 8.

51. Pree, *Memoir,* pp. 75, 78, 79.

52. WGS:Interview, 7/25/88.

53. Selcke, *Memoir,* p. 20.

54. WGS:Interview, 5/9/86.

55. U.S. Bureau of the Census, *Census of Population, 1960,* Vol. 1, Pt. 15, Illinois (Washington, DC: GPO, 1962), pp. xiii, 8, 267, 274.

Chapter 13. Years of Trial

1. WGS:ISHL. Box 133, "1961 Pers. Corr."

2. *Chicago Sun-Times,* Jan. 22, 1965, p. 26. *Chicago Tribune,* Jan. 22, 1965, p. 5; Jan. 26, 1965, p.1.

3. Downey, *Memoir,* pp. 56–57.

4. *Chicago Sun-Times,* Jan. 25, 1965, p. 5; Jan. 28, 1965, p. 30; Feb. 2, 1965, p. 2. *Chicago Tribune,* Jan. 22, 1965, p. 5; Jan. 26, 1965, p. 1; Jan. 27, 1965, p. 1; Jan. 28, 1965, p. 5; Feb. 2, 1965, p. 1.

5. Ice, *Memoir,* p. 88. Norton E. Long, "A Day of Reckoning," *Chicago Sun-Times,* Mar. 25, 1962, Sec. 2, p. 1.

6. *Chicago Tribune,* July 12, 1961, p. 8.

7. WGS:ISHL. Box 133, "Pers. Corr."; "1961 Pers. Corr."; "1962 Pers. Corr."

8. *Chicago Tribune,* Feb. 2, 1965, p. 1. *Chicago Sun-Times,* Feb. 2, 1965, p. 26.

9. WGS:ISHL. Box 133, "1962 Pers. Corr."

10. WGS:ISHL. Box 134, "Dictate, Unfiled Letters, 1963."

11. [Springfield] *Illinois State Journal,* May 20, 1963, p. 19.

12. *Chicago Tribune,* Aug. 23, 1963, p. 4.

13. *New York Times,* Oct. 10, 1963, p. 37. *Chicago Tribune,* Apr. 16, 1964, p. 2.

14. WGS:ISHL. Box 134, "File [1964]."

15. *Chicago Tribune,* Apr. 15, 1964, p. 1.

16. *New York Times,* Apr. 16, 1964, p. 1.

17. Martin, *Adlai Stevenson of Illinois,* pp. 514, 580.

18. *Chicago Tribune,* Apr. 16, 1964, pp. 1, 2; Apr. 17, 1964, p. 9. *Chicago Sun-Times,* Apr. 16, 1964, p. 1; Apr. 17, 1964, p. 26.

19. WGS:ISHL. Box 134, "File [1964]."

20. *Chicago Sun-Times,* Jan. 6, 1965, p. 16. *Chicago Tribune,* Jan. 6, 1965, p. 1; Mar. 10, 1965, Sec. A., p. 1.

21. *New York Times,* Jan. 5, 1965, p. 19. *Chicago Tribune,* Jan. 5, 1965, p. 1. *Chicago Sun-Times,* Jan. 5, 1965, p. 6.

22. *Chicago Sun-Times,* Jan. 8, 1965, p. 3; Jan. 12, 1965, p. 4; Jan. 16, 1965, p. 12. *Chicago Tribune,* Jan. 8, 1965, p. 1; Jan. 12, 1965, p. 1; Jan. 16, 1965, p. 10.

23. *Chicago Tribune,* Jan. 13, 1965, p. 1. *Chicago Sun-Times,* Jan. 13, 1965, p. 30.

24. *Chicago Tribune,* Jan. 14, 1965, p. 1. *Chicago Sun-Times,* Jan. 14, 1965, p. 3.

25. *Chicago Tribune,* Jan. 15, 1965, p. 4. *Chicago Sun-Times,* Jan. 15, 1965, p. 4.

26. *Chicago Sun-Times,* Jan. 20, 1965, p. 20. *Chicago Tribune,* Jan. 20, 1965, p. 12.

27. *Chicago Tribune,* Jan. 22, 1965, p. 5; Jan. 28, 1965, p. 5. *Chicago Sun-Times,* Jan. 22, 1965, p. 26; Jan. 28, 1965, p. 30.

28. *Chicago Tribune,* Jan. 26, 1965, p. 2. *Chicago Sun-Times,* Jan. 26, 1965, p. 16.

29. *Chicago Tribune,* Jan. 25, 1965, p. 1; Jan. 26, 1965, p. 1. *Chicago Sun-Times,* Jan. 26, 1965, p. 16.

30. *Chicago Tribune,* Jan. 27, 1965, p. 1. *Chicago Sun-Times,* Jan. 27, 1965, p. 5.

31. *Chicago Tribune,* Feb. 18, 1965, p. 1; Feb. 19, 1965, p. 5; Feb. 20, 1965, p. 10; Feb. 23, 1965, p. 6. *Chicago Sun-Times,* Feb. 20, 1965, p. 5.

32. *Chicago Sun-Times,* Feb. 24, 1965, p. 22; Feb. 25, 1965, p. 18. *Chicago Tribune,* Feb. 24, 1965, p. 7; Feb. 25, 1965, p. 14.

33. *Chicago Tribune,* Mar. 10, 1965, Sec. 1A, p. 1; Mar. 12, 1965, pp. 1, 2.

34. *Chicago Tribune,* Feb. 25, 1965, p. 14; Feb. 26, 1965, p. 10. *Chicago Sun-Times,* Feb. 25, 1965, p. 18; Feb. 26, 1965, p. 17.

35. *Chicago Tribune,* Feb. 27, 1965, p. 12. *Chicago Sun-Times,* Feb. 27, 1965, p. 14.

36. Selcke, *Memoir,* p. 15.

37. Clabaugh, *Memoir,* p. 228.

38. *Chicago Daily News,* Mar. 2, 1965, p. 1.

39. *Chicago Sun-Times,* Mar. 2, 1965, p. 24; Mar. 3, 1965, p. 3. *Chicago Tribune,* Mar. 2, 1965. p. 10; Mar. 3, 1965, Sec. 2A, p. 4, 1965.

40. *Chicago Tribune,* Mar. 4, 1965, p. 3; Mar. 5, 1965, p. 15. *Chicago Sun-Times,* Mar. 4, 1965, p. 76.

41. *New York Times,* Mar. 6, 1965, p. 9. *Chicago Tribune,* Mar. 6, 1965, p. 1. *Time,* Mar. 19, 1965, p. 31.

42. *Chicago Sun-Times,* Mar. 6, 1965, p. 1. *Chicago Tribune,* Mar. 6, 1965, p. 1.

43. *Time,* Mar. 19, 1965, p. 31.

44. *Chicago Tribune,* Mar. 6, 1965, p. 1; Mar. 9, p. 2; Mar. 11, 1965, p. 1. *Chicago Sun-Times,* Mar. 6, 1965, pp. 3, 18; Mar. 9, 1965, pp. 3, 34.

45. *New York Times,* Mar. 11, 1965, p. 16.

46. WGS:ISHL. Box 134, "S. Pers. Corr. 1965."

47. *Chicago Tribune,* Mar. 11, 1965, p. 1; Mar. 12, 1965, p. 1. *Chicago American,* Mar. 11, 1965, p. 1. *Chicago Sun-Times,* Mar. 12, 1965, p. 1.

48. *Chicago Tribune,* Mar. 12, 1965, p. 1. *Chicago Sun-Times,* Mar. 12, 1965, pp. 1, 34. *New York Times,* March 12, 1965, p. 1.

49. *Chicago American,* Mar. 11, 1965, p. 1; Mar. 12, 1965, p. 1; Mar. 13, 1965, p. 1.

50. Selcke, *Memoir,* p. 15.

51. *Chicago Tribune,* Mar. 12, 1965, p. 2.

52. WGS:ISHL. Box 134, "S. Pers. Corr. 1965."

53. WGS:Interview, 5/9/86.

54. WGS:ISHL. Box 134, "S. Pers. Corr. 1965."

55. *Chicago Tribune,* Mar. 12, 1965, pp. 20, 57; Mar. 17, 1965, p. 16.

56. Pree, *Memoir,* pp. 81, 95, 96, 99.

57. WGS:ISHL. Box 134, "S. Pers. Corr. 1965.

Chapter 14. After Politics

1. WGS:ISHL. Box 134, "S. Pers. Corr. 1965."

2. [DuPage County] *Press Publications,* Aug. 24–25, 1965, p. 3.

3. WGS:ISHL. Box 134, "S. Pers. Corr. 1965."

4. WGS:Interview, 5/9/86.

5. Pree, *Memoir,* p. 79.

6. Selcke, *Memoir,* p. 22.

7. WGS:Interview, 5/1/87.

8. George W. Dunne, *Memoir* (Springfield, IL: Sangamon State Univ., Oral History Office, 1988); Cecil Partee, *Memoir* (Springfield, IL: Sangamon State Univ., Oral History Office, 1982); William Redmond, *Memoir* (Springfield, IL: Sangamon State Univ., Oral History Ofice, 1986).

9. Esther Saperstein, *Memoir* (Springfield, IL: Sangamon State Univ., Oral History Office, 1987), p. 267. Robert W. McCarthy, *Memoir* (Springfield, IL: Sangamon State Univ., Oral History Office, 1983), pp. 132–34.

10. Parkhurst, *Memoir,* p. 71.

11. Clabaugh, *Memoir,* p. 183. Immel, *Memoir,* p. 4. Lee, *Memoir,* p. 161.

12. O'Brien, *Memoir,* p. 139.

13. Scott, *Memoir,* p. 87.

14. Anthony Scariano, *Memoir* (Springfield, IL: Sangamon State Univ., Oral History Office, 1988), pp. 147, 153.

15. Frank Bane, "The Job of Being a Governor, *State Government,* Summer 1958, pp. 184–89; William H. Young, "The Development of the Governorship," *State Government,* Summer 1958, pp. 178–83.

Bibliography

Bane, Frank. "The Job of Being a Governor." *State Government,* Summer 1958, pp. 184–89.

Barrett, Edward J., Secretary of State, ed. *Illinois Blue Book, 1943–44.* Springfield: The Secretary, 1945.

"Billy the Kid." *Time,* July 13, 1953, p. 24.

Bird, Fred. *Memoir.* Springfield, IL: Sangamon State Univ., Oral History Office, 1984.

Clabaugh, Charles W. *Memoir.* Springfield, IL: Sangamon State Univ., Oral History Office, 1982.

"Dark Horses for '56." *Newsweek,* Oct. 17, 1955, p. 34.

Davis, Corneal. *Memoir.* Springfield, IL: Sangamon State Univ., Oral History Office, 1984.

Douglas, Paul H. *In the Fullness of Time.* New York: Harcourt Brace Jovanovich, 1971.

Downey, William "Smokey." *Memoir.* Springfield, IL: Sangamon State Univ., Oral History Office, 1984.

Dunne, George W. *Memoir.* Springfield, IL: Sangamon State Univ., Oral History Office, 1988.

Emmerson, Louis L., Secretary of State, ed. *Official Vote of the State of Illinois, 1928.* Springfield: The Secretary, 1929.

"First Attempt at Politics Lands Him in Congress." *Future,* Dec. 1940.

Fribley, John. *Memoir.* Springfield, IL: Sangamon State Univ., Oral History Office, 1981.

Fuller, Helen. "Report to Stevenson." *New Republic,* Aug. 31, 1953, pp. 8–9.

"High Cost of Politics." *Time,* Mar. 19, 1965, pp. 30–31.

Ice, Willard. *Memoir.* Springfield, IL: Sangamon State Univ., Oral History Office, 1977.

Immel, Joseph. *Memoir.* Springfield, IL: Sangamon State Univ., Oral History Office, 1984.

Jensen, Richard J. *Illinois: A Bicentennial History.* New York: Norton, 1978.

Kanady, Johnson. *Memoir.* Springfield, IL: Sangamon State Univ., Oral History Office, 1984.

Kennedy, Leland J. *Memoir.* Springfield, IL: Sangamon State Univ., Oral History Office, 1988.

Kenney, David. *Basic Illinois Government.* Carbondale: Southern Illinois Univ. Press, 1974.

Lee, Clyde. *Memoir.* Springfield, IL: Sangamon State Univ., Oral History Office, 1988.

"*Life* Goes to a Governor's Open House." *Life,* Mar. 30, 1953, pp. 146–47.

Lohman, Martin. *Memoir.* Springfield, IL: Sangamon State Univ., Oral History Office, 1980.

Long, Norton E. "A Day of Reckoning." *Chicago Sun-Times,* Mar. 25, 1962, Sec. 2, p. 1.

McCarthy, Robert W. *Memoir.* Springfield, IL: Sangamon State Univ., Oral History Office, 1983.

Martin, John Bartlow. *Adlai Stevenson of Illinois.* New York: Doubleday, 1976.

Michaelson, Ronald D. *Gubernatorial Staffing.* De Kalb: Northern Illinois Univ. Center for Governmental Studies, 1974.

Morey, Lloyd, Albert E. Jenner, Jr., and John S. Rendleman. *Reports and Recommendations to Illinois Budgetary Commission.* Springfield: The Commission, 1956.

O'Brien, Donald J. *Memoir.* Springfield, IL: Sangamon State Univ., Oral History Office, 1988.

O'Connor, Len. *Clout.* Chicago: Regnery, 1975.

Olson, Russell. "Illinois Faces Redistricting." *National Municipal Review,* July 1954, pp. 343–46.

"Origins and Inclinations of the New Men in the House and Senate." *U.S. News & World Report,* Nov. 15, 1946, p. 76.

Parkhurst, John C. *Memoir.* Springfield, IL: Sangamon State Univ., Oral History Office, 1984.

Partee, Cecil. *Memoir.* Springfield, IL: Sangamon State Univ., Oral History Office, 1982.

"Pass the Stratton Bill." *Nation,* June 17, 1947, p. 164.

Pree, Edward. *Memoir.* Springfield, IL: Sangamon State Univ., Oral History Office, 1984.

Randolph, Paul J. *Memoir.* Springfield, IL: Sangamon State Univ., Oral History Office, 1988.

Rayson, Leland. *Memoir.* Springfield, IL: Sangamon State Univ., Oral History Office, 1987.

Redmond, William. *Memoir.* Springfield, IL: Sangamon State Univ., Oral History Office, 1986.

Reum, Walter J. *Memoir.* Springfield, IL: Sangamon State Univ., Oral History Office, 1980.

Robichaux, G. A. "Springfield: Big Shoes, Middle-Sized Man." *New Republic,* Aug. 31, 1953, pp. 11–13.

Rowe, Harris. *Memoir.* Springfield, IL: Sangamon State Univ., Oral History Office, 1988.

Saltiel, Edward P. *Memoir.* Springfield, IL: Sangamon State Univ., Oral History Office, 1985.

Saperstein, Esther. *Memoir.* Springfield, IL: Sangamon State Univ., Oral History Office, 1987.

Scariano, Anthony. *Memoir.* Springfield, IL: Sangamon State Univ., Oral History Office, 1988.

Scott, Maurice. *Memoir.* Springfield, IL: Sangamon State Univ., Oral History Office, 1984.

Selcke, Frederic B. *Memoir.* Springfield, IL: Sangamon State Univ., Oral History Office, 1984.

Smith, Elbert. *Memoir.* Springfield, IL: Sangamon State Univ., Oral History Office, 1982.

Star, Jack. " 'Billy the Kid' Makes Good." *Look,* Dec. 15, 1953, pp. 75–78.

State of Illinois. *Financial Program for Illinois.* Springfield: The State, 1953.

Stratton, William G. "An Administration in Review." *Illinois History,* Oct. 1961, p. 5.

———. "The Business of Being Governor." *State Government,* Summer 1958, pp. 146–47.

Stratton, William J., Secretary of State, ed. *Illinois Blue Book, 1929–30.* Springfield: The Secretary, 1930.

"Stratton Bill." *Commonweal,* July 4, 1947, p. 46.

U.S. Bureau of the Census. *Census of Population, 1960.* Vol. 1, Pt. 15, Illinois. Washington, DC: GPO, 1962. Pp. xiii, 8, 267, 274.

U.S. Congress, 80th Cong., 2nd Sess. Doc. No. 198. *Summary of Legislation Enacted by the Eightieth Congress.* Washington, DC: GPO, 1948.

U.S. Senate, Committee on Banking and Currency. *Hearing.* Sept. 6, 1956, Chicago, IL.

Van Der Vries, Bernice T. *Memoir.* Springfield, IL: Sangamon State Univ., Oral History Office, 1980.

Verbatim Record. Meeting of the Executive Committee of the Republican County Chairmen's Association with State Treasurer William G. Stratton, Dec. 16, 1943. In WGS:ISHL. Box 12, "County Campaign Chairmen."

Votaw, Albert N. "Chicago—The Machine Has Run Down." *New Republic,* Aug. 31, 1953, p. 10.

Young, William H. "The Development of the Governorship." *State Government,* Summer 1958, pp. 178–83.

Index

Abney, Arthur E., cabinet appointment of, 109

Akers, Milburn, view of Stratton trial of, 203

Allison, Charles, 11

Altorfer, John H., 189, 308; gift from, to Nancy, 187

Amberg, Richard, support of, 184

Austin, Richard B.: background of, 145–46; defeat by Stratton of, 149–50; selection as gubernatorial candidate of, 145

Baker, Charles W., 39

Banking and Currency, U.S. Senate Committee on, 94, 138; investigation of Hodge case by, 146–47

Banta, Parke, 56

Barnett, William A., service to Stratton as defense attorney by, 188

Barrett, Edward, 146; as candidate for secretary of state, choice of, 33–34

Barrett, George, 20, 108

Barrett, Robert E., cabinet appointment of, 108–9

Becker, Conrad, 49, 186

Benson, Arnold P.: defeat for secretary of state of, 34; for secretary of state, candidacy of, 29, 31; success against Stratton in 1944 primary of, 32

Bettag, Otto L., cabinet appointment of, 108

Bibb, Joseph D., cabinet appointment of, 107

Bidwell, Arthur J., evaluation of Stratton by, 159

Bippus, Rupert: advice of, 29, 39, 40–41, 45; background of, 26; death of, 109; letters of, 26; support of, 38; views of, 31–32, 53

Binks, Vera M., cabinet appointment of, 107

Blackwell, Kent, 43

Bloomington Pantagraph, support of Stratton by, 134

Bond issues: for education, 165, 173; for mental health, 165, 173

Bost, E. L., advice of, 177

Boyle, Leo M., cabinet appointment of, 108

Breckenridge, Shirley: friendship of, 71; marriage to Stratton, 72. *See also* Stratton, Shirley

Bricker, John W., 48

Brooks, C. Wayland, 38, 39; advice of, 28–29; background of, 12; election to the Senate of, 13; factional alignment of, 20; loan to Stratton by, 19; loss of Senate seat by, 61; reelection to the Senate of, 24

Broyles Bill, Stratton veto of, 120

Budgetary Commission, Illinois, 138

Burgess, Charles, 69, 72; advice of, 43, 49–50, 56–57, 176; criticism of Emily Taft Douglas by, 45; emergence in politics of, 41; Toll Highway Commission, chairman of, 164; views of, 38, 41, 47, 49, 56–58, 60–61

Index

Burton, John M., 8
Byerly, Clyde, 43

Campaigns: Democratic, 1950, problems
of, 70; Republican, 1950, tone of, 70–
71
Carpentier, Charles, 101, 171, 175;
election as secretary of state, 102;
reelection, 150, 177
Carroll, Kenneth B., testimony at Stratton
trial of, 192
Castle, Latham, 140; election as attorney
general, 103; reelection, 150; role in
Hodge case, 139–40
Castle, Ward, advice of, 155
Centralia mine disaster, 50
Chapman, John W.: defeat of, 177;
election as lieutenant governor of, 102;
reelection of, 150
Charlesita, Sister Mary, view of Stratton
trial of, 200
Christenson, D. C., 180; Navy service
with Stratton of, 42–43
Civil Service Commission, 154–55
Clabaugh, Charles: opinion of Hodge of,
144; opinion of Stratton of, 209; views
of, 59–60, 128, 196
Clinton, Claude E., 4
Commission to Study State Government
Personnel Administration, 120
Conn, Perry, 4; advice of, 69
Connell, Francis X., testimony at Stratton
trial of, 196
Coutrakon, George, role as Hodge
prosecutor of, 139
Craggs, Clinton, testimony at Stratton trial
of, 192
Cross, Hugh, 20, 39, 41; withdrawal from
politics of, 59
Cross, Roland R., cabinet appointment of,
108
Crowley, George D., service to Stratton as
defense attorney of, 188
Crowley, John P., prosecution of Stratton
by, 190
Cummins, Roy, cabinet appointment of,
108

Daley, Richard J., 166, 168, 176, 182,
210; background of, 127; efforts to
elect Austin of, 150; role in

determining Democratic candidate for
governor in 1956 of, 145
Davis, Corneal, 241; opinion of Hodge of,
137; views of Bibb appointment of, 107
Davis, Dwight, 38
Day, Stephen A., 18; defeat of, 34;
election to Congress of, 11, 13;
reelection of, 24
Dearing, Charles L., 164
Dehen, Leo: testimony at Stratton trial of,
193; visit to Stratton for IRS by, 180–82
Delta Chi Fraternity, 8
Democratic State Central Committee: appointment of Edward J. Barrett as
candidate for secretary of state by, 33–
34; choice of gubernatorial candidate in
1956 by, 145
Dempsey, John T., 30, 68; involvement in
patronage of, 19; opposition to Stratton
in 1944 of, 32
Dibble, Howard, 10
Dirksen, Everett, 174; election to Senate
of, 72, 150, 186; testimony at Stratton
trial of, 198–99
Displaced Persons, Commission on,
Illinois, 66
Displaced Persons Bill: groups in favor of,
55, 57; introduction of, 51; letter from
DPs in favor of, 54; passage of, 59;
summary of arguments pro and con, 54;
views of journals of opinion toward,
51–52. See also HR 2910; Public Law
774
Dixon, Sherwood, gubernatorial candidacy
of, 101, 102
Doctoroff, John, testimony at Stratton trial
of, 192
Douglas, Emily Taft, 40, 41, 43–45, 48,
182; defeat by Stratton of, 47; election
to Congress of, 34; salient facts about,
44–45; target of Stratton campaign, 46
Douglas, Paul, 40, 124, 146, 182; call for
investigation of Hodge case by, 147;
election to Senate, 61, 177; salient facts
about, 45; views on the defeat of Emily
Taft Douglas of, 47
Downey, William W. "Smokey," 39, 42,
101, 106, 107, 118–19, 140; advice of,
20–21, 28–29, 32–33, 49; assistance to
Stratton in 1946 of, 45; cabinet, views
toward, 110; early career of, 20; guilty
plea of, 174; Hodge, views of, 140;

Index

indictment of, 172; IRS investigation of
Stratton, view of, 181; legislative
interaction of Stratton, view of, 116; as
press secretary, 71, 106, 153; Stratton's
third-term candidacy, view of, 169

Downs, Thomas J., 183, 185

Drach, George R., testimony at Stratton
trial of, 196

Dreiske, John, 167; testimony at Stratton
trial of, 198

Dresden nuclear power station, 168

Dunne, George W., 209

Dyas, Robert, testimony at Stratton trial of,
194

Edgar, Jim, 62

Eisenhower, President Dwight D., 213,
253; Chicago visit of, 165; host of
Republican strategy dinner, 124–25; at
Springfield, 122–123

Elmwood Park, Bank of, 144

Emanuelson, Chester A., defense attorney
for Stratton, 190

Emmerson, Louis L., 12; running for governor, 3

Eovaldi, William G., 70

Epping, Edward A., 162; imprisonment of,
146; indictment of, 141

Erickson, William N., 68; withdrawal from
gubernatorial race by, 95–96

Fasseas, Andrew, 38, 71, 95, 102, 186,
197; cabinet appointment of, 153;
support by, 61; testimony at Stratton
trial of, 191; views of the DP bill of,
53–54

Fleck, Charles J., 95

437 Vine St.: in Morris, purchase of, 19;
sale of, 205

Francisco, Charles, IRS visitor, 180–82

Franklin Life Insurance Co., 64

Friedrich, Dwight, testimony at Stratton
trial of, 197

Frisch, Frank A., testimony at Stratton
trial of, 197

Fulbright, Senator J. William, 138–39

Gerber, Joseph S., cabinet appointment of,
152

Governors Conference, 120–21, 122;
meeting in Chicago of, 133; Stratton
chosen to chair, 160

Graham, John O., 8, 23–24, 34–35, 49,
109; advice of, 66; congressional
secretary to Stratton, 14; failure to
rejoin Stratton team, 43–44; views of,
41–42, 62

Graves, W. Brooke, 183

Greek Star, The, 53

Green, Dwight H., 11, 33, 39, 42, 44, 46;
background of, 12; congratulations to
Stratton by, 69; election as governor of,
13; entertained by Strattons, 121; factional alignment of, 20; feeling toward
Stratton of, 38; Hodge, involvement
with, 142; lack of popularity in 1947,
49–50; opposition to Stratton in 1943,
28–32; Stratton endorsement by, 56;
third-term candidacy of, 59–60

Guild, William L., testimony at trial of,
195–96

Handley, Harold, views on Stratton trial
of, 188, 202

Hanrahan, Thomas, prosecution of
Stratton by, 188

Heidinger, James, 85

Higher Education Commission, formation
of, 122

Hintz, Edward A.: background of, 141;
imprisonment of, 146; indictment of, 141

Hodge, Orville, 25, 26, 101–2;
background of, 137–38; election as
auditor of, 102–3; embezzlement
system of, 142; indictment of, 142;
investigation of, 138; resignation of,
140; sentencing and imprisonment of,
143–44; testimony to Senate committee
by, 147

Hodge case: revival of, 170–71; summary
of impact of, 211

Hoffman, Elmer, 189; election as treasurer
of, 103; views toward Personnel Code
of, 156

Hoffman, Leonard, view of Stratton trial of,
201

Holderman, James, testimony at Stratton
trial of, 197–98

Holderman, S. James, testimony at Stratton
trial of, 197

Hollingsworth, Morton H.: cabinet
appointment of, 108; resignation of, 173;
views on third-term candidacy of, 169

Index

Hook, Marion, marriage to Stratton of, 9. *See also* Stratton, Marion

House, Judge Byron, testimony at Stratton trial of, 198

Howell, Evan, 163, 164; Toll Highway Commission, chairmanship of, 129

Howlett, Michael: defeat of, by Stratton, 72; election as auditor of, 177, 189

HR 2910, 51, 57. *See also* Displaced Persons Bill

Hughes, Edward J., 28; death of, 33

Ice, Willard, opinions of, 11, 95, 99, 121–22, 153, 182

Illinois, state of, characteristics of, 105, 179

Immel, Joseph: alliance with Stratton of, 94; background of, 93–94; opinions of, 65, 93, 94–95, 100, 109, 209

Indiana Society of Chicago, 183, 185

Ives, Elizabeth, 111; criticism of Stratton by, 148–49

Jewish Community Council of Peoria, urging admission of DPs, 52

Judicial reform: adoption of, 186; defeat of, 165; nature of, 117–18

Jurgensmeyer, John E., 185

Just, F. Ward, 187

Kanady, Johnson, 127; background of, 153; opinions of, 97, 153; press secretary, appointment as, 153

Kaplan, Stephen, prosecution of Stratton by, 190

Keevers, Marion: assistance from Stratton to, 185; congressional staff, member of, 14–15, 48–49; correspondence of, 186; executive secretary role of, 93, 105–6; secretary to Congresssman Howell, 35; support of Stratton by, 67, 71

Kelly, Edward, 26, 39, 202

Kemper, James, 183, 185, 187

Kennedy, John F., 48, 177, 178, 182

Kennedy, Leland, evaluation of Stevenson by, 98

Kennedy, Robert, 182

Kerner, Otto, 176, 184, 203, 204; election of, 173, 177; reelection of, 189

Kingsley, Austin, views of, 41, 183

Klein, Julius, testimony at Stratton trial of, 196–97

Klingbiel, Judge Ray, testimony at Stratton trial of, 198

Lee, Clyde: opinion of Stevenson of, 99; opinion of Stratton of, 209

Legislative Budgetary Commission, recommendations of, 154

Leopold, Nathan F., Jr., parole of, 164–65

Lewis, John W., testimony at Stratton trial of, 196

Lewis, Paul O., views toward the DP bill of, 56

Lindsey, Edward, correspondence of, 16–17

Littlewood, Thomas B., 11

Livingston, Park, 96

Lodge, Henry Cabot, Jr., 48; nomination for vice president of, 174

'Lo Franco, Niccolo (ed. of *L'Italia*), support by, 70

Lohman, Joseph, 146; candidacy for Cook County sheriff of, 124; elected treasurer, 165

Lohman, Martin, evaluation of Stevenson by, 98–99

Lynch, William J., evaluation of Stratton by, 159

Lyons, Richard, 11, 95; cabinet appointment of, 107; candidacy for the Senate of, 20, 34; death of, 152–53; performance of, 114

McAdamis, Donald, cabinet service of, 155, 157

McBroom, Victor, 63, 95

McCarthy, Joseph R., 48, 123

McCarthy, Justin, cabinet service of, 109, 152

McCarthy, Robert W., opinion of Stratton of, 209

McCormick, Robert R., 15

McLaughlin, Joseph K., cabinet service of, 108, 109

Madigan, Earl, 38, 61, 62, 67, 146; advice of, 49, 50, 56, 64, 69–70; chief clerk in treasurer's office, 93

Madigan, Edward, 39

Madigan, Robert, 39

Mason, Charles, view of Stratton trial of, 188

Index

Meek, Joseph: candidacy for Senate of, 123; opposition to optional city sales tax by, 128

Menard Penitentiary, 100

Michaelson, Ronald, staff of Stratton, view of, 114

Mitchell, Stephen, 145

Moore, Edward R., Personnel Code, views of, 156

Morey, Lloyd, service as auditor, 141

Morris, IL: characteristics of, 9; Community High School band of, 95; site of announcement for office, 95; Stratton move to, 9

Munyon, Marion, testimony at Stratton trial, of, 191–92. *See also* Hook, Marion; Stratton, Marion

Murray, Sinon, 50, 66, 67

Myers, Maude, 111; as survivor, 157–58

Nelson, Louis, candidacy for treasurer of, 66–67, 68

Newspapers, Chicago, political alignment of in 1952, 96

Nickell, Vernon, 39, 49, 52, 95; election as superintendent of public instruction of, 47; reelection of, 70, 72

Nixon, Richard M., 48, 168, 174, 176, 178, 179; gift from, 184

O'Brien, Donald J.: evaluation of Stevenson by, 99; opinion of Stratton of, 210

Office building, state: construction of, 120, 122, 133; plaque to Stratton hung in, 212–13

Ogilvie, Richard, 122, 178, 205

Overacker, M. B., 62

Page, Ray, 185; election as state superintendent of public instruction, 186

Palmer, Glen D., 29, 60, 65, 161, 168; advice of, 21, 38, 49, 50; background of, 21; cabinet appointment of, 107–8; friendship of, 184

Parkhurst, John: opinion of Stratton of, 209; view of Stratton's staff of, 106

Parr, Sam, 50

Partee, Cecil, 208

Paschen, Herbert C., 139; gubernatorial candidacy of, 134, 144–45; Hodge case, involvement in, 144

Patton, Francine, testimony at Stratton trial of, 191

Patton, Robert, 161; testimony at Stratton trial of, 192

Percy, Charles, 185, 186; defeat for governor of, 187, 189

Perrine, George: advice of, 38–42, 49; cabinet appointment of, 109; views of the DP bill of, 52–53

Personnel Advisory Board, 154–55

Personnel Code: implementation of, 154–56; nature of, 130–31

Personnel, Department of, creation of, 154–55

Perz, Robert, 156–57

Peters, Everett R., 202

Peterson, William, 22–23, 60; staff service of, 49

Phillips, Frank, 31

Powell, Paul, 116, 117, 129, 131, 187; donation to expenses of Stratton trial by, 202; election as secretary of state of, 189

Pree, Edward, 104, 108, 118, 144, 175; background and characteristics of, 106, 159–60; cabinet, view of, 110; campaign in 1944, view of, 33; campaign in 1946, view of, 45; candidacy in 1968, view of, 205; election of 1948, view of, 62; Hodge case effects, view of, 160, 178; patronage, role in, of, 112; Personnel Code, view of, 131; resignation of, 159; Stratton's performance, view of, 68, 114, 116, 121; Stratton trial, view of, 203

Prehn, Paul, view of Stratton trial of, 202

Public Law 774, 59. *See also* Displaced Persons Bill; HR 2910

Randolph, Paul, 122; interaction with legislature, view of, 116

Randolph, Ross, Hodge as convict, view of, 171

Rayson, Leland, evaluation of Stevenson by, 99

Redistricting, 116–17

Redmond, William, 208

Republican County Chairmen's Association, Executive Committee of, conference with Stratton in 1943, 29–30

Republican leaders in Illinois, in 1950, 72

Index

Republican National Convention, in 1960, Stratton role in, 174

Reum, Walter, view of Stratton on education matters, 122

Robertson, Hayes, 175; candidacy for governor, 171–73

Roosevelt, Eleanor, 56–57

Rosenstone, Edwin A., cabinet appointment of, 108

Rowe, Richard Yates, 37–38, 50, 59, 96; campaign strategy, suggestions of, by, 44; candidacy of, 59; factional alignment of, 20; retirement from politics of, 97; state treasurer, election as, 47

Russo, Vincent P., prosecution of Stratton by, 188

Saltiel, Edward: opinion of Stratton of, 95; view of the 1954 campaign of, 123

Saperstein, Esther, opinion of Stratton of, 209

Scariano, Anthony, opinion of Stratton of, 210

Schaefer, Judge Walter, 118, 146

Schuey, Wilma, testimony at Stratton trial of, 197

Schupp, Alfred F., 9, 30

Scott, Bill, 187, 203; election as treasurer, 186

Scott, Maurice, 173; opinion of Downey of, 154; opinion of Hodge of, 137; opinion of Stevenson of, 99; opinion of Stratton of, 210; Personnel Code, view of, 131

Searcy, Earle B., 25, 95; candidacy in 1950 of, 70

Selcke, Fred, 109, 143; on Bibb appointment, 107; on cabinet, 153; on candidacy in 1968, 205; on Downey, 153–54; on election of 1948, 62; on Hodge, 144; on patronage, 113; on Pree, 160; on Stratton, 114, 116; on Stratton trial, 201; on use of political contributions, 196

Sheehan, Timothy P.: testimony at Stratton trial of, 196; view of Stratton trial, of, 203

Shull, Ben H., cabinet appointment of, 108

Simon, Paul, evaluation of Stratton by, 134

Simpson, Jim, 68

Small, Len, 12, 209; service as governor of, 3–4, 6

Smith, Clem, Hodge sentenced by, 144

Smith, Elbert, 162; background of, 141; defeat, 177; election as auditor, 150; on Hodge, 171; on Personnel Code, 131; on Stevenson, 98

Smith, John W. F., 144

Smith, Victor, 188

Southmoor Bank, 144; Hodge case liability of, 162

Stanard, Stillman: cabinet appointment of, 107; performance of, 114; views on civil service of, 111

State Fair, 121; patronage positions in, 132

State Racing Board, patronage positions in, 131

Stelle, John, opinion of Austin of, 146

Stevenson, Adlai E., 117, 127, 132; background of, 97; criticism of, by Stratton, 71–72, 135; death of, 204; defense of his administration by, 103; as Democratic presidential candidate, choice of, 100; election as governor of, 61; leaving office, 110; opinion of Stratton of, 103; performance as governor, 97–100

Storey, George, 38; advice of, 69

Stratton, Charles Kerwin: birth of, 2; death of, 30; early life of, 7–8; education of, 8

Stratton, Diana Joy, 27, 135; appearance in 1948 campaign of, 60; birth of, 10; custody of, following divorce, 65; marriage of, 175

Stratton, Marion, 19; appearance in 1948 campaign of, 60; assistance with congressional matters by, 56; Bippus letter, subject of, 40; letters of, 36–37, 40. See also Hook, Marion

Stratton, Nancy Helen, 187; birth of, 184; growing up, 212

Stratton, Sandra Jane, 27, 135; appearance in campaign of, 60; birth of, 9; custody of, following divorce, 65; letters of, 37

Stratton, Shirley: activities of, 135, 162, 169, 172, 175–76; illness of, 184; opinion of Stratton trial of, 193; role as first lady of, 111; support of Stratton by, 94. See also Breckenridge, Shirley

Stratton, William G.: administrative style of, 114–15, 121–22, 162; adult life begins, 9–11; birth of, 2; business career of, 204–5, 206, 212; cabinet of, 106–10, 153; campaign finances of,

181–82, 193–94; campaign of 1954, role of, 123–24; campaign style of, 101; candidacy of, in 1968, 205–6; college days of, 7–9; congressional campaigns and elections, 11–13, 43, 45–47; congressional work of, 14–18, 50; Council of State Governments, presidency of, of, 160; Daley, friction with, 169–70; Democratic criticism of, 96; Displaced Persons bill, sponsorship by, 51–59; divorce of, 64–65; education bond issue, support of, 158; evaluation of, by Godfrey Sperling, Jr., 132–33; evaluations by others of, 158–59; farm, purchase and nature, 161; Governors Conference, chairmanship of, 160; gubernatorial campaigns and elections of, 101–2, 148–51, 175–79; Hodge case, involvement of, 138–43, 147–48, 150–51, 162–63; isolationist views of, 15–18; judicial reform, interest in, 158; judiciary, relations with, 118; Kerner veto of redistricting, criticism by, 186; legislative accomplishments of, 115–20, 130, 159; lodge built by, 133, 161; Masonic Lodge, membership of, 133; Navy service of, 36–45; open house of, 110–11, 122, 165; parents' influence upon, 6–8; patronage, use of, by, 19–20, 25–26, 111–13, 122, 131–32, 157, 172; personal finances of, 27, 45; political life, summary of, 206–12; political parties, views of, of, 167; politics, early exposure to, 6–8; politics, entry into of, 10; Powell campaign for Speaker, support of, 166–67; presidential election results, 1960, certification by, 179; Queen Elizabeth, hosted by, 167; recreation of, 161, 166, 170; Republican national convention role of, in 1952, 100–101; Republican national ticket potential of, 124–25, 134–35; secretary of state, campaign and election for in 1948, of, 59–63; secretary of state, campaign for in 1944, of, 27–32; Soviet Union, trip to, by, 167; speeches and addresses of, 110, 118–19, 126–27, 152, 154, 166, 167; staff of, 106, 114; state government, view of in 1961, by, 183; state treasurer, campaigns and elections for, of, 18, 22–24, 25–27, 38, 66–72, 93, 94; Stevenson, criticism of, by, 70; tax increase agreement with Daley, of, 127–29; third-term candidacy of, 169, 171–77; travels of, in 1961, 180; trial of, 184–85, 187, 188–201

Stratton, William J.: death of, 5; forebears of, 1; political life of, 2–6; as secretary of state, 3–5

Stratton, Zula Van Wormer, 60, 161; early life of, 2; letters of, 21–22, 36–38, 40; marriage of, 2; presence at Stratton trial of, 195, 200; support of Stratton by, 68

Sullivan, John E., 144

Sulzberger, Frank L., views toward the DP bill of, 53

Tagge, George, 29; political columns of, 37

Tax increase, opposition to, 127

Thiem, George, 11

Todd, Chester, 38, 39, 42, 95; advice of, 41

Toll Highway Commission: difficulties with program of, 129–30; establishment of, 119–20; patronage positions in, 131

Toll highway system: opening of Northwest Tollway, 163; political liabilities of, 164; program of, 163–64

United Service for New Americans, 57. *See also* Displaced Persons Bill

Van Der Vries, Bernice, evaluation of Stevenson by, 99–100

Veterans in Congress in 1946, 48

Viereck, George S., 15, 17

Volz, Leslie P. "Ike," 21, 68–69

Walker, Dan, 203

Watson, Ken, 186

Weiskopf, Norman, marriage to Diana Stratton of, 175

West Frankfort mine disaster, 100

White, Henry J., 41

Wiles, Walter E., view of Stratton trial of, 188

Wilkins, George T., 165

Will, Judge Hubert L., 190, 192, 195, 201; assignment to Stratton trial of, 188

Index

Winsor, Chester P., view of Stratton trial of, 201

Wirtz, Leonard E., testimony at Stratton trial of, 197

Witwer, Samuel W., 168, 184, 196; candidacy for Senate of, 173, 177

Wood, Warren, 117, 131; evaluation of Stratton by, 97

Woodward, Robert B., cabinet appointment of, 109

Wright, Warren, 123, 124, 173; factional alignment of, 20; gubernatorial candidacy of, 133–34; political practices of, 23, 134; state treasurer, candidacy for, 163, 165; suspicions of Hodge of, 138

Wyman, Austin L., 164